ACKNOWLEDGMENTS

Writing a book sometimes feels like a singular, individual experience when you're staring a computer screen for days on end. However, the truth is that no book enters into existence without a team effort that combines the talent and support of many people. To those who have been a part of my team, I want to express my sincere gratitude.

Thanks to Phillip Sexton at Writer's Digest for his desire to partner with me in providing top-notch marketing instruction to authors around the world. To Scott Francis for his editing assistance and help with improving this manuscript.

Thanks to Alan Weiss for his incredible wisdom and willingness to pour insights into the growth of my business and personal life. So many pieces of the puzzle fell into place after we met.

Thanks to the hundreds of authors I've coached through Wild-Fire Marketing. You have challenged me to create the best instruction available, and watching you enjoy the results is incredibly satisfying.

Special thanks to my mother, an English major and book lover, who birthed in me an unending interest in the literary world. To my father, who had an incredible career as a salesman and passed on his marketing acumen to me.

Most of all, thanks to my wife, Ashley, for her unwavering support and love. You've been a God-given sounding board, soul mate, and best friend. I will always be thankful.

TABLE of CONTENTS

PREFACE

There are a ton of books written on the subject of marketing. Plus, there are thousands of authors interested in marketing their books. Yet, with all this expertise and desire, more than eighty percent of the books published each year fail to break-even financially. That number represents a lot of frustration, dashed dreams, and lost money. After working in the publishing industry for more than ten years as an author and a consultant, I've learned two things. First, authors who write books as an avocation just to have fun or tell people they're published rarely succeed. Secondly, authors who write books as a vocation and take their work seriously usually achieve their goals.

Therefore, this book was not written for the armchair author who chatters about becoming a bestseller someday but rarely takes action. There are enough books already available for beginners toying with the idea of getting published. This book is for the author who is dedicated to reaching a larger audience and changing thousands of lives through literature.

With over one million new books published each year, the world doesn't need more authors who just write more books. Rather, the world needs more authors who know how to get their books in front of more readers. This book is written as a guide to show you how to accomplish that task. My goal was to create a resource that does more than just tell what to do, but explains why you should do it and how do it effectively. For example, anyone will tell you that authors should have a website and use social media. But, few will tell you what makes a website effective and the principles that apply to building a fast-growing online community. Likewise, anyone will tell you that it's important to expand your author platform. Yet, few are actually successful enough to show you how.

I'm an author just like you. I started writing books in 2002, before the luxury of fancy technology, such as social media, blogging, or live webcasts. I was just a normal guy who had never written a book, had no fan base, and had no idea what an "author platform"

1

meant. Instead, I had a business background and the burning desire to share a message that I knew could help people. With a lot of determination and plenty of critics, I set out to try every strategy possible to sell my books. It wasn't easy, but within a couple of years I sold 13,000 copies on my own and built a nationwide following. I conducted more than 170 events across North America and spoke to more than 35,000 people.

Even better, I began to generate a six-figure income that allowed my wife to quit her job and stay home. Through that success, publishers began to court me, I landed a nice contract, and my first book was re-released with national distribution. Ten years later, you can still find it selling in major retailers. In truth, I never made the bestseller lists. However, I achieved something much more difficult. I made a great living as an author through writing, speaking, and spin-off products.

My success, though, led to an unexpected path. Authors began to call me out of the blue asking for marketing advice. I was more than happy to share my ideas. Soon, distress calls from struggling authors became so frequent that I realized there was a huge need for advanced-level information about how to market books.

To meet this need, I started my own consulting practice in 2007 called WildFire Marketing (www.startawildfire.com). Since then, I've consulted with numerous publishers and coached more than 400 fiction and non-fiction authors at all levels. My client list includes numerous first-time authors with no experience to numerous *New York Times* bestsellers, such as Dr. Gary Chapman, Lysa TerKeurst, and Wanda Brunstetter. I've helped beginning authors start out on the right foot, and I've helped established authors achieve the highest levels of success.

The reason why I share my background is because it's imperative that you take advice from someone who has actually achieved the goal you seek. As the old adage says, "Never take financial guidance from a broke person." Likewise, don't give credence to book marketing advice from someone who has never written a book or succeeded in selling their work. I see too much blind leading the blind in the publishing industry. Instead, follow a leader who has already gone down the road, knows the difference between the land mines and shortcuts, and has the experience to help you navigate a steady course.

This book was written to serve as your personal guide to help you sell more books. In the coming pages, I will dispel a lot of myths and offer a lot of new ideas. However, none of the information will benefit you unless you're willing to work at marketing your book. You cannot spend one hour a week on promotional activities and expect to grow. Neither should marketing get limited to only what you do when you're not writing. If you want to build a bigger following of readers, then marketing should become synonymous with your writing. You engage in both activities together throughout the course of your week and month.

Good writers will tell you that consistency is the key to honing their craft. Likewise, good marketers will tell you that consistency is the key to reaching a larger audience. Therefore, I hope you'll use this book on a regular basis as a practical guide to help upgrade your marketing efforts and keep you on track.

My desire is to help you light a fire under your marketing plan, get your book in front of more people, create a word-of-mouth wildfire, and enjoy the response of happy readers. When that happens, I hope you'll share your success story with me. That's the kind of tale that I relish reading the most!

Rob Eagar
WildFire Marketing
Atlanta, GA

CHAPTER 1

ESTABLISH YOUR EXPERTISE

Envision you're camping in the wilderness. The sun is going down, the temperature is dropping, and you're getting hungry. To make it through the night, you will need warmth, you will need light, and you will need a way to cook dinner. You need fire.

In the distance, you spot a fallen tree that is large enough to provide wood for weeks. Seizing the opportunity, you set up camp beside the tree and prepare to build a fire. But, if you light a match and throw it onto the big log, will it ignite? No. What if you light another match and try it again? *Nada*. Same result. You could light a whole box of matches, throw each one of them at the log, and never get a flame started. Tossing matches at a log simply leads to frustration and a long, cold night in a dark forest.

Why doesn't the big log cooperate? It's woody, flammable, and possesses the ability to combust. If you touch the wood with a lit match, shouldn't it light? Not necessarily. The problem is that the fuel inside the log is covered with a tough outer shell that's resistant to sparks. You can toss a match at a log, but the exterior bark is too hard for the flame to penetrate. The match just bounces off and fizzles out.

Even if it didn't, the flame from a match doesn't last long enough to create the heat and power needed for combustion to take place.

How does all this talk about fire apply to your desire to sell more books? Trying to ignite a big log represents the battle that authors and publishers face when launching a new book. The fire represents your book and the message you've written. You want it to spread. You want your book sales to get out of control and consume as many people as possible. You want to sell hundreds, thousands, even millions of copies.

To achieve that goal, however, you'll need to build the marketing equivalent of a massive wildfire that spreads fast and burns for a long time. Getting a flame to start is the key. And there's more than one way to do it. For instance, wildfires can start from both natural and man-made causes.

Natural wildfires are created by rare, catastrophic events, such as lightning strikes or volcanic eruptions. You can't plan or prepare for these occurrences, which are beyond our control. In the publishing world, a naturally started wildfire would be like a lightning strike, such as Oprah selecting your book for her famous book club, landing a guest spot on *Good Morning America*, or getting a random endorsement from the President of the United States. It's rare, and there's very little you can do to make it happen, but it does occasionally happen.

Unfortunately, some authors concentrate on trying to make such phenomenon happen. They hope, they pray, they read their horoscopes, but they do little to market their books. They seem sure that their big break is just around the corner. Or, they sit back and mistakenly believe that their publisher will do all of the promotional work for them.

This attitude is like standing out in the woods, trying to start a fire by waiting for lightning to strike. The odds that it will happen are absurdly low. Is it possible? Yes, but it's also unpredictable. You'll sit around waiting and hoping while nothing happens except the passing of time. In the process, the opportunity to start a better kind of wildfire is wasted—one that you can create on your own.

Contrary to natural causes, wildfires can also originate from man-made triggers, such as discarded cigarettes, sparks from equipment, acts of arson, or a deliberate burn that's meant to clear out dead growth and rejuvenate an old forest. It's surprising how a huge wildfire can start from one simple act. A casual match thrown into the woods can lead to a huge blaze that consumes thousands of acres.

As an author, you can start your own wildfire and use it for good. By taking intentional steps to ignite your readers, you can generate awareness and word of mouth that sweeps the country. As a marketing consultant, I've taught hundreds of authors how to start book-promotion wildfires from scratch and make them burn bigger and hotter.

The key to success is understanding how to build a fire, light it, and help it spread. This book will walk you through that process. Marketing a book is not as complex as you may think. You can boil it down to three simple questions:

1. What is my value?
2. Who needs my value the most?
3. Where do the people who need my value congregate?

I'll talk about the first question in this chapter and address the second and third questions in Chapter 2.

SO WHAT'S YOUR BOOK ABOUT?

Since the dawn of the printing press, authors have garnered a certain mystique within modern society. People tend to look at writers with fascination because of their ability to compose words that generate deep emotion or provide answers to frustrating problems. This mystique is similar to the interest that doctors bring about when they walk into a room and everyone starts describing their aches and pains. People marvel at the talent and intellect in their midst. Fair or not, this fascination creates a unique credibility factor that authors experience simply because they have written a book.

When people find out you're an author, you will eventually be asked this common question: "So what's your book about?" This inquiry may sound simple, however, it is one of the most difficult questions for most authors to answer. And this creates a fundamental book marketing problem. The difficulty arises because authors tend to misunderstand the question the other person is asking. This misinterpretation leads to a generic response that generates a disinterested look on the other person's face or a quick change of subject. And once you miss an opportunity to capture someone's interest in your book, it's tough to get it back.

Though our culture is fascinated with authors, this question doesn't give you carte blanche to babble about what you've written. There's a deeper principle at work that trumps a person's curiosity about a book. It's the principle of self-interest. Every human being lives from a mind-set of protecting his or her own interests and making decisions for personal benefit.

For example, you buy a new outfit because it makes you look good. You buy a certain car because you believe it will keep your family safe. You go to a restaurant so that you don't have to cook. You buy the latest technological gadget because it makes you more efficient. More often than not, people buy things according to what's in their self-interest, including when they purchase books.

Though people might think it's cool that you're an author, it doesn't mean they will buy your book—unless there's a reason that appeals to their self-interest. If you miss this fundamental principle, you will fail to create the sparks needed to sell books like wildfire.

In contrast, if you keep the concept of self-interest in mind, you will see readers and book shoppers in a whole new light. When they ask, "So what's your book about?" you'll be able to turn the question to your advantage. Remember, you will face this inquiry, or various versions of it, from everyone you meet face-to-face, or when buyers encounter your message online and in bookstores. And here's the interesting part: That's not really the question they're asking you. Actually they are wondering, "What's in it for me if I buy your book? Is it in my best interest to read what you've written?"

You want to publish and sell as many books as possible, right? Here's the bottom line: You will maximize the power of your marketing when you take the focus off yourself and place it on satisfying the self-interests of others. Let go of the idea that the public may be fascinated that you're an author. Concentrate on answering their internal question: "What's in it for me?"

TRUST ME, I'M AN EXPERT

Besides making decisions according to self-interest, most people buy products and services from someone they trust. For instance, most consumers shop at a grocery store that exhibits consistent cleanliness and low prices. People want to know their food is fresh and inspected. Likewise if someone needs surgery, she seeks out a trained medical professional for help, rather than asking a next-door neighbor to do the procedure. Part of making decisions based on self-interest means discriminating between who we trust and who we doubt.

As an author, you can use this dynamic as a way to generate interest in your books. People tend to regard authors as experts due to the time, thought, and research that many put into their manuscripts. This case is especially true for nonfiction subjects but applies to fiction as well. So if you want to sell books like wildfire, position yourself as a trusted expert. Doing so will naturally build a credibility factor that helps people feel more comfortable purchasing from you.

Being an expert doesn't mean you have to get a PhD in a specific field or have a high IQ. To be an expert, you simply need more successful experience than the average person. You need to be farther down the path than your readers and provide the capability to lead them in a beneficial direction.

For a nonfiction author, you build expertise by researching particular topics, gaining knowledge, conducting research, testing your findings, and gathering experience. Then you take your acquired wisdom and teach other people how to overcome a problem or learn a new subject. If you successfully lead other people to obtain a new perspective and they experience sought-after results, then you are an expert.

If you write self-help books, you might be an expert at helping people solve specific challenges. If you write memoirs or biographies, you might be an expert at teaching people to learn from history. If you write textbooks, you might be an expert at helping students master new skills. So how are *you* an expert at making someone's life better?

If you are a fiction author, establishing your expertise is just as important as crafting a great story. Consider the success of acclaimed novelist, John Grisham. Before he wrote books, he went to law school, practiced criminal law for a decade, and served in Mississippi state House of Representatives. Each year after being elected to serve as a representative, Grisham would spend January to March in the state capitol dreaming of a big case.

In 1984, a big case came through the court system. As Grisham was hanging around the court one day, he overheard a twelve-year-old girl telling the jury her painful story of being attacked and abused. It intrigued Grisham, and he began watching the trial. It was then that the story for his first book was born. He wondered what would have happened if the girl's father had fought back and murdered her assailants. Using his firsthand experience of the legal system, Grisham poured himself into the retelling of the story. It took him three years to complete his first book, *A Time to Kill*, which eventually became a runaway bestseller.

Grisham's novels appeal to millions of readers because he approaches his stories from an expert's point of view that provides unique details and behind-the-scenes insight. Likewise, if you're a novelist, use your background and the research you conduct to build your expertise. Maybe you write fiction in genres, such as fantasy or children's books. If so, you still need to become an expert storyteller, dialogue writer, entertainer, or interpreter of human nature. If you're not an expert, people will wonder why they should listen to you.

Expertise builds credibility. Credibility builds trust. Trust breeds comfort and confidence. Comfort and confidence breed book sales. Any questions?

ALLOW ME TO STATE MY VALUE
Since most people purchase books based on the principle of self-interest, the key to powerful marketing is to show how you meet other

people's needs. Therefore your promotional efforts should be audience focused, rather than self-focused. All of your book marketing materials, such as your website, back cover copy, personal bio, bookmarks, newsletters, and even social media posts, should explain how you can improve a reader's life.

More important, if you want people to pay money for your book, then you owe readers a return on their investment. A financial transaction is literally taking place. However, authors have an advantage in that consumers usually have to purchase books prior to reading them. Otherwise some books might never earn a penny.

I'm not trying to be harsh. I just want you to understand the reality that an author faces. More than 500,000 new books are published each year. Yet the average title only sells around five thousand copies in its lifetime. In addition, more than 40 percent of newly manufactured books never meet the publisher's sales goals. Worse, the industry return rate is over 35 percent for hardcover and 25 percent for paperback. If you want to make a living as an author, you must convince readers that your book is worth the investment. And it's your job to make this distinction, not your publisher, literary agent, or anyone else.

I'm surprised, however, by how many authors are unaware of this fact. They market books by focusing on their self-serving personality or harp on features within the pages, such as study guides, seven nebulous steps, or bonus chapters. Nobody cares about features. They care about themselves.

Readers are asking you, "If I give you my money first, will your book give me something in return?" That return can be increased knowledge, a problem solved, or hours of pure entertainment. But it better be something that the reader deems as worthy of their purchase. If you create a positive result, you'll win the exciting prize authors and publishers crave called "word of mouth."

Don't take your responsibility as an author lightly. Think of your audience's needs as much as your own. To identify the value of your books, start by asking yourself these questions:

1. How do I specifically improve the life of my readers?

2. What tangible results do I create for my readers?
3. How do I help leaders meet the needs of their organization?

HOW TO WRITE VALUE STATEMENTS

When I teach my author clients how to answer the questions above, I encourage them to write out their answers in the format of a value statement. A *value statement* is an individual sentence that describes a specific result you know you can create for your readers. You should have many value statements. Your goal is to clearly explain how your message will improve a reader's life.

Here's an example of four value statements that I wrote for you as the reader of this book:

- I will help you sell more books.
- I will help you secure more speaking engagements.
- I will help you create raving fans who spread word of mouth.
- I will help you increase your author income.

Do those results sound good? They should, because it's what every author wants. How do I know? Because I'm an author myself, and I want the same results you desire. How do I know that I can create these results for you? Because I've already trained more than four hundred authors across America and successfully helped them experience these results. My statements are based on fact, not hypothesis.

A value statement isn't a guess of what you think you can do. It's a declaration of your track record helping other people. Remember that you're supposed to be an expert. Experts are people who possess experience creating positive outcomes for others. Writing value statements is a way to show the public that you can give a return on their investment if they buy your book.

I'll talk about how to use value statements in your marketing strategy later. First, I'll walk you through a step-by-step process to create these statements for your books. Follow along with a pen and paper, or set up a new file on your computer, and take a few minutes to complete this exercise.

1. List the common results you create for readers

Write out separate sentences that explain individual results you've created for your readers. Don't make guesses. You should be stating actual fact. Recall how readers have described the ways in which you have improved their lives. How are people better off after having read your book? What is your track record of improving the condition of others?

Don't confuse stating your results with making a guarantee. Writing a book isn't a legal contract that binds you to certain obligations. It's the reader's responsibility to create the positive outcome by applying the message of your book. You need to assure the reader that results are possible, but you don't have to make a guarantee. The burden is always on the reader to make change happen.

Avoid trying to cram several results into one sentence. Break each result into a separate statement. You may end up with many value statements for each book (or each chapter) that you've written. The more, the better—but focus on the results that appeal to the largest segment of your book's intended audience.

If you're a novelist, this exercise applies to you as well. Fiction has the advantage of helping people experience powerful results by showing how central characters overcome difficult situations. That's why *The Lord of the Rings* by J.R.R Tolkien is such a popular trilogy. Even though its fantasy fiction, readers feel inspired to look at life from a new perspective of hope, courage, and respect for others. Following the adventures of the Hobbit, Frodo, serves as an example for readers to follow.

WD **BONUS ONLINE CONTENT:** Download the article "What If I Don't Know the Value of My Book?" at bookwildfire.com and writersdigest.com/book-wildfire-downloads

2. Complete the sentence: I will help you _____

Since value statements describe a result that your book creates for other people, try starting sentences with the phrase, "I will help you

_____." Then, fill in the blank with your specific result. The concept of providing help is a convincing motivator that can cause others to seek out and purchase your resources.

You can also try a different approach by starting with the words, "Imagine what your life would be like if _____." The goal is to get the attention away from you as the author, and redirect the focus on how you improve the reader's condition. If you don't want to help people, why write a book? Believe me, there are much easier ways to make a living and enjoy your life.

3. Use specific and emotional language

Besides using value statements to state your result, you should also attempt to generate emotional interest. For instance, if I say, "I will help you increase your author income," I know that idea is emotionally appealing, because it connects with your deep desire to be financially stable. In contrast, if I said, "I'll help you understand new marketing principles," you would ignore me, because people don't care about principles. They care about the beneficial results that principles will produce.

One of the best ways to make your marketing more effective is by making an emotional connection with your readers. Logic makes people think, but emotion makes them act. So if you want people to purchase your book, you need to explain your value on an emotional level. Therefore, avoid writing value statements that use generic language. For instance, ask yourself if the statements below sound appealing:

- I help people feel better.
- I help businesses run smoother.
- I will help you live with confidence instead of fear.

These statements sound beneficial, but do they move you emotionally? Probably not. Those sentences are about as bland as a vanilla wafer. To engage a reader's emotion, the value must be described more specifically. Take a look at these powerful statements some of my clients wrote:

- I will help you regain the pain-free life you used to enjoy.
- I will help your company build teams that finish tasks faster with less conflict.
- I will help you learn how to trust others and no longer feel alone.

Notice the emotional energy in these statements. If you're not captured by the result that's offered, check your pulse.

4. Employ the power of quantifier words

A great way to enhance the impact of value statements is by using *quantifiers* that describe positive change. A quantifier helps legitimize your value statements because it shows how you increased something good or decreased something negative. Moving a person from point A to point B in a beneficial manner represents a helpful result. For example, observe how the following value statements utilize quantifiers to reflect positive change. I will help you:

- *Strengthen* the ability to express genuine love to your spouse.
- *Decrease* conflict by learning to build trust and resolve disagreements.
- *Improve* productivity among employees with proper motivation.
- *Enhance* your people skills to foster encouraging relationships.
- *Restore* adventurous dreams you may have postponed

Below is a list of fifteen quantifiers that can help spark ideas for your value statements:

increase	decrease	enhance
improve	renew	strengthen
negate	diminish	reduce
expand	raise	heighten
double	boost	lower

5. What if you get stuck?

If you experience difficulty writing out specific value statements, I recommend the following ideas as sources for inspiration.

A. Review any thank-you letters and e-mails that you've received from fans and readers. Sometimes people will send you a testimonial that spells out a unique result that your book created for them. If you see a pattern in the testimonials that you get, that's a sure sign of consistent results. Use those comments to create value statements.

B. Examine the reviews that your books receive on popular book-selling websites, such as Amazon.com or BarnesandNoble.com. Most reviews are usually too generic to provide much insight. However, occasionally you'll find a review that is specific enough to describe a result that your book produced in a reader's life. Use the details in those reviews to write specific value statements.

C. Reflect on the personal reasons you chose to write your book. What was the big reason that drove you to expend so much mental and emotional effort? Consider the central reasons you were motivated to write your book. Had you recently overcome a challenge? Did you see injustice that needed to be addressed? Were you moved by headlines that laid the foundation for a compelling story?

If you experienced a personal result in your own life that led you to write your book, then that same result is probably true for many of your readers. As the common adage says, "Practice what you preach." Thus, examine how the message of your book improved your own life. Then use that knowledge to write powerful value statements for others.

D. If you write nonfiction, another way to uncover possible results that your book creates is by interviewing leaders within your target audience. Ask them to describe specific problems that their organizations or communities face. Then connect how the information in your book offers solutions to those issues. This is a helpful way to assure that your book can provide value to the groups that really need it.

6. Avoid these value statement pitfalls

Value statements are the foundation for an effective book marketing campaign. Thus, they need to be compelling. Otherwise your promotional efforts could be wasted. Steer clear of the actions that can steal the thunder from your statements:

A. Avoid using clichés and ambiguous phrases, which assure your book gets lost in the crowd. Examples include, "I will help you find peace in your heart" or "I will help you live in harmony with others." These statements aren't specific enough to draw attention. Always use language that separates you from the pack and makes your books sound unique.

B. Avoid writing value statements that are teaching points. For instance, the statement, "My book will help your kids behave better when they go out to dinner," can come across as preachy or condescending. Your value statements should not make the reader feel guilty or embarrassed. Instead, your goal is to describe a positive result that you know readers want.

C. Avoid using technical terminology or religious expressions that might confuse a mainstream audience. For instance, some spiritual authors make the mistake of using unfamiliar language, such as "justification," "sanctification," "quiet-time," or "the world." These words are confusing to the uninitiated. Your book sales will increase when your value appeals to as many readers as possible. Make sure people who aren't a part of your religion or particular business niche can understand your statements.

D. Avoid negative statements. Most people are more intrigued by a positive result than advice on how to prevent something bad. The following value statement is too negative to gain attention: "I will help you steer clear of destructive dating relationships." People would rather know how to find the best relationship than how to avoid a bad one.

E. Avoid long sentences. The principle of less is more applies to your value statements. If you take too long to describe your result, you'll probably lose the reader's attention. I suggest that you keep all of your value statements to less than thirteen words in length. Why? Most of your marketing materials won't provide enough space to list a long sentence. So keep your value statements short and sweet, and use brief, punchy phrases that grab the reader's attention.

Before you continue reading this rest of this book, I encourage you to try the following exercise. Take each of your books, and write three to five value statements for each one. Start your sentences with "I will help you ..." Then list your results as bulleted sentences under each book title. If you come up with more than five, that's great. Just make sure that your statements represent real results that you've created for people—not hunches, guesses, or wishful thinking.

HOW AND WHERE TO USE YOUR VALUE STATEMENTS

Now that you've learned how to create powerful value statements, the next step is learning how to use them. Below are six essential ways every author can use their value statements to immediately improve their book marketing.

1. Author website

Post your value statements all over your website, including the home page, about page, and books page. You need to remind readers of the value that you can bring to their lives. Don't hide your value. Keep it up front and use your bulleted lists of results on a repeated basis. The more you make the reader feel an emotional desire for your book, the quicker they will purchase it.

2. Personal bio

Incorporate your value statements into the text of your author bio. Instead of bragging about your history and accomplishments, write your bio in a way that reflects your value and credibility. For instance, write your introductory paragraph, and then list of three to five value statements that best sum up the benefit of your books. Turn an otherwise boring bio into a supplementary marketing tool.

3. Newsletters
If you send out regular print pieces or newsletters, it's important to remind the recipient of your value. Therefore include a small area of text that provides a mini bio with a list of your strongest three to five value statements. Remember that some people will receive your newsletter because it was passed on to them. Therefore they won't know who you are. Use your value statements as a friendly explanation.

4. Event promotional material
If you conduct regular speaking engagements or book signings, value statements can help you draw a larger crowd. For instance, no one will attend your event if they don't see a valid reason to pay money or take time out of their schedule. Therefore all of your event promotional materials need to concisely answer the question, "What's in it for me?" An easy way to satisfy this question is by putting a few value statements on your event posters, brochures, and flyers. Spell out the results that the reader will receive by attending your event.

5. Back cover copy
When consumers walk into a bookstore, they usually pick up a book, look at the front cover, then turn it over and read the back cover copy. This is a crucial moment to grab the reader's attention. However, most authors and publishers use bland text that describes the book's topic or the author's bio. No wonder so many books never break even. The reader is never engaged on an emotional level to feel a need for the book. Make your book capture the reader's attention by listing several value statements on your back cover. Doing so implies the result that the readers can experience and answers the question, "What's in it for me?"

6. Personal conversations and media interviews

Some authors mentally freeze when people ask them about their books. However, these are important marketing opportunities, especially if you're talking with an influential leader or making a media appearance. Use your value statements as the perfect fallback position. People don't want a boring description of your books. They're looking for an answer that will overcome their skepticism. Memorize a few of your value statements, and be ready to recite them at a moment's notice. This will prevent you from getting a glazed look if someone suddenly asks, "So what's your book about?"

Examine all of your current marketing materials to see if you describe the results that your book can create for readers. If your materials are missing this element, revamp them by including a bulleted list of your three to five strongest value statements. Use them everywhere, and don't worry about repeating your statements. Readers need to be consistently reminded of your value.

SUMMARY

Never answer the question, "So what's your book about?" Remember that no one cares. Instead, they want to know, "What's in it for me?" Thus, redefine yourself from an author who writes books to an expert who helps people. Use value statements to capture the public's attention and light a flame of desire for your book. Turn to the next chapter, and I'll explain how your value serves as the best fuel possible to ignite a marketing wildfire.

CHAPTER 2

LIGHT A FIRE IN YOUR READERS

When you want to start a fire, there's a strange paradox that must be remembered. Bigger is not necessarily better. You can't ignite a large log on fire with matches, no matter how many you throw at it or how much lighter fluid your pour on it. You may get a quick flare-up, but the fire will soon die out and send you back to square one. There's only one way to start a lasting fire that easily spreads. You must find some kindling.

Kindling consists of small branches, sticks, and dry vegetation that easily light with a single spark. Once you start a fire by using kindling, you can add larger logs that will burn hotter, brighter, and longer. And if the fire gets out of control, you could even wind up with a full-blown wildfire on your hands.

As I mentioned in Chapter 1, marketing your book is similar to starting a fire, and you can break the process down to three questions:

1. What is my value?
2. Who needs my value the most?
3. Where do those who need my value congregate?

We've already addressed the first question in Chapter 1. So, let's focus on the second and third questions in this chapter, and build a roaring fire for your message.

IDENTIFY YOUR KINDLING

Authors and publishers can throw book advertisements at the masses, but nothing happens. When most people see promotional material for a book, they tend to act like the big log in our earlier example. They may see an ad, but it simply bounces off of them, the promotional flame flickers out, and everyone moves on unaffected.

People in the real world are like hardened logs in the forest. They're tough. They're weathered. They're skeptical. They've seen a lot, and they're not interested in being interrupted with a promotion for your book. Instead, they're going about their day, making decisions according to their self-interest. Fortunately there's a way to break through their tough exterior. You can overcome a person's skepticism by showing how you can improve his life.

As discussed in Chapter 1, your value is your single most powerful marketing weapon. That's because it's hard for people to feel antagonistic when they realize you're trying to help them. Your book doesn't look like just another product to purchase. Instead, a nonfiction book is regarded as a helpful source of information. A novel can be seen as a beneficial source of entertainment, escape, and inspiration.

When you possess a crystal clear understanding of your book's value, your marketing will naturally become more effective. Why? Your marketing will also naturally become more focused. It's counterproductive to market a book to everyone all at once. There are over three hundred million people in America. Yet the top-selling books only capture a few million readers. So don't write a book and say, "My book is for everyone!" It's not, and it never will be.

However, your book may be perfect for thousands, and eventually millions, of readers who desperately need your value. Thus, once you know your value, start your marketing plan with the next logical question: Who needs my value the most?

When answering this question, you must resist the temptation to cast too wide of a net. Without focus, you will harm your marketing efforts. Your goal isn't to define everyone who may buy your book. Instead, you want to identify the people most likely to buy your book at first exposure, because they are in desperate need of your value.

Let's go back to our example of building a fire. In order to get one started, experts agree that the best first step is to gather together kindling. Once you light a pile of this tinder, the result is a flame so intense that it quickly spreads and ignites the larger branches around it. As the larger branches catch fire, they generate enough energy to ignite a large log. And if that resulting fire is left uncontrolled, the flames can get so powerful that they create a wildfire that sweeps through the entire forest.

If you want to sell books like wildfire, utilize the same principle. To start a fire, you need to identify and ignite an initial group of readers who will get so excited that they turn into raving fans. I like to call them "Word-of-Mouth Warriors." These are people who will forcefully take up the cause to tell others about your book. You don't have to ask them to promote. They will do it willingly, because your value touched an emotional fuel that lights them into action. They want to tell others how your book improved their life. Or they want the joy of being the first person to tell others about your book, which makes them feel cool (never underestimate a person's desire to be seen as influential).

A "kindling" reader is a person who feels so excited or grateful for your message that they want to share their experience with others. This excited influence acts like a flame that spreads interest to new and larger groups of people. A domino effect occurs, and the excitement about your book expands outward from your raving fans to other readers they know.

One of best examples of this wildfire principle in action is a book called *The Shack*. Originally this novel was rejected by more than twenty publishers and destined for the slush pile. So the author, William Paul Young, decided to self-publish, because it was the only way to print the story he had written for his children. He had no name recognition, no platform, and no aspirations to be a big-time author.

However, as Young gave away initial copies of his book to friends, they were amazed by the unique power of his story. The value of his book was so unusual that they couldn't help telling others about what they had read. One friend told ten other friends, and so forth.

Soon Young was receiving orders for caseloads of his self-published book. People started buying books in bulk and giving away copies to friends, family, neighbors, and co-workers. Some began to call his book a work of genius. Others called it heretical. But the word of mouth spread so fast that big bookstores made exceptions to their "no self-published books" policy and began stocking copies on their shelves.

Within two years, Young sold more than one million copies and became an American literary sensation that captured the media world and blogosphere, and sparked huge controversy across the country. Major publishers swooped in to take advantage of the income opportunity. Young signed a contract with Hachette, the second largest publisher in the world, which re-released his novel under their distribution. As of this writing, *The Shack* has more than fifteen million copies in print and held the No. 1 spot on the *New York Times* bestseller list for fifty weeks. Talk about a wildfire! It all started because Young's book gave initial readers a sense of value that they couldn't keep to themselves. His kindling group lit others on fire, and their enthusiasm spread across the nation.

To create a similar dynamic for your book, the question you must ask is, "Who needs my value the most?" You could even turn the question around and ask: "Who stands to lose the most if they never get my value?" Your answers to these questions help identify the people most likely to read your book, burn hot with excitement, and enthusiastically tell others. They define the tinder needed to start your own wildfire.

Here's an example to help walk you through the process. Say an author writes a book about how to navigate the dating world and build a successful marriage. If you're that author, who do you think would need the book's value the most?

If you answered single adults and college students, you're on the right track. But that's a large, generic group. Not all of them would constitute kindling for this book. For instance, some single adults aren't interested in getting married. And many college students feel they won't be ready for marriage until they settle down and get a job. Thus, this book wouldn't appeal to them. You could market the book to this group, but it won't respond.

To find the kindling, you need to narrow down this large crowd to a more focused group of singles who could immediately appreciate the value of the book. Think of the process like creating concentric circles that get smaller and smaller. Narrow your target audience until you identify the group most likely to respond when they first hear about the book.

A great way to narrow the focus is by concentrating on any strong emotions that might be affecting your target audience. Logic makes people think, but emotion makes them act. Think about the inner turmoil, challenges, joys, or needs that would make people take action to buy your book.

For instance, if a single adult feels lonely or frustrated over a bad breakup, then she would be more likely to want dating advice. If she's constantly badgered by a parent who wants to see her married as soon as possible, then she may feel more inclined to take action.

You're not trying to judge your readers or criticize their behavior. You're identifying the fuel within them that motivates action. Remember that people act according to their self-interest. If you fail to engage their internal motivation, then they won't catch flame when exposed to your book. They will fizzle out, and you're marketing efforts will be in vain.

In the case of our example, you could narrow down a broad group of single adults to find kindling in the following manner:

Value of the book: Helping readers find the right person to date and build a lasting, satisfying marriage.

Let's narrow down that audience to identify find the kindling:

- All single adults in America.
- Single adults in America near or past a certain age, who want to get married.
- Single women in America near or past the age of thirty, who want to get married soon.
- Single women in America near or over age thirty, who feel tired of the dating scene and watching all of their friends getting married, and are sick of their mother asking, "When are you going to get married?"

There's a theme that characterizes this final group. The last bulleted statement defines readers who feel something so strongly that they're likely to take action. Thus, they're less skeptical and more open to making a purchase. When these ladies recognize the value that's available in the proposed book, they'll feel drawn to buy it. The book provides value by satisfying a felt need in their lives. If they read the book and experience a positive outcome, they will excitedly tell friends who may be in the same struggle—thereby activating word of mouth.

I chose this example because you can apply it to both fiction and nonfiction. For instance, our sample book could be a nonfiction self-help manual that walks readers through the dating process. Or the book could be a romance novel about a girl who endures a complicated relationship struggle. No matter what genre your book fits, you can always identify the kindling.

This process may lead to identifying several different types of specific kindling groups. That's fine. It's okay to have two or three diverse groups that need your value the most. However, guard against creating so many kindling groups that you lose focus. Otherwise you'll wind up back in a position of trying to be all things to all readers. This will lead to a watered-down marketing plan that smothers your attempt to start a wildfire.

In addition, don't confuse this process with limiting your total audience. The goal isn't to alienate readers. The goal is to give your book the best chance to catch fire by identifying the people most likely to purchase and share it with others. Pursue the readers who have the desire and the money to buy your book first. That's your tinder, the group who can provide the essential momentum needed to get book sales rolling.

In the example just mentioned, you could market that book to groups besides single women, such as single men, young adults in their twenties, and parents of adult children. However, your marketing efforts will be the most efficient when you focus your initial efforts on those who need your value the most.

In addition, I recommend that you occasionally revisit how you identify your kindling. You may find that your initial assumptions are incorrect. Or an unexpected group may reveal itself to be raving fans for your book's value. Never assume you've figured it all out. Marketing is a constant process of monitoring who needs your value, who responds the best, and who is most likely to help spread the word.

Too often authors and publishers don't take time to identify and ignite the kindling groups for their books. Instead, they usually publish a new title, market it to a mass audience with a cookie-cutter strategy, and hope the excitement catches on. That's like trying to start a fire without gathering any tinder. You can't light just anything on fire and expect it to burn. The right fuel must be present.

Without kindling, there is no fire. Without kindling readers, there is no wildfire ... no word of mouth ... no spreading book sales. However, once you've identified your kindling, the marketing process gets a lot easier. The next section explains how.

FIND WHERE YOUR KINDLING GROUPS CONGREGATE

It's important to identify your kindling readers. But it's all in vain if they never identify you. It's one thing to differentiate the people who need your value the most, but the trick is getting your value in front of them. You can't light a fire without gathering enough tinder first. Fortunately the task of finding large groups of like-minded people is easier than ever before.

As humans we are relational beings who like to congregate based on interest and need. For instance, people who like the same sports teams fill huge stadiums to cheer together. People who share similar political views tune in regularly to the same radio and television programs. People who share similar religious beliefs join large churches and mosques to worship en masse. People who battle cancer join support groups to encourage each other. People who like computers get together at massive conferences and act geeky. People who write books congregate at writers conferences and moan about the publishing industry.

In other words, people will generally organize themselves into a kindling group for you. This is great news, because you don't need to cajole people to get organized around your book's subject matter. They've probably done it already. You just need to find them.

In his book, *Pyromarketing*, author Greg Stielstra says, "Instead of promoting to more people, promote to people who are more interested." I agree that this approach is much better use of time and money for busy authors with a limited budget, which is almost all of us. Thanks to the Internet, it's quicker and cheaper than ever before to locate large groups of people who share the same interests. Simply type a topic into your search engine of choice, and you'll find numerous links to groups organized around that issue.

For instance, a publisher hired me to work with a first-time fiction author who wrote faith-based novels set in the English Regency time period. She possessed an expert level of understanding of this era and conducted significant research for her stories.

During our initial meetings, we defined this author's kindling group as Caucasian women in America, ages twenty-five to seventy-five, who like to read for pleasure, prefer clean stories free from vulgarity, and especially enjoy historical romances set in the English Regency period. When we made this distinction, however, the author worried that she would have a difficult time locating where her kindling readers gathered in groups. So I issued her a challenge.

I guaranteed this author that she could find at least twenty-five to fifty specific groups if she followed my strategy. I gave her two weeks to conduct an Internet search using the description of her kindling and to make a list of any groups that she found.

When we later talked, she exclaimed, "You were right. In fact, I found over one hundred groups dedicated to the exact kind of reader I'm trying to reach!"

She found these groups using Internet search terms, such as "historical romance," "Regency lovers," "Jane Austen," and "clean romance." She produced a long list of specific historical societies, online reader forums, book clubs, chat groups, social media pages, websites, and blogs—all connected to the theme of her new book. With that kindling information, she was armed and ready to light a fire under her readers.

Once you've defined your kindling group, I challenge you to take the same step and ask where they congregate. I'll bet there are more than fifty places, online or off-line, where your kindling congregates right now. Use the list of questions below, and you will find that it's easier to identify them than you probably think:

Online:
- What websites do my kindling readers visit?
- What groups on Facebook, Twitter, LinkedIn, and other social media match my kindling audience?
- What active forums discuss my book's topic and value?
- What blogs do they read?
- What news sites do they frequent?
- What online book clubs are they members of?

Off-line:
- What professional or social organizations do my kindling readers join?
- What print magazines do they read?
- What television shows do they watch?
- What radio shows do they listen to?
- What religious groups or events do they participate in?

- What newsletters do they subscribe to?
- What hobbies do they enjoy?

You may conduct research using these questions, yet still wind up scratching your head. Don't assume that you have no kindling. Instead, find some men and women who represent your target audience and ask them the above questions. Look for patterns in their responses that help identify where they get together in concentrated groups. And avoid broadening your search just to find an answer. Stay focused on locating groups that closely fit the definition of your kindling reader.

You can't start a fire based on assumption. Combustion happens according to facts. A real spark from a real match lights real tinder. Oxygen combines with the vegetation and a real fire starts to burn. Likewise, don't assume that you know where your kindling exists. Take steps to verify where your readers get together. A few simple questions and a few hours of research can help produce long-lasting results for your book sales.

LIGHT YOUR KINDLING ON FIRE

Once you've identified where your kindling readers congregate, the most important step is getting them connected with your value. This action is like lighting a match and placing it into a pile of dry leaves and sticks. The spark connects with the flammable tinder, and it bursts into flame. Now you've got a hot fire with the power to spread.

When you present your book's value to the people who need it most, you create a dynamic for emotional combustion. People are looking for entertainment, inspiration, and life change. When they realize your book offers a needed solution, they will feel an internal interest toward purchasing it. And if they buy your book and read it with a positive result, they will burn with enthusiasm and tell others.

For instance, consider what convinces you to pay money for the products that you buy. Most people are fairly skeptical and hate to waste money. We must be mentally and emotionally convinced that a product is worth the price. We can make this decision in a split second, but it happens prior to every purchase. If we can be persuaded that a product will satisfy a need, we'll buy it in a flash. If it's good, we'll tell others.

Let me give some personal examples. I must admit that I'm a sucker for Bruster's real ice cream, especially for the flavor called chocolate raspberry truffle. This ice cream is so unbelievably delicious that I feel like I'm eating heaven on a waffle cone. My brain gets dizzy and my knees go weak whenever I pass by a Bruster's store. I'm so in love with their creamy desserts that I've urged my friends, family, neighbors, and even strangers to try it. Bruster's successfully lit me on fire, and now I'm a word-of-mouth warrior for their ice cream. Silly, I know. But, it's true.

Here's the same dynamic from a more serious point of view. I went through a painful divorce at age 28 that left me devastated. My wife walked out on me, and I walked down a difficult road for several years. That situation led me to question everything I knew about relationships. How do you recover from such pain? How do you pick up the pieces and move on? How can you allow yourself to be vulnerable again after you've been hurt? Is it possible to make love last?

Along came a book called, *Safe People*, by Henry Cloud and John Townsend. A friend who knew my struggle recommended it to me. I went into a bookstore and found the book on the shelf. As I flipped through some of the pages, I began to read answers to some of my questions. So I bought the book, took it home, and devoured it in a matter of days. By the time I was finished, the authors had helped me create a new, wiser view of relationships. A fresh sense of hope and discernment boosted my confidence to interact with people. To this day, I credit that book as one of the tools that helped rally me out of despair and build an incredible new marriage with my wife Ashley.

Looking back, you can see how I was prime kindling for the book, *Safe People*. I was in a desperate situation and needed what the authors could provide. Once I was exposed to the authors' principles, my life changed and burned hot with enthusiasm for their message. My appreciation for the results they helped me experience has never weakened, and I've recommended that book to literally hundreds of people. I don't take credit for the book's success. But I do take credit for helping spread their wildfire to a wider audience around me.

Whether you write fiction or nonfiction, marketing your book is much easier if you spend your time marketing to the people who are most interested in your value. By lighting little pockets of kindling across the country (even around the world), you set the stage to build a massive wildfire that consumes as many people as possible.

If you're still skeptical, let's look at this idea from the opposite point of view. You could spend your time and money promoting your book to large masses of people everywhere who don't need your value. For example, you could buy advertising space on television, purchase a full-page ad in *The New York Times* (over $50,000), or blanket the country with media kits and postcard mailings. The problem with that strategy is twofold. First, those tactics are extremely expensive. You must pay big-time for that kind of large-scale exposure. If you fail, you will lose a ton of money. Second, the consumer is now in control of the advertising world. We live in a new age where people can literally tune out, delete, fast-forward, or ignore any advertising that doesn't interest them.

For instance, I hate most television commercials. They're loud, annoying, and rarely talk about a product or service that interests me. So when I watch television, I usually record all of the shows ahead of time and fast- forward through the commercials. In addition, I rarely listen to radio or read the newspaper. Instead, I listen to my own library of songs on my iPod and get the daily news from specific websites or apps on my iPad. And I'm not alone.

Consumers have the power to turn off the advertisements in their lives. We are in control of what we watch, hear, and read more than ever before. This new dynamic doesn't bode well for advertisers and authors who want to promote their books to a large generic audience.

This new dynamic explains why marketing your book via a targeted approach is a better way. Most people today respond less to advertisements and more to word-of-mouth recommendations and straightforward explanations of value. If you answer the question "What's in it for me?" you stand a better chance of grabbing the public's attention.

When you know your book's value, who needs it the most, and where those people congregate, you can light them on fire in several ways. Consider the following tactics and choose the options that make the most sense for your kindling group.

Sampling

The readers that make up your tinder are still a naturally skeptical audience. People tend to distrust what is new or what they don't know. This attitude is a natural part of our self-preservation system. If we're not familiar with something, we usually see it as a risk.

By offering your kindling group free samples, however, you allow them to overcome their skepticism on their own and recategorize your book from *risky* to *rewarding*. Rather than argue with your audience or attempt to coerce it to your point of view, sampling allows people to agree using their own will. This happens by creating methods or environments to let people experience your book in a positive light.

For example, the food industry realized many years ago that if you let people taste a new product, they're more likely to purchase it. That's why they offer free samples at grocery stores, fast-food restaurants, shopping malls, and concerts. With sampling, you can control a large part of the process and use it in your favor. You can choose what sample to offer, where and when to offer it, and how people can take the next step.

In publishing, the most common practice of sampling involves mailing advance reader copies (ARCs) to well-known reviewers and offering a sample chapter to the public via websites. These tactics are no-brainers and should be offered for every book you write. The question is, though, which chapter should you offer as a sample? With nonfiction, there's a frequent complaint among readers that a book's first chapter rarely offers any value. Too many opening chapters just set the stage without providing enough information for the reader to take the book from risk to reward. Thus, the author isn't really sampling. Instead, she's generating more distrust.

In some cases, it may be wiser to offer a sample chapter from the middle of your book. It must be one that provides more detail and tangible value. Another option is to group together compelling segments from several chapters throughout the book, rather than one chapter by itself. Try your sampling ideas on a few people and get their reaction before going public.

If you're a first-time unknown author with no platform, I recommend giving away your entire book for free as an e-book for a limited time, such as thirty days. The electronic version prevents you from buying hundreds of copies to hand out and allows word of mouth to happen faster. If you can't build buzz by giving away your book for free, then your book may not be very good.

Too many authors and publishers don't put enough thought into their sampling techniques. Don't make this mistake. When you engage in sampling, determine if you're giving real value for the reader to overcome their skepticism and taste the results your book can offer. I'm not suggesting that you give away the farm forever. There's a big difference between giving a sample and giving unlimited access to the restaurant. However, if your sample isn't perceived as tasty, no amount of sweet talk will win readers over.

Offer free resources

A great way to light up your kindling group is to give them free resources that highlight the value in your book. You could offer articles, videos, pictures, audio clips, maps, pictures, resource guides, and/or appendices. In Chapter 11, I'll go into more detail about how to create these important marketing tools. But, for now, follow this rule of thumb: Don't create a free resource unless it showcases your expertise. Thus, if the reader doesn't learn anything substantial, doesn't receive tangible entertainment, or wouldn't tell someone else about it, don't offer it. Otherwise your kindling group will snuff out the fire that you're hoping to start.

For example, if you wrote a romance novel that's set in Paris, use your research to provide articles that give helpful travel tips, little-known facts about the city, recommended restaurants to visit, recipes, videos, or historical background. If you want to be quirky, you could even offer a free resource that teaches the reader how to say romantic phrases in French, lists the best smooching spots in Paris, or explains how Parisian women plan a wedding.

The options for creating free resources are endless. You simply need to give value that convinces the recipient that your book is worth purchasing. You're on the right track if you can make people think, "Wow, I got so much value from this helpful resource for free. Imagine how much more value I'll get if I buy the author's book!"

Utilize endorsements and success stories

Another way to help people overcome their doubt about your book is by getting a recommendation from someone they trust. This is why you see major corporations hire well-known actors, athletes, and public figures to endorse their products.

For instance, one of my clients wrote a book called *Made to Crave* that deals with the subject of food addiction and weight loss. Through her personal connections, this author created focus groups and sought testimonials from her early readers. In the process, she received incredible word of mouth via a heartfelt success story from *American Idol* contestant and award-winning gospel singer, Mandisa. After reading the author's book, Mandisa achieved and maintained her desired weight for the first time in many years. The author used this success story to gain credibility with her kindling group by using Mandisa as a person they could trust. Women who see her success think, "If that book helped Mandisa, maybe it will help me."

To ignite your tinder, you don't have to get a national TV personality or famous musician to endorse your message. But you do need to get someone that your kindling group respects. Doing so helps grab awareness, removes skepticism, and fosters word of mouth.

HOW TO STRIKE THE MATCH

Once you've identified your kindling group and created tools to ignite them, heed these words before you try to light the fire: Don't talk about your book. Yes, that's what I said. I know it sounds counterintuitive, but don't push your book, plug it, promote it, or hassle people about buying it...unless someone asks you first. Instead, talk about the value that you enjoy helping people experience.

I've watched too many authors blow great marketing opportunities by acting like shameless, multilevel marketers. They find an audience who seems like a perfect fit, and then they proceed to unload a guilt trip or used-car salesman tactics on those poor individuals. For example, I've seen authors join groups and immediately tell everyone that they're a writer, drop hints that they have new book, pass out coupons, beg people to help spike their Amazon ranking, or spam people with annoying e-mails on a daily basis. The people in these groups recoil because it's uncomfortable to watch the author act like a fool. The author, after all, is supposed to be an expert. Don't reduce yourself to a cheesy book hawker.

You won't start a fire with your kindling group by throwing a match in their face. You've got to light a fire in their minds by appealing to their self-interest. Put yourself in the position of a reader and ask, "What would make my book appealing to me? What value can I offer that meets their needs?" Will this approach take longer than blatant self-promotion? In the short run, yes. But in the long run you'll gain their trust.

Position yourself as a partner, an ally, or an expert who can help. This stance will create a perception of trust, rather than someone who is using a group just to get book sales.

For example, if your kindling group belongs to a specific organization, such as a worker's union, pastors network, college fraternity, or business trade association, don't blanket the group with advertisements and solicitations. Instead, try these ideas to garner legitimate exposure:

- Offer to provide free articles for the group's newsletter.
- Ask to be a speaker at the group's next conference.
- Provide a specialized resource or exclusive discount for the group.
- Provide free Q&A to the group's members.
- Volunteer your time and expertise at one of the group's events.

In places where your kindling group may congregate online, such as forums, websites, or social media pages, take the same approach. Remember that social media is meant to be social, not commercial. People don't want to endure an appeal to buy your stuff. Instead, join the group, lay low, and act like one of the members. Take part in some online conversations and build rapport. If people ask what you do, it's okay to mention that you're an author. But, focus on your value and expertise, not your latest book to sell. Use these ideas to gain trust:

- Offer interesting or humorous videos that the group can enjoy and share.
- Supply sample chapters and free resources for everyone to download and distribute.
- Talk about the research you conducted for your book and share it with the group. Give links to websites that supply more detail. Act like an expert within the group.
- Host online discussions or Q&A sessions based on your book's topic and provide assistance.
- Provoke opinions with counterintuitive remarks from your book to back up your point of view.

You might be thinking, "But, my kindling groups congregate in hundreds of different places. I don't have time to join a bunch of clubs, try to become everyone's buddy, and gain their trust." I understand your concern. All of us are busy. However, you can maximize your efforts by doing similar tactics for each group. You don't have to offer exclusive advice or specific content for each organization. It's okay to use the same approach to help connect with as many people as your time allows—as long as your value actually impresses them.

I'm not advocating that you join every Facebook group, Google+ circle, or trade association imaginable and spend all of your time trying to befriend everyone. Just concentrate on the largest groups that are desperate for your value and possess the means to buy your book. Make genuine contact with these groups as a partner who has their best interests in mind. The world doesn't need more authors. The world needs more experts and entertainers who can truly stimulate the mind.

Summary

Millions of people around the world congregate based on shared needs and interests. Thus, they usually interact with other people and know like-minded groups with the same need. If you work to gain trust with one group, they will likely pass word of mouth about you to the other groups whom they know, thereby helping to market your book for you. A wildfire doesn't spread because someone lights a match a thousand times in the woods. Wildfires occur because one spark ignites the tinder, which kindles the surrounding vegetation, sticks, and trees.

Likewise, if you identify the kindling for your book, find where that group gathers, and light it with a matchstick of value, your book sales will take off and a wildfire will spread on your behalf. The next chapter will explain how to turn up the heat even more and make sure they never forget who you are.

MAKE YOUR MARK WITH AN AUTHOR BRAND

Imagine this situation happening to you:

- Author gets on a plane.
- Person sitting in the adjacent seat strikes up a conversation.
- As they talk, the author is asked what she does for a living.
- Author doesn't mention that she writes books. Instead, she replies, "I'm the Manners Mentor. I help parents train their children in manners to become respectful adults, and I help business people move up the corporate ladder by applying proper etiquette."
- Person on the plane happens to work for a daily TV show syndicated across America.
- Person gets off the plane and tells his boss the next day, "I just met the Manners Mentor. She could provide a lot of value to our television audience as an interesting guest."
- Boss of the television show says, "Let's book the *Manners Mentor* on our show right away."

- Author receives request to be interviewed on national television three days later.
- Author appears as the Manners Mentor and provides helpful information to viewers.
- Impressed, the boss of the television shows says, "You did a great job! Would you like to become a regular guest on our show and feature your expertise on our website?"
- Author now has steady opportunities to promote her resources to a nationwide audience.

This true story illustrates the inherent power of a great brand. It happened to an author I know who realized the importance of standing out from the crowd. By creating a personal brand, she no longer became just another author. Instead she is recognized as the go-to girl for a specific type of expertise. Her value-based brand as the *Manners Mentor* acts like a magnet that draws people to her.

If you create a dynamic author brand, you no longer get lost in the shuffle with thousands of other writers. Instead you become a leading source of information or inspiration for leaders and readers, regardless of whether you write fiction or nonfiction. Building a powerful brand will help you reach a larger audience with less effort.

BE INTERESTING OR BE INVISIBLE

In his book, *Word of Mouth Marketing*, Andy Sernovitz states:

"Advertising is the price of being boring."

I couldn't agree more. If you're an author who is considered interesting, memorable, and full of value, you won't need to advertise because people will naturally tell their friends about your books. You will get all of the word of mouth you want. However, this process won't take place if people do not associate you with something positive in their mind.

First, make sure you have the proper understanding of a brand. As human beings, we are finite people with limited brains who can't remember everything we see. Nor can we recall everything we learn. Yet, we live in a society that bombards us with overwhelming amounts of information. How do we make sense of it all? Branding.

When you think about the concept of branding, you might hearken back to the Wild West days when ranchers branded their cattle. This process still happens today, because it helps both the owner and the public identify whose cattle belongs to whom. Using a hot brand to sear the ranch's logo onto the side of a cow leaves a lasting mark that everyone can see and remember. Fortunately building an author brand isn't as painful, but it creates the same benefit.

Since people can't remember everything they encounter, authors need a way to stay stuck in the public's mind—ready to be recalled at a moment's notice. But the average person's brain is swirling with so much information that they can't keep track of everything. So a brand creates a mental shortcut that's easy to remember.

Unless you're a household name, most people don't know you exist. So when someone first hears about you or your books, they have no context for who you are or the value you might offer. This uncertain position puts you at a disadvantage in the public's mind, because their uncertainty creates a hesitancy to buy your books. In contrast, when you build a brand that explains your value up front, people who have never heard of you are able to feel a positive connection to you from the very beginning.

For instance, I don't have to try and remember that the *Manners Mentor* is an author named Maralee McKee. I don't have to recall that she helps businesspeople move up the corporate ladder, apply proper etiquette, or train children to be polite. That's too much information to memorize. Heck, I probably wouldn't remember how to spell her name correctly. It's her brand that reminds me how she helps people. With three simple words, I know who Maralee is, the expertise she provides, and the results she can deliver.

The benefit of a strong brand is that it creates a positive impression on your audience and stays lodged in their collective subconscious, ready to be recalled. Since it's easy for me to remember the *Manners Mentor*, it's easy for me to spread word of mouth and tell others about her. For instance, anytime I meet someone who's looking for a job, I can recommend that they check out the *Manners Mentor* to prepare for their next interview. If I meet a parent who is struggling with a misbehaving child, I can point them to the *Manners Mentor* for assistance. Her brand has been seared into my mind as a shortcut that I can quickly remember.

Your goal as an author should be to create the same dynamic. There's so much competition in the marketplace, you can easily get lost in the noise of voices and choices. By building a brand that generates a positive association that lasts, you help prevent people from forgetting about you.

Consider how major corporations spend millions of dollars to build a strong brand. If they can get you to keep a positive connection locked in your mind, then you'll be more likely to purchase their products. For instance, here are some examples of famous company brands:

Walmart: "Save money. Live better."

Maxwell House: "Good 'til the last drop"

National Geographic Channel: "Live curious."

Lowe's: "Let's build something together."

What do these corporate brands have in common? They're short, memorable, and they answer the all-important question that consumers ask, "What's in it for me?"

Brevity, remembrance, and value are critical to creating a powerful brand. Keep in mind, however, that your focus should lie primarily on explaining the value that you provide. Cleverness is cool, but companies know that it takes more than just a witty phrase to satisfy today's savvy consumer. Your job is no different. Read on about the process of developing a compelling author brand.

SEVEN PRINCIPLES FOR CREATING
AN EFFECTIVE BRAND

Your personal name is ultimately your best brand, because it's a direct reflection of you. For instance, as your career grows, you hope people will eventually say, "Give me any book by Jane Doe, and I'll read it." However, if you're not yet a household name, then creating a value-based brand is the best option to help make a name for yourself. Below are seven principles designed to guide you through the process:

1. YOU ALREADY HAVE A BRAND WHETHER YOU LIKE IT OR NOT, AND IT'S USUALLY NEGATIVE UNLESS YOU TAKE PRO-ACTIVE STEPS TO CONTROL IT. In his book, *How to Establish a Unique Brand in the Consulting Profession,* management consultant, Alan Weiss says:

> "Branding will occur by default, whether you intend it to or not. Therefore, it's imperative to create the brand that will provide the maximum possible marketing benefit. To believe this to be unimportant is equivalent to believing that your attire or letterhead is unimportant."

People are branding you every day, because their finite brains need ways to remember everything around them. Thus, a brand taps into the mental function of memory. However, if you let other people brand you, the outcome will usually be negative. That's because people don't fully know who you are. They're working off of limited information. Therefore, you must actively manage your brand to create a perception among readers of your book's uniqueness, value, and expertise.

2. A GREAT BRAND MAKES YOU STAND OUT FROM THE MYR-IAD CHOICES OF OTHER AUTHORS. This may sound obvious, but many writers still overlook the fact. You need a brand that is memorable and makes it easy for people to pass on word of mouth about you. For instance, the *Manners Mentor* beautifully illustrates this point.

3. A GREAT BRAND GENERATES A SENSE OF APPEALING CURIOSITY THAT MAKES PEOPLE WANT TO FIND OUT MORE ABOUT YOU. If you can't make readers and leaders feel a magnetic attraction to you and your books, your brand isn't working. Start over and develop a better one.

4. A GREAT BRAND COMMUNICATES THE KIND OF RESULTS THAT YOU CAN PRODUCE FOR YOUR READERS. It's not enough to simply have a clever catchphrase or tagline. Your brand must express how you make other people's lives better. In the corporate world, top brands achieve this goal. For example, Walmart's brand is "Save Money. Live Better." This phrase implies that my life will be better if I shop at Walmart, because I'll be saving money.

A great brand focuses more on communicating value, rather than cleverness. A catchy phrase is helpful, but not if it fails to communicate the help that you and your books provide. Readers need to know the return on investment they'll receive from buying your books. Thus, your brand must explain how you will improve the reader's condition. For instance, I helped an author named Mary Southerland develop the brand tagline, "The Stress-Buster," which is easy to remember. But more important, readers know exactly how their life will be improved by reading Mary's books: We all need less stress in our lives.

5. A GREAT BRAND SHOULD ESTABLISH YOUR BOOK AS THE BEST CHOICE IN THE MARKETPLACE. Household names, such as Martha Stewart, Dave Ramsey, and Dr. Phil, are powerful brands because they're considered the best in their business. They're regarded as the go-to guy or girl for home decorating, personal finance, and counseling. Likewise, your brand should position you as the best option. When your brand becomes synonymous with quality, you've got a powerful marketing force at your disposal.

6. A GREAT BRAND SHOULD REFLECT YOUR PASSION, BECAUSE YOU ARE SOLELY RESPONSIBLE TO GET IT IN FRONT

OF THE WORLD. No one else can promote your brand better than you. It's like trying on a new dress or a suit. You buy the one that best fits you and makes you feel confident. When you create your brand, you should feel comfortable, positive, and excited to use it.

7. YOUR BRAND SHOULD ALSO APPEAL TO THE PEOPLE WHO HAVE THE DECISION-MAKING POWER AND MONEY TO BUY YOUR BOOKS. If your brand appeals to influential leaders, media producers, literary agents, and publishing editors, then you're especially on the right track. They are the individuals who can open doors to larger opportunities for exposure.

WD **BONUS ONLINE CONTENT:** Download the article "But I'm a Bestselling Author; Isn't That My Brand?" at bookwildfire. com and writersdigest.com/book-wildfire-downloads

HOW TO CREATE AN AUTHOR BRAND

By now, I hope you're convinced of the importance of having a strong author brand. But you could be wondering how to utilize the preceding principles to build a new brand from scratch. Here's a step-by-step process that I've used successfully with many of my fiction and nonfiction clients.

Step 1—Create value statements for all of your books.

The most effective brands focus on the benefits that the author's audience receives. Likewise, your brand should communicate the positive results that readers attain from purchasing your books. In Chapter 1, we discussed how to create value statements that identify those particular results. Therefore, your first step to building a brand is to identify and write specific value statements for each of your books. The more statements you create, the more clearly you'll be able to express your value.

Keep in mind that your brand needs to focus on your future, not only the past. So write value statements for any upcoming books that you have contracted or planned with your publisher or literary agent. This may be difficult if you haven't had an opportunity to test your material on readers. However, you should have a basic grasp on the results that you're trying to create, because that's one of the reasons behind writing your book in the first place.

To offer an example, I've displayed a sample from one of my nonfiction clients. Below are ten of the fifty value statements business author, Dr. Paul White, wrote:

> Dr. Paul White will help you:
>
> 1. Boost workplace trust by helping co-workers genuinely value one another.
> 2. Improve your employees' ability to deal with difficult colleagues.
> 3. Improve the quality of work performed by your team members.
> 4. Lessen fatigue created by the revolving door of losing staff and training new employees.
> 5. Make your organization the top choice where volunteers want to serve.
> 6. Assist confused individuals with developing a successful and satisfying career path.
> 7. Reduce the amount of "headaches" created by disgruntled employees.
> 8. Enjoy your next job better by understanding the factors that create satisfaction and success.
> 9. Decrease workplace cynicism by training supervisors to express authentic appreciation.
> 10. Create a more positive work environment that reduces apathy and frustration among staff.

Step 2—Analyze your value statements for a central theme.
After you've generated a list of specific results for all of your past, current, and future books, analyze your list for common themes. Take your value statements and mix them up, so that they become

one, long, bulleted list that's not associated with any particular book. Then read over this list repeatedly and look for distinct patterns. Usually there will be a thread that runs through your value statements and reflects your brand.

For instance, when you read Dr. White's value statements, what patterns do you see? As he and I worked together, we noticed several recurring themes, such as:

- Making office environments more satisfying places to work
- Creating a more positive overall attitude among employees
- Handling difficult people and preventing employee turnover

One pattern really jumped out: In most of his value statements, Dr. White's results pertained to *improving business relationships and helping co-workers get along better.* When executives and employees mutually support one another, the organization becomes more productive. We agreed that this idea was his main theme and moved to the next step.

Step 3—Create a short phrase that sums up that pattern.

Once you've identified a central theme that describes your overall value, the goal is to sum it up in a short phrase. This phrase, sometimes called a tagline, serves as the foundation for your new brand. To succeed at this step, you must draw on your creative ability with words. Your phrase should be no more than seven words, riveted on your value, and easy to remember. Below are some of the ideas that Dr. White and I generated together:

- Growing the People Side of Business
- The Workplace Whisperer
- Powering the Relationships of Business
- Powering Business by Empowering People
- Making Work Relationships Work

Which of these phrases do you like best? The process isn't a question of right or wrong. The goal is to build a brand that explains your value in the most captivating and memorable manner. In Dr. White's case, he felt that the tagline, "Making Work Relationships Work," best reflected his expertise and desire to help people. His response was, "When I say that phrase, it makes me feel proud and excited to tell others about what I do." However, this feeling may not occur immediately, which leads to our next step.

Step 4—Test your new branding phrase for emotional fit and appeal.

When you create a new tagline, you may instantly fall in love with an idea and feel like you're done. If you rush the process, however, you could damage the full potential of your brand.

Think of building your new brand like buying new clothes. When you go shopping, you see various options hanging on racks in the store. You choose some outfits that look appealing, but you try them on before you decide to buy. The next part is the real test. You take the desired outfit home and wear it in public.

The first time you wear a new outfit in front of other people is actually the most crucial moment of the decision process. If the outfit makes you feel comfortable and confident, then you'll continue to wear it over and over. In contrast, if the outfit makes you feel embarrassed or awkward, then you'll probably return it or let it gather dust in your closet.

Take this same approach when creating your brand. As you develop a new tagline, try it out on people. Say it aloud to your friends. Put it in your email signature file. Tell your publisher or literary agent. Ideally you want people whom know you well to respond, "Yes, that's an accurate summation of the value I've seen you create for me or other people."

Examine whether you feel comfortable saying your brand in front of others. If it's a struggle, that's a problem because your brand can't help you sell books if you don't like to use it. You may be introverted, but this trial period is a time to muster up some initiative because developing a brand is crucial to your success.

In addition, beware of how you gauge the feedback that you receive. Do NOT create a new tagline and just test it on a few friends and family members. That's too narrow, and you won't get honest or professional feedback from that group. You need to test your new brand on actual readers and people within your target audience. They're the ones who can actually buy your books, so their opinion should matter most. Get their input by bringing it up in conversation, posting the idea in a newsletter, or mentioning it on your social media page.

Listen to the feedback, and pay attention to the majority. Don't let a few negative critics kill your options. You will never please everybody. Don't base your decision on waiting for a unanimous response. Listen for consistent patterns in people's reactions.

Consider these questions:

- Is your brand tagline easy to say out loud, or do you trip over the words in the phrase? A good tagline should flow easily out of your mouth without having to think about it.

- Do most people understand what your brand means, or do you have to explain the phrase after you say it? If you have to explain yourself, then you need to come up with a better option that prevents confusion.

- Can people remember your brand if you ask them a day or a week later? If your brand is hard to recall, it won't be very effective.

- Do people agree that your brand answers the question, "What's in it for me?" Your brand needs to communicate the results that people will receive.

If you can answer yes to these questions, then you're on the right track. If not, take time to analyze your value statements again and create some new options to test. Don't rush the process. You may need a few weeks or a few months to gain clarity. Take time to build your brand on a solid foundation.

EXAMPLES OF EFFECTIVE AUTHOR BRANDS

Below is a list of well known fiction and nonfiction author taglines that are good examples of value-based brands. Respect the work of these authors by not copying them. Instead use them as a guide to create an equally powerful tagline for yourself.

Fiction:

Patricia Cornwell—Forensic Fiction
Debbie Macomber—Wherever You Are, Debbie Takes You Home
Brandilyn Collins—Seatbelt Suspense
Wanda Brunstetter—Lose Your Heart in the Amish Life
Susan Meissner—Fiction for the Restless Reader

Nonfiction:

Hal Runkel—ScreamFree Parenting
Cesar Millan—The Dog Whisperer
Dave Ramsey—Financial Peace
Dr. Mehmet Oz—The YOU Doctor
Rick Warren—The Purpose-Driven Life

WD **BONUS ONLINE CONTENT:** Download the article "Will a Brand Fence Me In?" at bookwildfire.com and writersdigest.com/book-wildfire-downloads

SPREAD YOUR BRAND ACROSS THE LAND

Once you've created a brand that communicates your value to readers, you must use it or lose it. Consider the story of Maralee McKee at the beginning of this chapter. She could either tell people that she's the *Manners Mentor* or say she's an author who writes books on etiquette. Which option do you think will stick in people's minds and generate curiosity?

If Maralee doesn't use her brand, it will eventually disappear into oblivion and stunt her marketing efforts. You're in the same position. Once you have an author brand, you must use it consistently with conviction in order to reap the benefits. Otherwise people won't know your brand exists, so they won't be able to remember you or your value.

If you're an introverted author, I understand that you may struggle to express your brand publicly. If you struggle in this manner, look at it from two viewpoints. First, you may have an ineffective brand that fails to provoke your passion. In that case, try constructing a better option. If you still find yourself hesitant after a few tries, you may need to address some shyness or self-esteem issues that could be holding you back. Unless you're a world-class writer who can capture readers with your prose, you must get comfortable marketing your message. Many of my introverted clients found it easier to promote their books when they focused on their value, rather than themselves.

I'm not suggesting that reticent authors start acting cheesy or try to conjure up false bravado. When you're in public, focus on working your brand smoothly into conversation, such as saying, "I write books that help people live their calling with confidence" or "I write stories about characters who turn trials into triumph."

Whether you are shy or bold, a brand will work only if the public hears it repeatedly. Here are several ways to put your brand into action.

1. Business correspondence

Make your brand synonymous with your name so they are always mentioned together. For instance, put your brand on all of your printed promotional items, such as business cards, flyers, bookmarks, and newsletters. In addition, include your brand tagline on all of your electronic correspondence, such as e-mails, texts, Twitter, and Facebook posts. If you want to appear professional, I suggest finishing your e-mails with a signature file in the following format:

Rob Eagar (Your name)

WildFire Marketing (Company name if applicable)

Spread Your Message Like Wildfire (Brand tagline)

Phone: 1-800-267-2045 (Business or cell phone number)

Web: www.StartaWildfire.com (Website address)

Email: Rob@StartaWildfire.com (E-mail address)

Twitter: www.Twitter.com/robeagar (Link to your social media page)

2. Website banner

Your website is one of your most important marketing tools, so place your brand in a prominent place within the top header of your home page. Most authors arrange their head shot, name, and tagline as a connected group in this top banner. Use that banner consistently throughout your website. Keep your brand consistent online by using the same website artwork on your social media pages and e-newsletters.

3. Personal bio

When people read your bio, they should be impressed by your value, not your credentials. So start your bio with your brand tagline. Then use the rest of your bio to describe the results you've created for people via your accomplishments, publishing history, media appearances, and education. You want people to read your bio and finish with your brand lodged in their mind.

4. Spin-off products

Don't limit your brand to just your books. Create accompanying products that utilize the power of your tagline. For instance, author and family therapist, Hal Runkel, took his best-selling book, *ScreamFree Parenting*, and turned it into a wide range of complementary products and services. If you visit his website, www.ScreamFree.com, you will find choices, such as:

> The ScreamFree Institute
> ScreamFree Parenting book
> ScreamFree Parenting video study kit

ScreamFree Parenting study guide
ScreamFree Marriage book
ScreamFree Marriage webinars
ScreamFree Marriage audio downloads
ScreamFree personal coaching

If you have a powerful brand, parlay it into an information empire. How many related spin-off products could you create right now?

5. In conversation

Besides putting your brand on all marketing materials, don't forget to use it in conversation with others. When someone asks what you do or what you book is about, respond by stating your brand and explaining the specific results you create for people. Say your brand a few times so that people can remember it. Don't be tacky, but don't be shy either.

You can't help, entertain, or inspire people if they don't know that you exist. And they can't spread word of mouth if they can't remember who you are. Your brand can help attract readers to your books and prevent them from forgetting you.

When people ask me what I do, I don't say that I'm an author or a consultant. My initial response is usually: "I help people spread their message like a wildfire, whether you're an author selling books or a business executive selling services. If you have a message that needs spreading, I can help you turn it into a wildfire." You could debate whether my response is corny, but there's no debating the number of people who've approached me months after our first meeting and said, "I've never forgotten that you're the 'wildfire guy.' It's easy for me to tell other people about what you do." Those words are music to my ears. I want you to enjoy the same tune.

 BONUS ONLINE CONTENT: Download the article "If I Have a Brand Do I Need a Logo?" at bookwildfire.com and writersdigest.com/book-wildfire-downloads

Summary

You have an author brand whether you know it or not. If you don't know your brand, then you may be considered just another ordinary author writing books. Yet you have the power to positively influence the public's perception of who you are. When you create a powerful brand, you position yourself as the go-to person for a specific need, genre, or interest. This recognition helps separate your books from the pack and stand out in a crowded marketplace. Why be bland when you can have a brand?

CHAPTER 4

HOW TO BUILD BOOK-MARKETING TOOLS INTO YOUR MANUSCRIPT

I've got a little secret to share. Keep quiet and come closer to the page. What if I told you that selling books might be a lot easier than you think? I know you may not believe me. But pay attention, because here's the deal: Sometimes people don't need much convincing to buy a book. Sometimes they need only one little reason, and nothing more.

You might think I'm crazy, but I can prove this secret is true. For example, how many times have you ever waited to buy a book until you could read through half of the chapters at the library or a bookstore? Probably never. How many times have you ever bought a book without reading one page of it? Probably a lot.

I bet you've even bought a book without ever holding it in your hands. Instead you heard the author speak about it at an event or got a word-of-mouth recommendation that drove you to make the purchase online. Do you see what I mean? This is the secret: Many people will buy a book without ever seeing the content. They just need one convincing reason to buy. As the author, you can create persuasive reasons that tip the buying scale in your favor. This chapter will show how to utilize this little-known concept to your advantage.

THE POWER OF A BUILT-IN BOOK-MARKETING TOOL

There's an overlooked secret that many authors, editors, and publishers miss when it comes to marketing books. The secret is that you can put tools within a book manuscript that act as lighter fluid to help ignite word of mouth and the purchasing process. I call them "built-in book-marketing tools." These tools are nuggets of content designed to spike reader interest that you place in your manuscript deliberately.

Here's an example: Many years ago, I began my author career by writing a book called, *Dating with Pure Passion*. As the title conveys, the book helped single adults navigate the complex dating process and build a passionate, lasting marriage. As I traveled across North America promoting this book, I stumbled upon an unusual marketing phenomenon.

When I had written the manuscript, I haphazardly inserted a short section of content in Chapter 9 called, "31 Character Questions." The point of this section was to help the reader manage the awkward process of determining if the person they were dating exhibited integrity. I added this material, because I found that many single adults didn't know how to ask tough questions and make this critical distinction. So I took the notion of character, broke it into different components, and included a list of four or five questions under each component. In all, the list totaled thirty-one questions. I thought it was a nice section, but I initially didn't regard it as anything important.

As I began to promote my book at speaking engagements, something interesting happened. In one of my presentations, I briefly mentioned my list of thirty-one character questions. I didn't go through all thirty-one questions, just four or five, and then moved on to my next topic. When my presentation was over, attendees started rushing over to my resource table saying, "I'd like to buy your book...I *need* those 31 character questions!" And, this didn't happen just once. It happened over and over as I traveled across the country.

In addition, I began to see a similar spike in sales when I mentioned the thirty-one character questions during a media interview or gave them away as a free handout on college campuses. In essence, that little list of thirty-one questions turned into a convincing reason for people to buy my book.

You could argue that people were responding to an emotional by-product of attending my event or simply following a herd mentality. That's when I would argue back that the positive response whenever I mentioned those thirty-one questions occurred too frequently to be mere coincidence. Through this process, I realized that many people need only one good reason to pull the trigger and buy a book. In my case, that list of thirty-one character questions was the one good reason for a lot of people. Looking back, if I had not put that list of questions in my book and had not mentioned it to the public, I shudder to think how many book sales I would have missed out on.

This example represents the power of building marketing tools into your manuscript. And I stress the word *tools* in the plural sense, because you should increase your odds of success by inserting as many as possible. You won't always know ahead of time which one may create the biggest response.

I'm the first to admit that this idea may be more feasible for nonfiction books than fiction. But there's more potential than a novelist might think. Even better, I've dedicated all of Chapter 14 in this book to highlighting additional ways to market fiction. So don't worry, I've got you covered.

I placed this chapter early in the book, because you need to think about creating built-in marketing tools early in your writing process. Too many authors write their manuscript, turn it in to their editor, get the book printed, and then wake up months later wondering how they can increase book sales.

I suggest that you consider the idea of creating marketing tools long before you turn in your manuscript. Consider the following three reasons: First, I haven't met many editors who understand this promotional secret and encourage their authors to build marketing tools into a manuscript. Second, the earlier you look at creating these tools, the easier it will be to come up with numerous ideas and options for their use. Third, you need time to let your ideas percolate—time to develop and determine the best tools to persuade potential readers to purchase. If you wait until the last minute and rush the process, your creativity will be limited. I was lucky that I stumbled across this secret midway through my promotional tour. Imagine what could have happened if I had harnessed its power from the beginning.

I'm such a believer in this concept that I encourage all of my clients to use it in their books. I worked with a licensed counselor named Leslie Vernick, who wrote an excellent book called, *The Emotionally Destructive Relationship*. Leslie took the time to identify helpful content that could be built in to her manuscript as marketing tools. One of my favorites was a sidebar quiz in her first chapter entitled, "Are you in an emotionally destructive relationship?" Her quiz uses a simple question-and-answer format with a self-ranking scale. In a matter of minutes, readers can determine if they're in a damaging relationship and need Leslie's help.

From Leslie's account, she heard from many people who took her quiz as they browsed through her book in bookstores, downloaded it off her website, or received it as a free handout. By taking the quiz, people realized their relational predicament and quickly convinced themselves that Leslie's book was worth purchasing.

However, Leslie didn't stop with just a quiz. She also loaded her manuscript with other valuable marketing tools, such as a breakout article on "Successful Confrontation." In addition, she developed a simple guide called, "When a Relationship Becomes Destructive," plus a helpful appendix called "A Special Word to People Helpers."

All of these nuggets of content acted as persuasive elements meant to convince readers to purchase her book. Did it work? Leslie's publisher went into six printings during the first year, and the book outsold her five previous books, which didn't have built-in tools. Need I say more?

WHAT IS A BUILT-IN BOOK-MARKETING TOOL?

Building a marketing tool into your book that impresses readers means more than creating a few sidebars, setting up a quiz, or adding an appendix. Success hinges on putting yourself in the position of the reader. Follow these guidelines to assure maximum impact:

1. A built-in book-marketing tool is a concise segment of content that provides the reader with immediate value. And, I stress the word *immediate*. The user must receive direct benefit in that moment to capture his interest. Benefits could include learning something new, solving a problem, getting behind-the-scenes access, or enjoying humor.

2. A built-in book-marketing tool must consist of specific content that the reader can appreciate as is. The tool must be self-contained and provide stand-alone value. In the examples I mentioned earlier, notice how each item was able to work persuasively by itself. The marketing tools were able to provide value independent of the actual book. In contrast, if your marketing tool requires something more in order for the reader to experience value, many will think you're pulling a bait and switch. Thus, your tool won't create the intended result to drive sales. Make sure the tool can impress people on its own.

3. A built-in book-marketing tool should be written in a format that's easy for readers to forward to others. You insert the content into your manuscript. But you will get greater response if you also turn the same tool into a separate promotional piece outside of your book, such as a handout, website quiz, free ar-

ticle, checklist, and/or resource guide. When you put these tools in a portable format, you enable people to spread word of mouth and drive sales.

Keep these three guidelines in mind, and use the following fifteen ideas to help build distinctive marketing tools into your next manuscript.

FIFTEEN WAYS TO BUILD MARKETING TOOLS INTO YOUR BOOK

Each idea that follows represents a separate tool that you could insert into your book. Many will work for both fiction and nonfiction. I encourage you to include as many ideas as possible. Leverage the odds in your favor by using a variety of tools.

1. Reader quizzes

A well-crafted quiz can build emotional curiosity and desire within people to buy your book. Quizzes can convince readers that their current position needs to be adjusted, which helps capitalize on their interest and move them toward making a purchase. The key is to make your quiz concise, easy to understand, and simple to score. You can also suggest recommended next steps once the reader has determined her status. Use your quiz to reveal a misconception, point out an unrealistic perspective, or challenge people's understanding of a specific issue, thereby creating the need for your book.

2. List of helpful questions or communication scripts

Oftentimes people don't know what they don't know. In other words, they're unaware of their ignorance and need someone to spell it out and, further, tell them what to do in a specific situation. You can use your expertise to educate and assist people by providing a list of specific questions to ask or a script to follow that guides them down the right path.

As mentioned earlier, this idea worked well for me when I created my list of "31 Character Questions." I've seen authors use the same idea to provide questions that help readers know what to ask when buying a car, talking with their doctor, purchasing insurance, meeting with a counselor, communicating with their spouse, or joining a new organization. Take some portion of the expertise within your book and break it into a separate element that helps the reader solve a specific problem.

3. How-to articles
Most people appreciate brief articles that explain how to do something in a simple, straightforward manner. In most nonfiction books, there are usually several places where you could insert a separate instructional article that acts as a built-in book-marketing tool. As you research and write your manuscript, take note of the most frequently asked questions or problems you run across. If you find that many people are perplexed by the same issue, write a brief, stand-alone article that directly tackles the issue.

Be sure you give a complete answer in your article, rather than making the reader need the rest of your book for the solution. You want to maximize the power of the article and increase your ability to use it as a portable marketing tool that can work in different formats, both online and off. If your article is good, it will lead the reader to believe that your book is even better.

4. Bonus back matter and appendices
You can insert marketing tools into the back section of your book, such as an appendix, special report, or bonus materials section. Seed business books with sample scripts that readers could use with clients, diagrams and worksheets for strategy meetings, resource and vendor guides to find outside labor, or employee hiring questionnaires.

A book that's famous for top-notch back matter is the perennial bestseller by Richard Bolles titled, *What Color is Your Parachute?* The back of this book is filled with thorough appendices that cover topics, such as "Finding Your Mission in Life" and "A Guide to Choosing a Career Coach or Counselor." Prospective buyers consider these materials as big plusses, because they view the author as doing some of the work for them. It's comforting for people when they see that they don't have to figure out the next step on their own. Thus, the extra value of your back matter materials can be worth the purchase price alone.

5. Study guides
An integrated study guide can also be used to boost group sales of a book. I've personally used this idea in my previous books and it resulted in a great response. I recommend putting study materials or discussion questions at the end of each chapter, rather than the appendix because it's easier for the reader to follow along.

Depending on the nature of your content, you could also include a separate guide that helps leaders foster group interaction with your book. Some groups don't like having to purchase both a book and a separate workbook. By integrating the two, readers perceive a beneficial cost savings. With that mind-set, it can be easier for leaders to justify buying your book in case quantities.

6. Key research or statistics
If your book is focused around important research, consider creating a stand-alone marketing tool based on the summary of your key findings. In addition, you could highlight the most fascinating statistics, graphs, or charts that prove the importance of your investigation.

Too many research-based books emphasize the problem without providing concrete answers. Avoid this situation by offering a separate section that tells the reader what he can do to help right now. Provide explicit steps and resources that assist the reader to take action. Format the content so that someone who doesn't have your book could be empowered.

7. Exclusive or rare content
If your manuscript is a memoir or biography, you could include a section of exclusive photos, letters, or documents made available

only within your book. For instance, tennis superstar Andre Agassi, inserted several pages of rare, behind-the-scenes photos in his popular biography, *Open*. The pictures helped walk the reader through different time periods in his life as the book progressed.

By "leaking" a few of these previously restricted items through the media or social networking sites, you can help build buzz for your book. Emphasize the rare quality and quantity of this content. When the public realizes they can get their hands on the exclusive content only by buying your book, they'll be more inclined to purchase.

8. Author interview or Q&A section

Book shoppers appreciate authors who explain why they wrote their book, what drove them through the process, and what led them to the book's conclusion. This content acts like a sneak peek into the mind of the author. People enjoy understanding how the creative development and writing process operates for other people.

You can take advantage of this consumer desire by including a "Q&A with the author" interview section in your manuscript. Be sure to give depth to your answers and allow yourself to be vulnerable. Readers enjoy feeling like they're getting to know the author personally. The benefit of creating this tool is that you can make it available to the public as a marketing aid that draws people and also rounds out the reading experience for those who purchase your book.

9. Add bits of humor: cartoons, jokes, top ten lists

Humor can be an incredibly powerful book-marketing tool. If you have funny jokes, cartoons, pictures, or top ten lists pertinent to your book's theme, you can build them into your manuscript. For good examples, check out books by TV comedy personalities Jon Stewart and Stephen Colbert. Their books, such as *Earth: A Visitor's Guide to the Human Race* and *I am America (and So Can You)*, are filled with zany vignettes, images, and diagrams.

Before you attempt to include humor in your book, make sure that you have a solid grasp on the type of audience you're trying to reach. If people fail to connect with your style of wit, this strategy could backfire and hurt your book's word of mouth. However, if you have funny content, don't make the laughs hard for people to find. Help them stand out by using sidebars, dedicated pages, or jokes grouped together in a distinct section. Doing so allows you to export the humor from your book in a separate format that you can give to people to forward to their friends.

10. Maps, drawings, or illustrations

We live in a visual society with 3-D movies, home theater systems, and on-demand television. When you consider those options, no wonder so few Americans like to read books. Fight back by using more visuals in your manuscript.

Cookbook, fashion, and decorating genres rely heavily on strong images to engage readers. Yet any manuscript can benefit from pictures. Authors can include maps, behind-the-scenes photos, drawings, how-to illustrations, or pictures of the book's main settings. Use black-and-white photos if you need to keep printing costs down.

New York Times best-selling author, Jeff Kinney, made a name for himself with his book, *Diary of a Wimpy Kid*, by including doodled images and cartoons throughout the chapters. The pictures from the author offered a window into the main character's eccentric mind and added a unique element that helped capture young readers. It also gave them a reason to talk about the book.

11. Resource guides

You can also add value to your book by offering a guide to additional resources. For example, if you write history books or textbooks, people may appreciate having a categorized list of all the national organizations, clubs, or research groups associated with your particular topic. By supplying their name, description, and contact information, you're providing a helpful service to the reader. If your list is personal and reveals access to hard-to-find organizations or individuals, your resource guide alone could be worth the book's purchase price.

12. Secret codes to web-based content

The more our society lives on the Internet, the more the line blurs between print and digital content. Consider crossing this line by creating a unique website or set of hidden web pages that is only available to those who buy your book. For instance, if you write children's books, you might connect an accompanying game or teaching section that's only accessible online via a "secret code" listed in your book. Or you might entice readers with the chance to locate buried treasure from your book only available online. Promote this web-based feature on your book cover as a way to separate your book from the competition and stimulate sales.

Another idea is to provide a unique code that allows readers to take a special online assessment. For instance, I worked as a marketing consultant on the book, *The 5 Languages of Appreciation in the Workplace*. The author and publisher created a special bonus feature for this book that directs the reader to a test that teaches their workplace appreciation language. In order to access the test, the reader must provide the unique code found in the back of the book. This feature saves the reader the $20 he would pay to buy the test separately. It also helped personalize the book.

13. Bonus audio and video content

Why limit your book's content to a paper page when you can offer extra content via audio or video? It's the same principle Hollywood studios use when they include bonus content on their DVDs. You can provide readers with a behind-the-scenes look at your life, author videos, instructional audio tracks, lost chapters, success stories, or artwork. Create the bonus content and insert it on a CD or DVD within your book, or make it available as a digital download.

A Korean publisher purchased the foreign rights to my first book, for example, and released it with a complimentary CD of related songs glued inside the front cover. I'm surprised more American publishers and authors don't do the same thing. These days, almost anyone can get CDs and DVDs duplicated for less than a dollar each. That's an amazingly low price to add an extra layer of value and differentiation in the marketplace. If your publisher won't include disks with your book, you can sidestep the problem by offering free downloadable files of the same content on your author website.

14. Teasers and cross-promotion

Many companies engage in the tactic of teasers and cross-promotion to help boost sales. For example, Amazon frequently entices shoppers with targeted offers such as "If you like book X, you might like book Y." Likewise, when you buy a new computer, it usually comes preloaded with free software, music, and videos from companies trying to gain awareness.

Take this idea and use it to promote related items that you sell. For instance, you might insert a chapter from one of your backlist titles or a forthcoming book in the back of your current book. If people are fans of your current book, they'll be more likely to purchase your other books (or products). If you've written a series of books, you could include coupons or discount codes that invite readers to acquire the whole set. By including cross-promotional content within your book, you make it easier for readers to discover your other works and make a purchase.

15. Integrate multimedia with QR barcodes

Modern technology has made it possible for authors and publishers to incorporate audio, video, website links, and imagery directly onto a printed page. This feature is based on using QR, or quick response, barcodes embedded in your manuscript.

When readers scan a QR barcode with their smartphone, such as an iPhone or Android, a video, audio track, special text message, or website instantly appears on their screen. With this technology, you can literally make the pages of your book come alive. Readers can watch videos from the author, meet the book's characters, view images that represent the settings in your book, or download bonus content. The options are endless. Even better, the creation and use of QR codes is free. To learn more, visit the extras page for this book's website at: www.BookWildfire.com

HOW TO USE YOUR BOOK-MARKETING TOOLS

Using the fifteen previous ideas, you can build many book-marketing tools into your manuscript. However, if nobody knows that your promotional tools exist, you won't get much return on your extra efforts. You must openly mention the tools within your book or create stand-alone versions of them and give them to your audience. Here are a few ways to make sure your tools grab the readers' attention.

Public appearances

Use speaking engagements and book signings to make your audience aware of the marketing tools you created for them. Don't expect people to figure it out by themselves. State the obvious. If I had never mentioned the "31 Character Questions" page in my book at my seminars and conferences, I would have sold a lot fewer copies.

The key to success is in the manner in which you mention your marketing tools to the audience. I instruct my clients to incorporate their tools into the natural flow of their presentation. For example, you could:

a. Open your speech with a quiz.
b. Show exclusive imagery when telling a personal story.

c. Make a how-to article part of your speech's answer to a problem.

d. Offer a free resource as an application step for the audience to use the next day.

Your marketing tools will have a stronger effect when your audience can see the immediate benefit from using it. Thus, you need to make the value apparent by openly mentioning your tool, showing it from the stage, and encouraging the audience to use it. This approach allows you to generate interest without being pushy because you incorporate the tool seamlessly into your message.

You could also place a copy of your marketing tool in every attendee's seat, give it away from your book table, or have someone pass it out after your presentation ends. Just make sure everyone in the room gets a copy. If your marketing tool is free and offers standalone value, no one should be offended to take it. Tell people that you like to be generous, then give away your free resource and ask them to share it with a friend.

Media interviews

Radio and TV interviews are great opportunities to get hundreds of people quickly excited about your book. However, most people won't immediately make a purchase. In reality, most people will forget about your interview in the course of a busy day and never think of your book again ... unless you give them a reason to do so.

Built-in book-marketing tools can be your best friend during an interview by highlighting specific nuggets of value that are easy for the audience to access. For instance, some people find it daunting to consider reading your entire book. Circumvent their concern by concentrating on one or two areas where you can really help or entertain them. When viewers sense that a small part of your book is valuable, they're more likely to perceive the rest of your book as worth purchasing.

As you prepare for an author interview, choose one of your book-marketing tools to mention during the conversation. If your promotional tool is an article, describe it to the listeners and tell them that they can get it for free at your website. Or you can arrange a way for the host program to make it available on their website. It's unrealistic to expect people to buy your book when they don't know what's in it. In contrast, you make it easier for consumers to purchase when you give something of value for free first. That tool helps build a positive relationship with you in their mind.

Websites

Another great way to get your marketing tools into reader's hands is by making them available on your author website. I encourage my clients to feature a value-laden resource, such as a free article or download, on the home page of their website at all times. I also recommend creating a separate free resources page that highlights several of your book's marketing tools. The goal is to take compelling nuggets from your book and get them in front of readers to convince them of your book's value. Stay tuned, I'll cover the details of building a powerful author website in the next chapter.

If your publisher's website receives a lot of traffic, encourage him to offer your book-marketing tool on his home page or your specific author or book page. Don't keep your promotional tools to yourself. Get them in front of as many people as possible.

If you're a well-known best-selling author, some retailers will offer your book-marketing tool as extra marketing content through their site to help build buzz or as incentive to buy. For example, Barnes & Noble has been known to give customers a free audio download from the author when they buy a book online. Contact your publisher to find out how you can partner with major retailers to expand awareness for your book.

You might be thinking to yourself, *But if they can get this tool for free, they won't buy my book.* But that's not necessarily true. In Chapter 11, we'll talk about the flammability of free and how it encourages, rather than cannibalizes sales.

WHAT IF YOUR BOOK IS ALREADY FINISHED?

Some of you may be reading this chapter and thinking, "My book's already printed. It's too late for me to take advantage of these book-marketing tools. What can I do if the window has already closed to put them in my manuscript?"

Use this awareness to make sure you create tools for your next book. You must plan during the writing and editing phase of your manuscript. And don't give up or assume defeat for your past books. There are still plenty of ways you can utilize the ideas in this chapter now.

First, go through your books and find concise segments of content that you can turn into any of the preceding fifteen ideas. You probably have sections in various chapters that can be turned into informative articles, how-to guides, listings, or a frequently-asked-question resource. Comb through your books' pages for nuggets of information that you can turn into a high-quality stand-alone pieces. You may need to rewrite your opening and closing paragraphs and smooth out some transitions. But, hey, you're an author. That part should be easy.

If you have trouble finding parts of your book that can be naturally retrofitted into a marketing tool, then consider creating something from scratch. Examine what areas of your book readers seem to appreciate the most. Which chapters or sections tend to generate the most positive feedback? Those parts probably include the ingredients for a good promotional tool.

Finally, if your book has been out for a while, you could write articles with information that's been updated since the book's publication. Provide a running list of revisions or extras on your author website that keep readers up-to-date. Just because your book is in print doesn't mean it is outdated. Keep it fresh by creating new elements and making them available in person and online. If you've already planned a sequel for your book, consider giving out previews and start the buzz-building process early.

Summary

The best time to start marketing your book is before you finish the manuscript. As you focus on writing a great book, put the same effort and detail into building nuggets of value that act as powerful stand-alone promotional items. These tools will make it easier to capture the attention of readers, influential bloggers, and media producers when your book launch occurs.

You may be wondering if I practice what I preach. Absolutely. In fact, I've loaded this book with marketing tools strewn throughout the manuscript. For example, I plan to use these sections of content that you've already read as part of my book-marketing tool arsenal:

- How to write value statements
- Seven principles for creating an effective brand
- How to create an author brand
- Fifteen ways to build book-marketing tools into your book

In addition, I'll use several other parts of this book, such as "Ten requirements for your author website" and the last chapter on how to market fiction.

Too many authors forget to consciously develop marketing tools for their books. Then they wonder why it's difficult to promote their message. Avoid this problem by brainstorming during the manuscript stage, and insert as many appropriate ideas as possible. I've just given you fifteen. That ought to be enough to light a fire under you.

CHAPTER 5

START A WILDFIRE
WITH YOUR AUTHOR WEBSITE

A real wildfire can consume over three thousand acres of land per hour. This ability to burn and spread so fast is what gives wildfires the respect they deserve. That speed also represents what many authors wish would happen with their books. They want to see cash registers firing up and sales sweeping across the country as fast as possible.

Thanks to the Internet, authors have the power to create a digital wildfire, an online blaze that spreads just as fast as those in the forest, without charring the landscape. And the best tool to help fan the electronic flames is an author website.

No other marketing tool can help boost your book sales in such a direct manner. Yet many authors miss the opportunity to fuel their sales because they never set up a website. Or they cut corners by getting an inexperienced intern or relative to do them a favor and create a shoddy web page. On the other hand, some authors spend thousands of dollars to create a glitzy image online, and their book sales remain stagnant. Why? The truth is that image only plays a small role in the book-selling power of a website.

For example, at the time of this writing, Stephenie Meyer is one of the top-selling authors in the world with her wildly successful Twilight series of novels. In my opinion, though, her author website (www.StephenieMeyer.com) has an unattractive homemade appearance that doesn't dazzle you with fancy bells and whistles. Nevertheless her website gets more traffic than most authors combined, which goes to show that looks aren't a primary factor. That's because the reading public demands more from an author than just image. It demands substance, and Stephenie delivers.

You may not be a blockbuster author with books turned into hit movies. Maybe you're a first timer just getting started. Or maybe you're a midlist author struggling to impress your publisher. Regardless this chapter will show how you can build a website that boosts book sales, whether you're a beginner or a bestseller. It's easier than you think!

THE POWER OF AN AUTHOR WEBSITE

In 2008, the publishing research firm, Codex Group, surveyed nearly twenty-one thousand book shoppers across America. The objective of their study was to understand the relative effectiveness of author websites among shoppers and determine the elements that keep them coming back to a site. Here are some interesting facts Codex uncovered.

1. Visiting an author's website is the No. 1 way that book readers want to get to know and support their favorite authors. And this desire is true regardless of age. What does this mean to you? If you don't have an author website, you're literally preventing your books from reaching their full sales potential.

2. Fans are much more likely to visit an author's website, rather than the author's page on a publisher's website. Readers don't care about publishers; they care about authors. So don't expect your publisher to shoulder the responsibility. Build your own author website.

3. When this survey was conducted, book shoppers who had visited an author website in the past week bought 38 percent more books, from a wider range of retailers, than those who had not visited an author site. What's the takeaway? Frequent visits to your website can directly influence the number of your books people buy. The more a reader visits you online, the higher likelihood that she will purchase your books—both online and at retail stores.

Source: Codex Group; Market Partners International Newsletter; December 2008

 BONUS ONLINE CONTENT: Download the article "What Makes Book Shoppers Return To An Author Website?" at bookwildfire.com and writersdigest.com/book-wildfire-downloads

FOUR GOALS FOR YOUR AUTHOR WEBSITE

Since it's proven that readers who frequent author websites tend to buy more books, what can you do to increase your website traffic? The answer is to build a website that accomplishes the following four goals.

Goal #1—Credibility: Establish your expertise

As stated in Chapter 1, most people feel uncomfortable buying a product from someone they don't trust. Thus, the first goal for your author website should be to build trust with visitors. A primary way to accomplish this objective is by highlighting your expertise. This doesn't mean you need a PhD or certain letters behind your name. Those things help, but they're not mandatory. Remember, the word *expert* comes from the word *experience*. You must adequately show that you possess more successful experience in a particular area than the average person.

When people visit your website, they're questioning your credibility. For example, they're silently wondering:

- Does this author have the ability to help me overcome a problem?

- Can this author entertain or inspire me to see the world in a new or different light?
- Has this author experienced tangible success with her own advice?

If your website doesn't answer yes to these questions, your credibility will remain suspect. Therefore many people will stay on the fence and hesitate to buy your books.

I've seen this dynamic play out in my consulting practice. Many of my author clients initially felt skeptical about hiring a marketing consultant, so they went to my website to "check me out." After reading my bio, numerous client success stories, and over twenty free articles, their trust level increased. This gave them the peace to contact me so we could start working together. If my website had failed to communicate my expertise, my credibility would have suffered. Instead, the opposite happened, and I've gained a lot of new customers over the years.

As an author, you face the same credibility battle. How do you overcome the skepticism? Give people what they need to feel comfortable about you. Examples include testimonials, free resources, sample chapters, and a bio that presents you as an expert who likes to help people.

If you write fiction, don't forget that you're dealing with the same problem. However, you can enhance your credibility by sharing the research you use to create your novels. Readers are more likely to bond with a writer who takes the time to add depth and authenticity to their stories. Use your website as a tool to convey the respect you feel for your readers.

Goal #2—Content: Offer value-laden information for free

Your author website should do more than simply broadcast your background and personality. Your site should offer visitors free samples of your expertise to show how their lives will be improved if they purchase your products. Potential readers must be convinced they'll get their money's worth. Therefore give your website visitors a taste of your expertise, or a sample of the power of your books to convince them of your value.

Your goal is to create the following dynamic in a visitor's mind: "Wow, I can't believe this author gave me this article/download/ sample for free! It's really good. Imagine how much more value I'll get if I buy their book!" This doesn't mean that you give away the farm. But, you do need to give away enough free nuggets of value to convince people of your nonfiction expertise or fiction story-telling skills.

The food industry uses this principle to turn prospects into customers by using free samples. For instance, Chick-fil-A has grown into one of the most popular fast-food restaurant chains in America. They grew their success by giving away free chicken nuggets in their mall food court locations across the Southeast. Their samples were so tasty that people wanted more. Chick-fil-A's marketing materials even proclaimed, "Taste it, and you'll love it for good." Soon skeptical shoppers turned into regular customers. The samples didn't cost Chick-fil-A much money to give away, and enticing people with free value led to billions of dollars in food sales.

Your author website needs to do the same thing. Let people taste the message of your book. If they like it, they'll be more likely to make a purchase. However, this idea entails more than just offering a simple sample chapter. That's too cliché. I'll explain more about how to give away free resources on your website later in this chapter.

Goal #3—Community: Create a reader fan base

Earlier I mentioned the Codex research that reported people who had visited an author website within seven days before the survey bought 38 percent more books than those who hadn't visited an author site. Therefore increasing repeat traffic to your website is a crucial component to boosting your book sales. Your goal is to get more people visiting your site and returning on a regular basis.

A great way to get return visitors is to provide an online community that lets readers connect and share with each other. Tools to create online communities include blogs, forums, e-mail newsletters, Twitter accounts, Facebook fan pages, and links to fan sites.

People like to congregate with like-minded individuals who share similar interests. Your website should serve as the gathering place for people to congregate around your books. The more that people enjoy talking about your book with others, the more likely they are to make a purchase, spread the word to others, and invite friends to join them on your website.

As I mentioned previously, best-selling author Stephenie Meyer doesn't have a fancy-looking website, but it serves as the linking hub to literally hundreds of fan sites around the world. When readers want the latest news about her books, they visit her website and then continue the conversation online at one of their favorite fan sites. It's an elaborate community of personal blogs, forums, and discussion boards that connect thousands of readers and keep them excited about Stephenie's books.

Readers set up these fan sites of their own volition, because they want an outlet to discuss their thoughts with like-minded people. As an author, you can't control these sites, but you can harness their power by searching for them and acting as the central hub of connection. In addition, you can offer free resources and exclusive content that keep people talking. You don't need hundreds of fan sites, but you do need the power of community to help promote your book.

Goal #4—Contact Information:
Invite visitors to let you stay in touch

An effective author website should also do more than passively offer content and community. Smart authors use their site to get visitors to voluntarily give them their contact information. Doing so allows the author to stay in touch and build the relationship through newsletters, RSS feeds, updates, and more. Contact information is the equivalent of marketing gold, because you're more likely to sell books to someone who willingly requests regular information from you.

One author I've worked with mails a monthly print newsletter to over ten thousand people. It costs him several hundred dollars to print and mail each issue. But the return on investment is worth it. He's told me that his office staff is able to correlate major book orders to the release of his newsletter. His success stems partly from the good content he writes for his newsletter, but more important, is the size of his list. He's spent years gathering voluntary contact information from thousands of people.

You should use your website home page to invite people to sign up for a newsletter, contest, regular updates, and other things. You can do this by including a small pop-up window or an easy-to-see box on the top of your site that asks visitors to sign up. Give visitors incentive to register by offering a small gift for joining your list, such as a free article, special report, exclusive resource, or other product of value. As you build the size of your list, you collect the kindling necessary to start a wildfire around your book.

WD **BONUS ONLINE CONTENT:** Download the article "A Free Blog Does *Not* Count as a Professional Author Website" at book-wildfire.com and writersdigest.com/book-wildfire-downloads

TEN REQUIREMENTS FOR AN AUTHOR WEBSITE

Now that I've established clear goals for your website, you need to examine ten essential elements that your site must include, why you need them, and some the details for each that you'll want to consider.

1. Home Page

Your home page is the most important page on your website for two reasons. First, it's most often the initial page visitors see. Second, it's one of the best tools to get people to return to your site for future visits.

The problem with many author websites is that they resemble boring, online brochures. I've seen a lot of websites that look as if the author took his printed media kit or a promotional brochure and typed the same text on his website. Why is that a problem? Once people read a brochure, there's no reason to read it again. It's a one-and-done situation. If you create this same feel with your website, it will kill your repeat visitor potential.

One of the best ways to overcome this problem is to create an active, frequently updated home page. Here are some different ways to create a dynamic feel:

- If you like to blog, incorporate it into the main part of your home page. Let it take center stage, so that people regularly return to your home page to read your blog posts. Blogging experts suggest posting at least two to four times a week to keep people interested. Don't start a blog if you're not committed to staying consistent.

- Create an easy-to-see section that offers informative Q&A, inspiring thoughts, or devotional text. You can update this area daily or weekly depending on how much content you have.

- Set up a "Latest News" section that keeps people informed on upcoming books, speaking engagements, media appearances, new product launches, and anything else that's newsworthy.

If you attempt any of the ideas listed above, here's the cardinal rule: You must update on a frequent basis. Find a balance that feels comfortable. At the very least, update your home page two to four times per month. If you don't update at least that frequently, your website will appear static, and nobody returns to a website that rarely changes. If you want repeat visitors, you must give them a reason to come back.

Lysa TerKeurst (www.LysaTerKeurst.com) is one of my *New York Times* best-selling author clients who really learned how to harness the power of her author website. To help boost repeat visits, she incorporated a blog into her home page. Each day, she writes about interesting situations that happen in her life and family. Her blog posts make you laugh, contemplate, and become more aware of the spiritual side of life. This attraction to her blog keeps people coming back in droves. On average, she draws over forty thousand readers per month. This allowed Lysa to build a huge author platform that helped place her book, *Made to Crave*, on the *New York Times* Best Seller lists for over twenty-five weeks.

You, too, must keep your website active in order to keep visitors returning. However, don't forget the importance of layout and navigation. When most people surf the Internet, they don't want to read a lot of text crammed onto a page, because it causes eyestrain and feels frustrating. When you develop your home page, keep it short on text and big on graphics. Avoid lengthy paragraphs, especially if you blog. Separate content into small chunks, which prevents people from just scanning your material or leaving altogether. Use your home page to introduce who you are and emphasize the benefits that your books offer. I recommend providing a mini-bio of less than 150 words, with an area that lists your value using bulleted statements.

Also avoid displaying overused stock photos. Instead, use images that convey a sense of your personality and the main topics of your books. Select pictures that make your website look unique.

Other items to avoid include videos or introductory screens that automatically appear when a visitor hits your home page. These are highly annoying because they waste time. Web designers like to insert these extra bells and whistles, but they're usually not worth the money. In addition, avoid using music that immediately starts playing. It's helpful to provide audio and video on your home page, but give visitors the choice to turn it on and off.

The ultimate goal of your author website is to help sell more books. So be sure to display your most recent book cover in a prominent area on the home page. If you have several books, you can place all of their covers in a rotating carousel that lets visitors click on a specific title for more details.

Finally, make sure that your navigation buttons are easy to find. These buttons are the links that take people to the other pages of your website. I suggest putting them across the top or down the left side of your home page. In addition, keep the look and position of these buttons consistent throughout the rest of your site.

2. Newsletter Sign-Up Box

Wise authors stay in touch with their readers by sending out a regular newsletter. Chapter 13 is dedicated to this topic. For now, remember that the biggest problem you face with newsletters is getting people to sign up in the first place. However, you can help overcome this dilemma by offering a newsletter sign-up box at the top of your home page. Make sure it's one of the first elements your visitors see.

If you want to grow your author platform, you must gather contact information from your website visitors. Thus, create an invitation for people to provide their e-mail or mailing address to receive your newsletter. Even better, encourage people to sign up by giving away something of value for free. For instance, if you visit this book's website at www.BookWildfire.com, you'll see a newsletter sign-up box that encourages authors to sign up for my free marketing tips.

Here's a time-saving tip: Ask your website designer to automatically connect your sign-up box to your newsletter management service, such as ConstantContact or MailChimp. I use Constant-Contact (www.ConstantContact.com), and their system provides a computer code that links my newsletter account with my home page sign-up box. This feature allows people to sign up or unsubscribe from my newsletter without my involvement. Also ConstantContact provides a free smartphone app that allows you to sign up new subscribers directly from your phone and even check the status of your current newsletters.

3. Free Resources Page

After training over four hundred authors, my experience with clients has shown that a free resources page is usually the second most popular page for readers who visit an author website. That's because people want the chance to test-drive your message. You wouldn't buy a car without taking it for a test drive. Likewise, you should use your website to let people get familiar with your message. If they like what they experience, they're more likely to purchase your books and return regularly.

How do you let people test-drive your message? Examine your website by putting yourself in the position of a skeptic. Consider whether your site would give a cynical person enough helpful information to overcome their resistance and get emotionally excited about your message. If you write nonfiction, develop an ever-growing library of articles or blog posts that expand on your book's message. (Yes, you can take material straight from your book and turn it into an article, but don't do it too often.) Here's a list of ideas to get you started:

Insightful articles, quizzes, assessments, special reports, study guides, sample chapters, past newsletter issues, recommended reading lists, relevant statistics and research, podcasts, video teaching lessons, top ten lists, product coupons, jokes and related humor, and appendixes. You can make each of these resources appear as a separate web page or as a PDF file that visitors can download.

If you write fiction, try the following list of ideas to create interesting free resources, such as:

Background information about your stories, sample chapters, insights from your novel's research, author Q&A, games, articles about current events that relate to your subject matter, a behind-the-scenes look at your writing life, character development information, alternate endings, lost chapters, artwork and downloadable images, maps, unpublished short stories, recipes and travel guides associated with your books, and especially sneak-peek chapters of your novel in progress.

Never be stingy with your expertise as an author. It's important to regularly add new material to your free resources page. Otherwise people will lose interest, and they will stop visiting. If you're an expert, you should have plenty of material to give away for free and plenty of material left that people are willing to buy.

If you're wondering whether I practice what I preach, visit my free resources page at www.BookWildfire.com. You'll find articles about book marketing, plus archived newsletters and a helpful resource guide for authors. For a deeper discussion on the power of giving away resources for free, see Chapter 11.

4. About Me Page

Many people will visit your website without really knowing who you are. They may find you through a random Internet search or a referral from a friend. So you need an about page that quickly reveals your author brand and the value of your books. (Refer back to Chapter 3 for details on the subject of building an author brand.)

Keep in mind that when most people read your bio, they don't care how many books you've written, how many copies you've sold, or how many awards you've won. Instead, the majority of website visitors want to know "What's in it for me?" So the trick to creating an effective bio page is to talk about your expertise without sounding narcissistic. Aim to describe your personal history in a concise manner (less than four hundred words) that reflects how you like to help other people.

Avoid describing yourself using such clichés as *authentic, genuine, sought-after, engaging*. Instead, focus your bio on the value you provide readers. But don't be stiff. It's okay to let your personality shine through and make fun of yourself, too. On this page, include both professional and casual head shots, so that visitors can see you as a professional person who's approachable.

5. Speaking Page

Public speaking is one of the best ways to grow your author platform, and Chapter 12 is devoted to the subject. However, it's tough to get more speaking engagements if people can't hear a sample of your speech in action. Your website can act like an online speaker's bureau to help line up new events. All you need is a speaking page that provides the pertinent information. The necessary ingredients for a speaking page include:

- Brief audio or video speaking sample before a live audience (three to five minutes in length).
- Testimonials from two or three leaders who have booked you in the past.
- Short descriptions of your top four to six presentations (include value statements).
- Contact information for someone to book you (e-mail address and phone number).

Your speaking demo should be professionally recorded with good audio quality. All you need is a five-minute sample from your best presentation. Just make sure those five minutes come from the strongest part of your speech. A strong first impression is critical.

A video speaking sample is preferred, but it can cost thousands of dollars to record yourself with the proper lighting in front of a large audience. Don't spend big bucks for a fancy demo if you're just getting started. A video sample must be top-notch, or it will do more harm than good. Wait to spend money on a video until your speaking skills are honed.

6 Events Calendar Section

Your author website should offer an updated calendar that keeps visitors abreast of upcoming events, such as speaking engagements, book signings, and media interviews. A busy calendar makes the impression that you're in demand, which enhances your credibility. You can incorporate your calendar into your speaking page, or set it up as a separate page.

I recommend displaying your upcoming events in chronological order, using a simple list rather than a monthly calendar format. Start listing your events at the top of the page, with January of the current year, and continue downward. If you spoke frequently the past year, it's okay to display that information as well. If it's a lot of text, put it on a separate page. Leaders like to see that you're active and experienced.

Don't forget to list the date, location, and contact information for your speaking events. Website visitors may want to hear you speak when you're in their area, or they may tell a friend that you're coming to their town. Above all, keep your calendar updated. Nothing says "dead book" like an old events calendar.

7. Endorsements

A great way to boost your author credibility is to provide testimonials from well-known people. I suggest sprinkling powerful endorsements throughout the different pages of your website. It can also be effective to dedicate a page on your website to at least five to ten testimonials. These endorsements can be praise for your books and speaking presentations. A comfort level is established when a leader sees that another leader went the extra step to publicly back you.

Keep in mind that most visitors are more concerned with who backed you than what the person said. Limit your endorsements to high-profile leaders and influencers that people would recognize, such as best-selling authors, business leaders, church pastors, celebrities, athletes, or politicians. If you don't have any endorsements, either you're not asking for them or you're not providing tangible value. Assuming that you write effective books, don't be shy to ask leaders for endorsements. Likewise, don't be shy to post them on your website.

8. Media Page

We live in an audio/visual media-based society. So including a media page on your website can serve two purposes. First, reporters and media personnel need a way to easily find your information in case they want to request an interview. I've heard several reporters complain that they were interested in contacting an author but gave up because that author's website lacked basic media information.

Second, it's wise to offer a media page that provides audio and video samples of past interviews or of you addressing your audience, such as a short frequently-asked-question video. For instance, many national radio and TV programs will not book an author unless they can first see a sample of that author on another program. Media producers have a reputation to maintain, so they will hesitate to contact you if they haven't seen a sample of your interview skills. To appease the media, include these elements on a page on your site:

- List any past national media appearances (radio, TV, newspaper, magazines). Don't display small town or regional shows, because they make you look small-time. To learn how to secure national interviews, see Chapter 6.
- Provide one to three audio or video samples of interviews you've done for a national program. If the quality is poor, don't post it on your website because it will work against you.
- Offer one to three brief videos that deal with frequently asked questions you receive. This gives you the opportunity to give visitors takeaway value and display your on-camera skills.
- Supply one to two professional-quality head shots that can be downloaded in color and black and white. Wear conservative clothing and a confident smile. Avoid one of my personal pet peeves: Keep your hands away from your face.
- List web links to any published magazine articles you've written or any appearances in a major newspaper.
- Downloadable media kit: This can be a PDF file containing a professional author bio, ten interview questions related to your book, three to five testimonials, author Q&A page, professional headshot, picture of your book cover, and full contact information.

You will attract more media coverage when you look the part: That is, you must appear to be a credible author who is experienced with the media. By including the elements listed above, you can help lure the larger radio and TV programs.

9. Books or Store Page

Your website is a prime vehicle to help sell books and related products, regardless of whether you direct visitors to Amazon.com or take orders from your site. However, don't confuse your store as the most important part of your site, because you won't sell many books if your visitors don't receive some value first. I've actually seen some well-known authors put their store page as the home page of their website—talk about a narcissistic turnoff.

You essentially have two options when advertising books on your website. You can create a books page that displays the related marketing text and purchasing links. Or, if you sell other products in addition to books, you might have a separate books page that links to a store page, with all of your products displayed together. For many website visitors, this format can help ease the purchasing process.

Regardless, people are more likely to buy from you when you pay attention to their needs first. So make your books available to buy, but keep it tasteful. Focus on the value that your products offer readers. Give a brief description and small picture of each book cover, and list your book's benefits in three to five bulleted statements. Focus on the results you create, rather than features. Don't tell people what they will learn. Tell them how your message will improve their lives.

If you choose to sell products directly from your website, feel free to offer coupons, discounts, and free shipping. But don't overcomplicate the system for the buyer. Keep your store simple, easy to navigate, and always accept credit cards.

If you need a free, easy-to-use e-commerce system that can connect to your website store, try www.E-Junkie.com or www.PayPal.com and their option called "Website Payments Standard." These systems allow your website visitors to buy a book using any major credit card. They give you the code to create "Buy" buttons that you place on your website. When people click on these buttons, E-Junkie and PayPal handle the order transaction securely. After an order is approved, you'll receive an e-mail notifying you of the order and the customer's shipping information.

After you ship product to the customer, you can log in to PayPal and wire money directly to your bank account for free. For an inexpensive fee, you can upgrade to "Website Payments Pro," which includes a feature called a "Virtual Terminal," which lets you gather a customer's credit card info either in person or over the phone. This system allows you to take credit card orders at your speaking events, book signings, via mail order, and over the phone. Once a customer gives you her credit card details, you log in to PayPal, enter the information on the Virtual Terminal screen, and conduct the transaction in less than a minute. I've used PayPal with great success.

10. Contact Page

Your author website isn't complete until you finish it off with a page that displays your full contact information. Do NOT put up a blank contact form that forces visitors to fill in their information and send you an e-mail. This is extremely annoying and makes you look like an amateur.

I don't care how famous you are, I suggest you give visitors a mailing address, business phone number, and working e-mail address. If you're worried about getting stalkers or dumb questions (you shouldn't be), then display a P.O. Box address or your personal assistant's phone number and e-mail. However, it is inexcusable to create a website and then hide from your readers and leaders. Give people the freedom to contact you. Relationships sell books.

BONUS ONLINE CONTENT: Download the article "A Word About Web Traffic and SEO" at bookwildfire.com and writersdigest.com/book-wildfire-downloads

HOW TO WORK WITH A WEB DESIGNER

Now that you know the ten essential elements for an effective author website, you need to find the right person to help you build it.

At the risk of offending some readers, I must draw a line in the sand about website development:

- Do not try to design a website by yourself. It will most likely look homemade and diminish your credibility.
- Do not let a friend or relative create a site for you. They may offer a "good deal," but they will rarely give you a good website. Several of my author clients have relatives who ruined their websites, which required a professional to come in and fix the mess.
- Do not use free website templates. Your website won't look unique, and when you use such templates, you're usually left with little or no follow-up support when problems occur.

The best way to find a good web designer is to seek out and hire a professional. Yes, they may cost more, but the investment is generally worth it. Here are some tips to ease your search process:

STEP 1: Spend time surfing the Internet and create a list of three to five author websites that you like. Write down what you specifically like about each site, because you'll need to explain your preferences to a prospective web designer.

STEP 2: When you see another author website that you like, locate that author's web designer contact information. There's usually a link at the bottom of the home page. Or ask friends or other authors you know to recommend names of web designers they respect. A web designer doesn't need to live in your area. Most communication is done via phone and e-mail.

STEP 3: Before you contact a potential web designer, go to his website first and look at his portfolio. Make sure it contains at least two sites that are similar to the style you prefer. If you skip this step, you could wind up with a web designer who is on a different wavelength than you, and that will cause trouble. You don't want to be a designer's first attempt at an author website. Being someone's guinea pig rarely works out well.

STEP 4: Once you locate a web designer with a portfolio that you like, initiate a phone call and describe the kind of website you're looking for. Tell them about the ten elements mentioned earlier in this chapter. (You're welcome to e-mail a designer my list.)

STEP 5: As you talk with the designer, pay careful attention to her ability to make you feel comfortable. Many web designers are so technology oriented that their communication skills are lacking. If you talk to a designer who uses techno-words that sound like a foreign language or is a spacey, creative type that's hard to understand, then walk away. Trust me, things are much easier when you are on the same page with your designer.

Your goal is to build a relationship with a web designer who talks like a normal person and pays attention to your needs. Be aware of any designer who tries to dictate what your site should be. Some web designers make great artists but ineffective business people. You don't want them to create a site that stifles your ability to build an author platform that sell books.

STEP 6: Once you've spoken with a web designer who makes you feel comfortable, ask him to give you a ballpark price and timeframe in writing before you agree to move forward. This step is critical, because some designers will add extra features or take longer than needed to build your site. Then they send you an inflated invoice for their work. Tell the designer up front what you're willing to spend and don't agree to a budget beyond your means.

A reasonable price for a basic author website should run around $3,000 to $6,000. Make sure this fee includes both web design and programming. Programming is the term used to describe the process of writing the actual computer code and building your site on the Internet. Don't let the price scare you. It's a wise investment that will pay for itself through additional book sales, speaking engagements, and media interviews. You have to invest money in order to make money.

STEP 7: You will need to decide who will update your site once it's finished, which is either you or someone else. If you're not Internet savvy, pay someone to make changes to your site when needed. Your web designer or programmer can usually do this for an hourly fee of $25 to $75 per hour. This is a reasonable cost if you only make a few updates per month.

In contrast, you may want total control of your website and all the future updates. If you don't mind learning new technology and doing it yourself, then tell the designer that you want a content management system (CMS) built for your site. The programmer can usually set up this system and train you to make changes on your own. This service will cost additional money, but it's usually a nominal fee.

BONUS ONLINE CONTENT: Download the article "Questions to Ask When Hiring a Website Designer" at bookwildfire.com or writers digest.com/book-wildfire-downloads

HOW TO TRACK YOUR WEBSITE EFFECTIVENESS

Just because you have a website doesn't mean it's effective. Fortunately there are easy ways to track the effectiveness of your website to build your author platform. I encourage my clients to monitor tangible factors, such as monthly visitors, popular pages, referring sites, and keyword search results. You can also manually track new subscribers to your newsletter, speaking engagement inquiries, media interview requests, or book sales from your website.

There are several excellent free tracking tools to help analyze your website statistics. My favorite is Google Analytics (www. Google.com/Analytics). If you're not familiar with using computer code, ask your web designer or hosting company to set up Google's service for you. Google provides special computer code that you embed into your website's individual pages. Once you do this, Google will track all of your website data for you.

When you examine your website statistics, however, make sure you concentrate on the right information. For example, basing your site's effectiveness on how many hits or page views you get is a flawed notion. These are inflated figures that don't provide accurate information about web traffic. A better guide is to track how many unique visitors your site receives. This number reflects how many different people actually visited your site, which is a better reflection of your real platform.

If you notice a decline in visitors, sales, sign-ups, or other factors, it could mean that people are bored with your website. Take time once a month to assess where you can add new content that provides value to your readers. If you run out of ideas, bring in guests with a similar message. People will appreciate your desire to help them, and they'll show it by returning to your website on a regular basis. The more often people return, the more likely they will buy your books.

Summary

A good author website can act like your personal marketing staff to promote your books 24/7. But your site won't be effective unless you meet the four goals and include the ten elements described in this chapter. Does it cost money to build a good website? Yes. Does it take extra time to update your site with new content? Yes. But remember that you're not flushing money down the toilet. You're investing in the growth of your author career. A wildfire can't spread without fuel. Think of your website as digital lighter fluid to boost your book sales.

CHAPTER 6

HOW TO CAPTURE MEDIA INTERVIEWS BY YOURSELF

One of the most thrilling experiences that an author ever gets to enjoy is the opportunity to appear on radio or television. There's no bigger boost to the literary ego than telling others, "I'm going to be interviewed on television." How can your friends top that?

The frustrating part is that landing an interview is easier said than done. There's a whole media world with its own rules that authors must learn to navigate. The good news is that it's possible to break into this world and secure radio and TV interviews on your own. I've taught numerous authors how to do it. Surprisingly almost every author I've instructed, fiction or nonfiction, has responded, "Wow, I thought I had to hire a publicist or rely on my publisher to get this kind of exposure." This myth, along with many others, is what led me to write this book.

In my opinion, it is vitally important for authors to learn how to take control over their career as much as possible. Yes, it's nice when publishers set up an author tour for you, or you have the financial means to hire third-party individuals to manage the details.

But there is nothing more satisfying than being able to oversee the process yourself. I say this for several reasons.

First, in the current publishing climate, publishers are off-loading more and more of the marketing responsibility to the author. This is primarily due to economic difficulties, slashed marketing budgets, staff downsizing, and increased competition. Thus, publicity is one of the first promotional tactics that publishers will drop and pass on to the author. These days, only a best-selling author gets a media tour arranged by the publisher. And even that experience isn't nearly as extravagant as it used to be.

Second, the more you delegate the responsibility of marketing your book to other people, the more you lose control over your own success. No one can be a better salesperson for your book than you, because no one else has the level of passion, connection to the audience, and intimate knowledge of the subject matter as you do. I've watched a lot of publishers and publicists ruin a book's sales potential, because they had no passion for the message. They treated the book like just another title to pump into the system.

Having said that, I'm not against authors hiring outside help. There are many professionals in the publishing industry who do dynamite work. And, in the case of some top national media programs, you simply cannot land an interview without some third-party representation. If fact, later in this chapter, I'll talk about how to work with a publicist, if you choose to get one. However, you will always be better off if you learn how to successfully implement specific marketing skills by yourself first, especially when it comes to publicity. That way, you can understand the process, work better in tandem with a publicist, and know how to hold others accountable without wasting your money.

If you aren't convinced, here are two more reasons why it's best for you to learn how to get media coverage on your own:

1. Most publisher publicity campaigns only last 90 to 120 days. That's right. Most publishers and publicity firms focus their efforts only on the first few months after your book initially releases. Once

those first ninety days are up, they move on to another author's book. The problem with this system is that it can take six to eighteen months for most books to build up enough word-of-mouth momentum to reach their full sales potential. In other words, just when a book is starting gain traction in the marketplace, most publicity campaigns stop and the book slides back into oblivion.

Publishers and publicists will argue that their system works, because they can generate enough buzz in ninety days to spike a book onto a bestseller list. However, this is only true for a few titles each year, usually those written by celebrities, politicians, athletes, and previous bestselling authors. Big media exposure is the exception for the average author, not the rule.

Publishers release hundreds of new books each year, so it's physically impossible for their marketing staff to give constant attention to all of them. Therefore, you're lucky to get a few weeks of love, and then they're off to help another book. Is it fair? No. Is it reality? Yes.

Here's my point. Let's imagine that you're lucky enough to receive media exposure through your publisher. Things go well for the first ninety days. Then, as planned, the media interviews stop. What are you going to do next? Since the publicist ended its campaign, are you going to stop marketing your book, too? Are you going to leave your book like an orphan in the marketplace and hope that it fends for itself?

Loving parents don't stop feeding their newborn baby after the first ninety days just because the process is hard, they lack sleep, or they feel too busy. They keep feeding a baby until it's mature enough to feed itself. Your book is your baby. Why would give up on it after only ninety days of publicity? By learning how to get media coverage on your own, you can keep feeding your book with constant exposure until it reaches marketing maturity.

2. Publicity firms are expensive.

If you want to hire a freelance publicist with a good reputation, you will usually pay around $2,500 to $10,000 per month. Over a ninety-day period, that's a total bill of $7,500 to $30,000. I don't know about you, but most authors I know don't have that kind of money lying around. Heck, think about how many books you'd have to sell just to break even.

Worse, there are a lot bad publicity firms who will take your money but yield little results. They'll promise to land you on big-time shows, charge you an arm and a leg for their services, but provide no accountability. Then they act offended when you question why you only got a few interviews on small radio stations or someone's unknown Internet radio show. If you're going to outsource publicity for your book, do your homework first.

This is why I recommend taking control of media interviews yourself. After you read this chapter, you'll be surprised (like many of my clients) by how easy it can be. In addition, the next chapter will describe how to maximize interviews once you've secured them. First, I'll tell you how to make contact with the decision makers who can make interviews happen.

HOW TO GAIN A PRODUCER'S INTEREST

In the media world, there's a hidden person who wields a lot of power. They're hidden because you rarely see these individuals on a TV program or even hear them mentioned on a radio show. This person is the producer. A producer is the one responsible for planning and executing each specific broadcast. They act as the behind-the-scenes manager who coordinates the actions of the host and the technical crew. Their job is to help make every show run smoothly.

A producer has power, because she is usually the person who researches and determines what show topics will be covered, and also decides which guests to book for interviews, when each episode will air, and how each program will be formatted. In many cases, the producer has more authority than the host when it comes to deciding who is interviewed on the program.

Therefore, if you want to get more media coverage for your book, your goal is to connect with producers. Each producer acts as the gatekeeper that can make interviews happen for each program. (In the print media world, the equivalent of a producer would be the newspaper reporter or magazine editor.) If you want to grab the attention of producers, though, you have to understand the rules that govern their world. Fail to abide by them, and you can find yourself running into a brick wall.

Rule #1—Producers live and die by audience ratings.

Radio, TV, and Internet-based programs are all graded by the size of the audience they can attract. This one issue drives the producer's decision making, because the larger the audience, the higher the ratings, which means the greater opportunity to sell expensive advertising slots. Thus, if a program consistently garners a growing audience, the company can generate enough advertising revenue to stay in business.

It is the producer's task to help create steady programming that draws more and more followers. If he succeeds, he's considered a hero. If he fails, he's eventually fired. What does this mean to you as the author? See the next rule.

Rule #2—Producers don't care about marketing your book.

Helping authors promote their books is the last thing on a producer's mind. They don't care about your book. Instead, they're focused on finding exciting guests who can help their radio or TV program maintain high ratings. If a producer brings in boring authors who just plug their books, the audience will tune out, the ratings will plummet, and that producer will lose her job.

Producers will cater to famous celebrities and well-known bestselling authors, because those individuals have the panache to attract a larger audience. That's why certain authors get more attention and time. Lesser-known authors may claim unfairness, but it's not unfair. The media does what's in their best interest.

Sometimes there are incentives for programs to emphasize certain authors and their new books. However, these situations are the exception, rather than the rule. For the average author, your name alone won't carry enough weight with producers to garner such favor. The fact is that you are one author among thousands. Fortunately there's another way to capture a producer's interest.

Rule #3—Don't push your book. Push an interesting topic.

To learn how the media landscape operates, put yourself in the position of a producer. Would you rather be approached by an author who is trying to get airtime to promote a book or one who is an expert on a relevant topic to the audience? From the producer's perspective, one approach is selfish, while the other is helpful.

Producers would much rather work with authors who are trying to help them achieve their goals. Radio and TV producers have no desire to turn their programs into annoying infomercials that plug an author's book. Audience ratings will drop if a show is too promotional. Nobody likes to be constantly sold.

Due to this fact, producers are constantly monitoring what topics might be of interest to their audience. If they can acquire guests who are experts on those relevant topics and who offer interesting discussion and are fun to watch, then the audience will tune in on a repeated basis. Producers dream of their show becoming the go-to source of information or the public's top entertainment choice. If they can achieve that position, their audience ratings will stay high.

If you want to get more media exposure, don't push your book. Instead, stress an interesting topic that would be important to the audience. Doing so gives you a much greater chance of grabbing the producer's attention. The next rule explains how.

Rule #4—Know the show and pitch a compelling idea.

Some radio and TV programs literally spell out how to qualify for an interview. You might see a paragraph on their website's contact page that says, "If you'd like to appear as a guest on our program, take the time to watch some of our past episodes to get a feel for topics and interviews that typically interest us and our audience." This is great advice that can prevent you from wasting time.

Heed this suggestion by doing your homework. Watch a few episodes, either live or archived, to identify what themes and topics the show likes to cover. For example, *The Oprah Winfrey Show* became popular because it was known for providing women with inspiring stories, self- improvement topics, and celebrity guests. *Good Morning America* is a blend of news makers, chefs, musicians, and experts on women's issues. Political programs, such as *Rush Limbaugh* and *Sean Hannity*, feature guests with a conservative point of view. Almost every program has a "sweet spot" that it tends to follow.

In some cases, though, you may not have access to the program in your area or be able to listen to archived episodes. In those situations, spend time surfing that program's website to see what kinds of articles and past guest interviews are listed. Look at the past few months of blog posts, articles, and discussions. This information can help determine what issues they prefer to highlight.

Next make a list of the central topics that your book discusses. For nonfiction, this should be straightforward. As you identify these core topics, examine which ones would interest a large audience and why. How would you need to discuss the topic in order to make an audience curious? In addition, consider how you can position yourself as an expert on the topic, rather than just an author.

If you write novels, identify the themes that surround your stories. For example, I consulted with *New York Times* best-selling author of Amish fiction named Wanda Brunstetter. She has no trouble getting media interviews, because America is fascinated with the Amish culture. People wonder why these families choose to live without modern conveniences. As a novelist who has researched the Amish culture, Wanda is an expert at explaining the misunderstood aspects of Amish society. Therefore, radio and TV programs regularly invite her to be a guest who can educate their audiences about the Amish way of life.

By identifying the topics in your book that would interest a particular program's audience, you stand a much greater chance to get that producer's interest. Write out a list of specific topics featured in your book and position yourself as an expert on those issues. Later in this chapter, I'll show you how to craft the actual pitch.

BUILD A MEDIA CALENDAR

The media industry depends upon a regular diet of guests to fill their interview slots, and they're always looking for someone new. This constant hunger for guests can work in your favor, especially when you plan ahead.

For instance, if your book focuses on the importance of patriotism, you could be considered as a good fit for a program around the July Fourth holiday or coverage during a congressional election period. If your book covers the struggle that moms make to hold a family together, then Mother's Day would open doors for media exposure. However, don't stretch the connection beyond realistic levels. There must be a legitimate link. Otherwise a producer will see you as just making a self-seeking attempt to get attention for your book.

I encourage my clients to get out a calendar and literally go through it month by month to brainstorm various connections that could arise. This exercise usually yields several applicable options throughout the year. Knowing these options ahead of time makes it easier to pitch media producers early and get in line before other authors clamor to fill open slots.

Even though the media world runs around the clock, producers usually work weeks or months in advance to prepare for featured shows, such as Christmas specials, back-to-school segments, or Valentine's Day. Thus, you need to plan your media calendar and contact producers early. If you want to connect your book's message to a specific holiday, the magazine industry works on a lead time of four to six months. Radio and TV generally prefer lead times of thirty to ninety days. Newspapers and blogs can thrive on shorter lead times, such as seven to thirty days.

WATCH THE HEADLINES AND ACT WITHIN 24 HOURS.

There is one exception to the media lead times that I just mentioned. When big news makes the headlines, programs that focus on news and pop-culture topics need guests who can appear on short notice to help round out a story.

For example, actor Alec Baldwin caught the nation's attention when the public got hold of an angry voice message he left for his daughter. Almost every news outlet and entertainment program covered the story. When this happened, one of my clients had just published a book called *When Your Marriage Dies*. In her book, she had devoted an entire chapter to handling common problems that parents face with their children after going through a divorce. When my client heard the news about Baldwin, she quickly put together a press release and e-mailed it to several radio stations. Within four hours, she received a response from the producer of a well-known radio program.

To maximize your reaction time to media headlines, predetermine what kinds of news would best fit your book's topic. Make a list of the issues, stories, situations, or natural disasters that would make your expertise valuable on short notice should they happen. Keep a running file on your computer and fill it in with discussion points that you could share. That way, when an appropriate headline comes your way, you'll be prepared to act fast.

This strategy is one of the best ways to get media exposure for new authors. Well-known authors tend to rest on their laurels after a while, so their reaction time may be slower. Their delay can open the door for hungry authors who take advantage of contacting producers first with relevant expertise to offer.

BUILD A MEDIA DATABASE

Knowing that producers are the individuals who determine interview bookings, it's another problem to figure who they actually are. More importantly, how do you get your topic in front of them in the first place? Most media producers and newspaper reporters are so busy that they rarely answer their phone. In addition, many receptionists are instructed to take a message for the producer in order to prevent authors from hassling them with cold calls. Trying to reach them directly can be a difficult task.

Fortunately e-mail has become a standard method to reach the media. And, most receptionists have no problem giving out the name and e-mail address of a producer or reporter, if you call and ask politely. In addition, you can usually find the same information on the website of most radio and TV programs as well as major newspapers. If not, get the main office number and talk with the receptionist or ask to speak to someone in the production department.

If you want to get regular media coverage on your own and save money, I recommend that you build and maintain your own database of producers and reporters. By researching online and making a few phone calls, you should be able to create a nice-sized database with just a couple of days effort. Yes, I know this may sound like grunt work. But, if you want to make money as an author, you've got to put in the work. Plus, a couple of days researching and compiling a database is a lot cheaper than hiring an expensive publicity firm. If you're truly strapped for time, this kind of project might better suit a personal assistant or college intern.

Store the names and e-mails that you generate in a notebook, on a computer spreadsheet, or in contact management software, such as ACT! or Goldmine. It doesn't matter how you collect the information, as long you do it and keep it current. There's a lot of turnover in the media industry, so it's wise to double-check the accuracy of your database at least once a year.

Try this idea if you're stuck and need to kick-start your media database research: Contact other authors whom you know and offer to manage a producer contact information swap. I did this as a Christmas present one year for all of my author clients, and it was a huge hit.

Each author submitted contact information they had for any producers or past programs that interviewed them during the past year. Then I verified all of the information that everyone submitted by calling the program's phone number. By the time I was done pooling everyone's information, I collected a list of over 125 legitimate radio and TV media contacts. My author clients used that database to land numerous interviews.

Allow me to throw in a bit of realism here. Is it possible to get booked on national radio and TV by yourself? Yes, many authors I know have done it successfully. However, keep in mind that most top-tier, national-level programs, such as *The Today Show, Dr. Phil,* and *Fox & Friends* have limited numbers of interview spots available. There is stiff competition from freelance publicists and publishing houses to land those valuable slots for the authors they represent. Personal relationships, firsthand experience, and money are involved that give the edge to those organizations.

Does this mean that you should forego pursuing national-level producers? No, by all means get their contact information and go for it. However, I am saying that you will typically have more success on your own when you pursue regional and local-level programs. It's better to get some media exposure than none at all. And regional shows can still generate real promotional power if you book's topic is a good fit for the listening audience. In other words, pursue every media opportunity that makes sense, but keep your expectations realistic so that you don't burn out after one attempt. Success will occur when you consistently provide the media world with value.

CREATE A MEDIA BLAST

So you've developed a relevant topic that would interest the media and have built a database of producer's names. You're ready to take the next step and make contact to generate interviews. The most common way to introduce yourself is by sending out a "media blast." Some people call it sending a "press release" or "news release." The bottom line is that you're sending a concise e-mail intended to capture a producer's attention and entice her to contact you for an interview.

This next section will walk you through each step to create your own media blast. Working from top to bottom, let's look at the key sections that must be included to make it effective:

Section 1—Attention-grabbing title

First things first. If you can't get a producer to read your media blast, then all your effort will be wasted. The trick to getting noticed is making sure you write a captivating title in your e-mail subject line. You must create a title that arrests the reader's attention and makes him think, "Wow, this sounds interesting. I've got to read the rest of this e-mail."

A big reason why so many authors struggle to get interviews is because they create a lame title that fails to charm a producer. Producers don't want bland guests. So if you send out a media blast with a bland title, you can pretty much guarantee that it will be ignored. Here are some examples of titles that will generally get trashed:

"Author available for interview"

"Exciting new book on secrets of parenting"

"Everything you need to know about finances"

"Great new way to lose weight"

Titles like these reek of the amateur, and producers will quickly delete anything that doesn't seem relevant and interesting to their audience. A great way to avoid this mistake is by creating an attention-grabbing title using a counterintuitive point from your book.

The sheer nature of counterintuitive points makes people take notice. Producers are no different. If your title makes them stop and want to know more, then your media blast has a much higher chance of getting read and leading to an interview. Compare the earlier boring titles with the media blast titles below:

"How to reward your employees without spending a dime."

"Mean girls come from mean mammas."

"Church attendance could increase your health risk"

"Is a late-in-life mom America's next best choice for president?"

Notice the difference? If producers see an e-mail with one of these subject lines, their curiosity should peak enough to inspire them to read the entire media blast. These titles automatically make you want to know more. You may even disagree with the title, but that's okay. The goal isn't to be right or appear politically correct. The sole purpose of your opening title is to get your media blast read by a producer.

As you create titles for your blast, gauge their effectiveness by trying them out on a few friends. If you can get them to say "Wow, what's that about?" then you're on the right track. If they hesitate, give you a glazed look, or don't show curiosity, go back to the drawing board.

Once you've developed a compelling title, display it in two places: your e-mail subject line and the top of the body of your main e-mail. If your title is really captivating, try just putting the phrase in your e-mail subject line. However, you could also state the intention of your e-mail blast by putting the words "Author Interview: then list your intriguing title" in the subject line.

Section 2—Opening paragraph

A great title can get your media blast read, but you're still a long way from securing an interview. Now you must prove that it's worthwhile to contact you. Put yourself in the producer's shoes and think about their needs. They're looking for an interesting guest who can keep an audience entertained and keep their program ratings high. How can you help a producer meet these goals? After training many authors at different levels, I've found two methods that work.

Start the first paragraph of your media blast with either a surprising statistic or a shocking story. The beauty of these methods is that they help prove you've got something to discuss that an audience would want to hear. Using a surprising statistic gives a sense of credibility that implies the following: "Hey, I'm an expert, and I've got evidence to support that interviewing me would be of importance to your audience."

One of my clients who wrote a health-related book started off her media blast with this statistic: "One in three American adults over the age of twenty has diabetes or pre-diabetes, and 80 percent of them have no idea!" This is a compelling fact that commands attention. A producer who manages a program that features health and wellness issues would see the benefit in having this author as a guest on their show.

If you use a statistic in your media blast, be sure to identify the source of your data. Producers don't want a guest who has invented facts in order to appear on their show. Your credibility is at stake, so notate where you gathered your facts in a footnote at the bottom of your media blast.

Another method to get a producer's attention is to start your media blast with a compelling story. The story could be about you or someone related to the main theme of your book. The key here is to convey a deep sense of emotion in just a few sentences. Your opening paragraph must be concise and draw the reader immediately, or your media blast will quickly get deleted.

If you want to use a story, keep this point in mind. Just because you think your story is great doesn't mean that a media producer will. If you've overcome a major challenge, such as cancer, depression, job loss, or infertility, many producers won't respond to your story because they've already heard such stories many times over. They don't want their show to sound like a broken record. Producers are looking for fresh stories that talk about issues from a new perspective.

Section 3—Bio paragraph with value statements

After you've grabbed a producer's attention with a convincing statistic or engaging story, you must establish your credibility. This does not mean stating you're the author of a new book. Remember, producers don't care a whit about your book. They care about entertaining and informing their audience. Thus, you want to transition from your opening paragraph into a second paragraph that describes your expertise.

In essence, you're writing a brief bio that explains how your background and experience can bring useful content to an audience. Use the most important aspects of your bio and condense the text down to less than 150 words. I also recommend that you refer back to Chapter 1 of this book and show a bulleted list of your top three to four value statements. These statements should help the producer understand what kind of positive results you can create for the audience.

It is allowable to mention your book title and show a small picture of the front cover in this section. If you're a best-selling author or have a well-known brand, include that information as well. Producers love booking famous people and established experts, because they draw more people to the program. Still, you must use your bio paragraph to communicate that you have information that can entertain or inspire other people. Otherwise a producer will write you off as just another desperate author begging for an interview. Don't be that author. Be the one that surprises producers by showing a sincere desire to help meet their goals.

Section 4—Closing paragraph with suggested interview ideas
As mentioned earlier, producers are extremely busy people who juggle a lot of responsibility. Because of this, one way to gain their favor is by doing their work for them. In other words, pitch a few ideas that portray what an interview segment with you could look like. If you do this step effectively, it can move your name to the top of their potential guest list.

The average author (or publicist) approaches a producer in an attempt to get some airtime for her book. Imagine being a producer who goes into the office every day and has to listen to many people say, "Pick me ... please pick me!" Producers like the power of controlling who gets an interview, but they also get tired of authors who care more about their books than inspiring an audience.

Therefore, set yourself apart by pitching a couple of ideas for a complete six- to ten-minute interview segment. This action saves the producer time by making it easier to see how they can fit you into an upcoming episode. I recommend that you create a clever title for each interview segment idea and list them in a bulleted fashion.

For instance, one of my clients is known as "The Stress Buster." She inserted the following interview ideas into her media blast to book interviews during the Christmas season:

- *Don't Let the Grinch Steal Your Christmas:* How to handle stressful family gatherings with difficult relatives or attend office parties with annoying co-workers.
- *Beat Holiday Stress and Shopping Mall Madness:* How to give ten meaningful gifts without spending a penny!

Section 5—List your contact information

No media blast is complete until you include all of your contact information. Producers will not hunt you down. They have too many other people begging to fill their open interview slots. So make it easy for producers to contact you via office phone, cell phone, e-mail address, and a link to your website.

Even though you're creating a do-it-yourself media blast, everything about it must communicate professionalism. Producers at well-known shows won't risk their reputation on inexperienced authors. Ease their mind by making your media blast look like you're ready to handle any opportunity.

HOW TO BLAST A MEDIA BLAST

At the time of this writing, most producers prefer to be contacted by e-mail. Fax is currently used by only a handful of programs and news outlets. The benefits of using e-mail to send out a media blast are numerous. First, e-mail is inexpensive and immediate. Second, you can contact as many producers as you desire without annoying anyone. Third, you can send your media blast via a reputable e-mail newsletter company, such as ConstantContact.com or MailChimp.com, which can help gauge the effectiveness of your blast by tracking how many producers read your e-mail. In addition, you can see if they clicked on the link to your website to get more information.

Finally, e-mail lets you test the waters by sending your media blast to a small test group of producers to see if they respond. If not, don't give up. Adjust your media blast by using a different title or pitch before sending it out to your entire database.

I also recommend ConstantContact and MailChimp because you can use their service to set up a separate database just for media producers. If a producer's e-mail becomes invalid, it will show up in the reports so that you can contact the program to find the producer's replacement. These services also provide a variety of great-looking e-mail templates you can use for your media blast. These services are affordable, and I've used them for several years.

When you're ready to send out your media blast, compose all of the sections I previously described into your e-mail template. Make sure the layout looks professional, and test it by sending a copy to yourself first. Once everything is to your liking, broadcast your blast by sending it to each media producer's e-mail address individually or as a group in the "Bcc:" blind carbon copy field. Never, I repeat NEVER, put a group of producers e-mail addresses in the "Cc:" copy field, where all of the other recipients can see it. That mistake is the height of amateurism and will disqualify you from interview opportunities.

After you've e-mailed your media blast, wait patiently for three to five business days and see if you get a response by e-mail or phone. If nothing happens after a week, you can try one of the following options: Tweak the title or opening section of your media blast and resend it to your database. Sometimes different wording, or just seeing your e-mail again, will get some producers to respond.

You can also try this option, which one of my clients, the former host of an afternoon radio program in a major city, recommended to me: Personally call and follow up by phone with the producers of the shows that you want to be on the most. In her years of experience, she said that hosts and producers respect an author who follows up by leaving a polite voice mail. Doing so reiterates the focus of your media blast and how you can serve their audience. In her opinion, authors who followed up exuded a passion for their message that garnered bonus points. If you want to try this step, use the following script to leave a message for producers:

> "Hi, my name is _____, and I sent you an e-mail a few days ago about the topic of _____. I would be delighted to appear on your program and talk about the importance of this topic with your audience. I've written a book based on this issue called _____, so I can bring expert-level knowledge to an interview. If you have any questions or would like more information, feel free to contact me at this phone number..."

WD **BONUS ONLINE CONTENT:** Download the article "How to Work With a Publicist" at bookwildfire.com and writers digest.com/book-wildfire-downloads

Summary

Using the strategies in this chapter, almost every one of my author clients has been able to land numerous media interviews on their own. They also report feeling empowered when a producer contacts them with an offer to appear on a program. However, the invitation is only half the battle.

The real fun starts when you show up in a studio and realize that thousands, even millions, of people could be listening to you discuss your book. If you don't have an effective interview strategy in place, you can quickly find yourself overcome by nerves and the sheer anxiety of being in front of a microphone. It's hard to sell books like wildfire when your mouth suddenly goes dry or the host asks you a weird question and you don't know what to say. Fortunately the next chapter is dedicated to helping you appear like a consummate media professional who can impress any audience.

CHAPTER 7

HOW TO TURN MEDIA INTERVIEWS INTO BOOK SALES

A few months after my first book was released in 2002, I received a surprising phone call. As I answered, I was stunned to hear the caller say, "Hi, I'm a producer for the *CBS Early Show*, asking if we could interview you on our national TV program." I was so shocked that I fumbled the phone and almost dropped it on the floor. I couldn't believe my ears.

"How did you find me?" I stammered.

The producer responded, "We were doing some research and ran across your website during a Google search. Can we send a camera crew to your office in the next six days?"

I was dumbfounded. The only professional thing I could think to say was, "Sure."

Six days later, a van loaded with equipment and technical people showed up and knocked on my door. "It's a beautiful day outside, so we've decided to interview you under a tree in your backyard. Is that okay?" "Sure," was my standard professional response. Within forty-five minutes, audio gear was set up, bright lights were blaz-

Ing, cameras were in place, and a famous network correspondent suddenly appeared to ask me a few questions. I tried to stay calm, but the whole experience was surreal. The interview lasted an hour, the crew thanked me, and the producer said the interview would air in a couple of weeks.

Ten days later, I turned on the television and saw my face and my new book being broadcast across the entire country. I was so excited by the exposure that I thought I had won the lottery! My mom was so proud, and my friends couldn't believe it. It felt like one of those life-changing moments.

I braced myself for an avalanche of fame and fortune. My author dream was about to come true. Then nothing happened. I woke up the day after my interview and the phone did not ring with book orders. I checked my Amazon ranking, but it had barely moved. The next day, the same thing happened again—no phone calls, no e-mails, no orders. The next week, it was same thing. Nothing.

It took a few weeks to accept reality and acknowledge my disappointment. I had landed an interview on a top-level national morning show and completely blown it. At first, I placed the blame on the program producers. I reasoned that it was their fault, because they didn't ask me better questions, they failed to show my book cover on the screen, they never mentioned my website, etc.

However, as I pondered what had happened, I realized the true source of the problem was me. It was my fault. I blew it, because I went into the interview without a plan. I was so awestruck that little ol' me was getting a chance to be on national TV that I failed to plan a strategy to maximize the opportunity. I simply assumed that my zeal would be infectious and a national TV interview would rocket me onto the bestseller lists.

Unfortunately I've discovered that I'm not the only author who has made this mistake. I've met authors who have appeared on *The Oprah Winfrey Show*, but for various reasons, their book sales never improved. Like my situation, nothing happened.

Has this same experience happened to you? Have you ever landed a major interview, but blown the opportunity? No boost in book sales...no major website hits...no speaking inquiries...just a congratulatory phone call from your mom.

Worse, are you too easily thrilled with getting on the air that you forget to be purposeful with the precious time you're given? Do you just show up and try to wing it because you hate to practice or sit down and build a solid game plan? Unless you're a celebrity, winging it is not going to help you sell more books. Sure it's fun to tell your friends that you'll be on the radio or TV, but don't let your ego get in the way of building your author platform.

In this chapter, I'm going to explain how to use media interviews to sell more books. If you give a great interview on a national-level program with thousands of people listening, your book sales should increase dramatically. The problem, however, is that too many authors obsess about getting on big-time shows, such as *Good Morning America, The Today Show, NPR, The Daily Show, The Colbert Report, Sean Hannity.* Meanwhile, the reality is that the competition to appear on those programs is fierce, which makes your overall chances of success pretty slim. Plus, just because you even get on a top-level show doesn't guarantee that you'll sell more books.

The wise approach is to garner as much media coverage as you can, regardless whether it's large or small, and learn how to use any interview to spread your message. If you focus on getting consistent exposure, you can build your platform and increase sales for your book.

To clarify, this session doesn't cover how to get more media interviews—that information was covered in Chapter 6. Instead, I will spell out how to help maximize book sales and platform growth once you've already booked an interview, even if you write fiction. That's right, novelists, everything discussed will apply to *any* author. Here's a look at the important issues I'll cover:

- How to prepare for an interview.
- How to control an interview—even with a difficult host.

- How to set appropriate goals and determine real results from your interview.
- How specific techniques can help an interview boost your amount of book sales.
- A secret that most interview hosts don't want you to know.

To start, let me give a brief example of what one successful interview can do for your book. One of my author friends wrote a book for women that focused on self-image issues and money-saving tips on cosmetics. Using her own contacts, she landed a phone interview on a major morning radio show in Atlanta. During her segment, she spent seven minutes sharing her expertise and advice. From that single interview alone, her Amazon ranking shot to #2 in the Health & Beauty category within forty-eight hours. Plus her author website was flooded with over 150 book orders in less than seven days, which yielded over $2,000 in personal sales. In addition, you can bet women were walking into bookstores asking for her book. All of those results stemmed from just one brief radio appearance.

As you can see, the media world offers an incredible amount of power to boost your book sales, but only if you know how to maximize the opportunity.

HOW TO PREPARE FOR A MEDIA INTERVIEW

Before we move forward, I need to bust a common misconception about author interviews. Some authors mistakenly believe that giving an interview is a prime opportunity to teach a large group of listeners. They see the microphone and think class is in session with a captive audience. This mind-set presents two problems.

First, your audience is not captive. They don't have to listen to you if they don't want to. They can change the channel, turn off the program, pay attention to something more interesting, or simply let their minds wander. It is your responsibility, not the host's, to keep an audience riveted on you and your book.

Second, most radio and TV author interviews last less than ten minutes, which isn't enough time to teach much material. You're especially lucky if you get anything over thirty minutes. That's because most programs are formatted for short, eight- to ten-minute segments with commercial breaks in between. So you generally have much less time on the airwaves than you think.

Therefore, it's crucial to use your brief interview to tease the audience, rather than teach the audience. I know the word *tease* may sound offensive. You might be thinking, "It's not right to tease my audience; that's manipulation or shameless self-promotion." In case you feel that way, let's discuss the most ethical action you could take toward your audience.

Let's say, for instance, you wrote a nonfiction book that helps parents communicate better with their children. Or maybe you wrote a fiction novel about a woman overcoming a deep tragedy. What is the best thing to do for your interview listeners? Is it wise to overwhelm your audience by trying to cover every teaching point that you can cram into ten minutes? You can try, but most people won't remember what you say. Wouldn't it be wiser to use your interview to motivate people to get your complete message?

My point is that it's actually more beneficial to your audience if you use an interview to lead listeners to what they really need—your whole book. You can throw a ton of information at people during an interview. But that's like a doctor throwing a box of Band-aids to someone with a serious illness. Band-aids won't cure the problem. Instead, a good doctor forgoes a short-term request and leads the patient down the long-term path to get cured.

Teasing your audience doesn't mean that you avoid giving listeners helpful information. On the contrary, you still need to provide helpful nuggets of value or inspiration to get people interested in your book. But don't try to cover your whole book in an interview. Tell the audience only what they need to know, rather than everything you know.

Most authors are shocked at how the time flies during a media interview. So you must use the brief moments you're given to engage the audience, get them interested in your message, and motivate them to buy your book. How do you do that quickly and effectively? Use this simple strategy. First, develop an interview structure based on a few main points. Second, create attention-grabbing answers to potential interview questions.

DEVELOP MAIN POINTS FOR YOUR INTERVIEW

Since most interviews last only a few minutes, your goal as a guest should be to engage the audience, give them enticing information, and lead them to take action. Most books contain too much information for the author to give a CliffsNotes review of each chapter. Instead, choose just two to four key points that you want to make sure your audience will remember. Key points could be based on the following kinds of important information:

1. If you write nonfiction, it's important to establish your expertise quickly so the audience feels it can trust you. For instance, you could share part of your personal story that captures the audience's attention and boosts your credibility. Present yourself as an interesting person who can relate to the problems that many people in the audience face. For example, award-winning chef and best-selling cookbook author, Paula Deen, is quick to share during her interviews how she once battled financial hardship, anxiety attacks in public places, and raising children as a single mom. Through this difficult period, she used cooking as a way to help rebuild her life and make ends meet. Her story has inspired many women who struggle with similar problems.

2. If you write fiction, you could share something that relates to the characters and situations in your novel. For instance, David Gregory, the best-selling author of *Dinner with a Perfect Stranger*, shares how he always wondered what it would be like to have dinner with Jesus Christ. So he wrote a short novella that captured that kind of situation. He engages his interview listeners

by suggesting what it would be like to find yourself in this interesting scenario.

3. Regardless of whether you write fiction or nonfiction, you must determine how your book can tangibly improve someone else's life. Then create two or three talking points that explain why. Don't waste precious time discussing nonessential background information or extraneous details. Keep your audience focused on the fact that your message can make their lives better. For instance, you could break down your information into interesting statistics, tell specific stories about how you help people, recite a useful resource list, or even conduct a brief quiz.

Whenever I conduct author interviews for my books, I generally try to cover three main points. My first point usually involves sharing my personal story to gain credibility with the audience. Then I attempt to provide at least one or two helpful teaching points, so that the audience feels like I truly helped them solve a problem. In addition, I may discuss new trends in society and show how my book should be considered as a go-to source for the latest information.

As you prepare for an interview, consider your book's primary topics and write out three or four main points that can guide you throughout the discussion. Your goal should be to cover that material before your interview ends. Don't worry, using this strategy won't make you sound canned. Instead, you will come across as organized, and you will feel more confident in front of your audience. It's better to be prepared and risk sounding canned, rather than wing it and blow a great book-selling opportunity.

HOW TO CREATE QUESTIONS FOR AN AUTHOR INTERVIEW

Once you've decided on your main points for your interview, the next step is to develop questions that will lead your host to ask about your main points. If you're new to the interviewing process, you may be thinking, "That sounds weird. Isn't the host supposed to come up with the questions?" You might think so. But in most situations, the hosts don't have time to read your book and create clever questions.

Most program hosts are happy to follow a list of questions that you give them. They may throw in a few questions of their own or cover issues out of order. But generally they will follow the road map that you provide.

This is good news, because it allows you to script your own interview and make sure you touch on your main points. It's like the host lobbing you softballs and letting you hit them out of the ballpark. The key, though, is to make your interview questions sound conversational. For instance, don't write "Question No. 1—Why did you write your book?" Instead, phrase your questions in a manner that a person would ask during a normal conversation. In addition, don't be afraid to make your interview questions sound provocative or controversial. You want people to stay glued to the program instead of changing the channel.

For example, you could write a question, such as, "I understand that you went through an unusual experience three years ago, what led you to write about it?" or "You believe most people are looking at their problem from the wrong angle. What do you mean by that?"

ANSWER YOUR INTERVIEW QUESTIONS WITH A SOUND BITE

Since most interviews are brief, you need to limit your answers to the most important information. I remember when I did a radio interview as a first-time author. I made the rookie mistake of going into deep detail when I answered the interviewer's questions. I talked on and on with a long, drawn-out answer. Then I tried to wrap it up with a clever statement. By that time, however, my audience was bored and disinterested. I had failed to capture their attention in the first place.

One of the best ways to grab your audience is to speak in sound bites, which are pithy statements that sum up your thoughts. Think about sound bites like a newspaper editor using a headline to introduce an article. When an interviewer asks you a question, start your answer with a sound bite. This approach will help keep your audience listening for the rest of your answer.

For example, the first book I wrote was about relationships, so interviewers used to ask me, "Rob, is it appropriate for a woman to ask a man out for a date?" My sound bite response was, "She can try. But, if a man isn't proactive in dating, then he usually won't be proactive in marriage. And, she'll wind up married to an insecure, passive guy." Now, you may disagree with my answer, but my bet is that I grabbed your attention. Plus you probably want me to explain my answer further. This should be your goal as an author: Answer with statements that grab the audience's attention and make them want to know more. Below are examples of sound bites that I've helped some of my author clients create:

- The goal of confrontation should always be restoration—not winning.
- Often, we're kinder to strangers than we are to our kids.
- Sex is like superglue.
- Forgiveness is a gift that you give yourself. As you forgive, you set yourself free.
- In the office, no man is an island. Real men need appreciation.

Logic makes people think, but emotion makes them act. So a good sound bite helps generate emotion in your listeners, such as laughter, curiosity, or even anger. When people feel a deeper interest in your book, they will want to buy it. Remember, someone may be listening to your interview while driving in his car or working at his office. Therefore, it may be quite a while before he gets a chance to purchase your book. If you find a way to stick in his memory, then you increase the likelihood that he will take action later.

USE VISUALS AND METAPHORS
Authors who know how to maximize media interviews are masters of metaphors and visual aids. It's not easy to discuss complex sub-

jects in a short amount of time. But you can help your audience recall your message by using word pictures and memorable objects.

I used to help listeners understand my book's message by combining metaphors with a tangible item. For instance, I would say, "Romance is like chocolate. Chocolate tastes good, and romance feels good. But both will eventually leave you unsatisfied and searching for more substance." Then I would hold up a giant 5-pound Hershey's chocolate bar as a visual aid. When I did television interviews, I could literally hear the studio camera crew gasp around me! As you can imagine, my chocolate prop made it easy for audiences to remember the main point of my book.

What kind of similar ideas can you create to make your message memorable? We live in a visually oriented society, and you need to consider the lowest common denominator of your audience. Using visual aids and word pictures makes it easier for everyone to understand the benefits of your book. One author I know uses a metaphor about blueprints and home construction to describe how his message can help couples build stronger marriages. Then he cleverly gives away a Home Depot gift card to his listeners as a prize. Listeners find it simple to remember his message.

Let me challenge you not to be cheesy when using metaphors or visuals. It's easy to copy another person's ideas, abandon creativity, or just throw something together. But if you do, you'll wind up hurting your credibility. If, for instance, your book discusses the various roles that women face, don't talk about wearing different hats or pull out something silly and put it your head. That's a stale idea. Instead, make the effort to create visuals that are memorable in a unique way.

As you prepare for an author interview, keep the previous points in mind. Create interview questions, develop sound bites for each answer, and incorporate visuals aids and metaphors. Then memorize your sound bites and practice out loud. If you do, you are more likely to appear professional and sound confident on the air.

THE MEDIA MIND-SET OF A PROFESSIONAL

Many authors mistakenly believe that just getting an interview automatically yields big book sales. This is a myth, because you can't show up as a guest and expect everybody to love your message. During every interview, there are several factors working against you, such as a short time limit, a bossy or disinterested host, other guests competing for attention, or a smaller audience size than anticipated.

To prevent these factors from diminishing your book sales, you must have a plan and be willing to work that plan with assertion. How do you assert yourself properly? Get over your awe of the media, and act like an equal.

Here's why your mind-set is critical. If you don't believe that you're an expert who deserves to be in front of an audience, your audience will sense your insecurity. Plus, if the host discerns your anxiety, she will be put in the difficult position of trying to make your interview sound professional. The host will feel like you have to be carried, which is a very annoying burden. Therefore, you must convince yourself that you belong on radio or television before you can convince other people.

The secret to acting like an equal is by treating your interview host as a peer. He isn't better than you, and you're no better either. You are equals, which means both parties can respectfully share concerns, ask for cooperation, and expect professional treatment from one another.

The reality is that the media industry needs authors as much as authors need exposure for their books. Radio and TV programs need a stream of lively guests with expert content for their audience. Likewise, you need a way to promote your message to a large group of people. You need each other equally. Consequently you are working together as partners to make something good happen. So don't cower like a beggar who's simply glad to be in the studio. Conduct yourself like someone who belongs in front of the microphone.

Besides exhibiting the right attitude, the best way to control an interview is to prepare for anything that might happen. This preparation includes creating effective questions, sending them ahead of time to the host, and practicing to answer any oddball topics that might arise. You don't need to prepare for every eventuality. But you want to have a working knowledge of your book, current headlines, and any related subject matter so that you're ready to offer an answer.

I used to sit in my office and practice my sound bites and interview answers out loud. In addition, I'd use a timer to rehearse how long it took to tell my main points and personal story. I practiced and made adjustments until I could clearly say all of my answers in less than two minutes. Remember that many of your interviews may be live. So you can't stumble through your answers and expect someone to edit your comments. You only get one shot to do it right.

As I continued to practice for my interviews, my comfort level and confidence shot through the roof. I no longer feared the microphone, bright lights, or TV cameras. Instead, I felt energized as an expert who could influence a lot of people with my message, because I knew I was ready to offer helpful information.

If you want to give a professional-quality interview, practice out loud by yourself beforehand. Only amateurs wing it, because they're lazy and inconsiderate of their audience. If you take a careless attitude to your interview, your audience will usually take it out on you by ignoring your book.

HOW TO CONTROL A CONVERSATION

A good way to gauge your interview prowess is to master the ability to steer a conversation to only the topics that you want to discuss. Just because a radio or TV host asks you a question does NOT mean that you must answer it. Sure it's polite to respond to someone's question. But if the host starts down a verbal rabbit trail, you're not obligated to follow. Doing so will take time away from talking about your main points.

Occasionally you may interact with a host who condescends to you or openly disagrees with your opinion. Don't let him or her bully you. Instead, sidestep the argument and redirect the question to a subject that you want to discuss. It's like steering a car. The host may ask the questions, but you're the one driving the direction of the conversation. Here are three different responses you can use when a host asks you something antagonistic or irrelevant:

- "Yes, that's an interesting issue. But, I've found that an even bigger issue is ..."
- "I'll be glad to answer that question. But, first, let me say something about ..."
- "You bring up a good question. But before I leave I really want to emphasize this point to today's listeners ..."

Remember: You're the expert, the host is not. Therefore, it makes sense for you rather than the host to control the flow of information to the audience. The host probably hasn't even read your book.

Try this exercise the next time you're channel surfing. Tune in to CNN or FOXNews. When an interview segment occurs, watch carefully how politicians or corporate executives control the interview. These people can take almost any question and steer their answer to the point they want to make. Sometimes it gets annoying, because they rarely say anything with substance. But they stay focused on their agenda, which is your goal as an author. With a little practice, you can develop a similar ability to keep the conversation focused on your book's message.

Before I leave this topic, let me clarify that I'm not advocating manipulation or impolite behavior on the air. However, I am stating the fact that getting on national TV or radio is hard for anyone to do. So don't take it lightly. You probably won't get a second chance to be on the show. If you fumble an interview because you weren't prepared or felt intimidated by the situation, then it's a disservice to your audience, your publisher, and your book sales. Only you can make an interview successful.

SMILE FOR THE CAMERA

At the beginning of this chapter, I shared the story of getting interviewed on the *CBS Early Show*. Up until that time, I had only done a couple of small-time interviews on cable TV channels that few people watched. So after the *Early Show* producer called, my jubilation quickly turned to anxiety. I had never been in front of an audience of millions.

My wife had the presence of mind to suggest I take a few practice runs. So I sat in my office one afternoon while she lobbed questions at me. After a few questions she said something strange. "You look too stern when you answer the questions. You appear defensive and anxious." I responded, "What do you mean? I feel confident and at ease with my comments." I was confused about what she was seeing until she said, "Go look at yourself in the mirror." Lo and behold, she was right.

When I watched myself answer her questions in the mirror (you could use a home video camera), I looked dour and uncomfortable. And, I had no idea that the image I was portraying appeared so negative. Without the mirror, I thought I had looked fine. That's when I learned the Golden Rule for TV Interviews—smile constantly.

I don't care if your face hurts or the host insults you. Never stop smiling on camera. You've probably heard that the TV camera adds ten pounds. Well, I believe that smiling on camera multiplies your credibility by ten times. And that will increase your book sales. Let me explain what I mean.

Years ago, I watched financial expert, Dave Ramsey, appear on *The Oprah Winfrey Show* to promote his new book, *The Total Money Makeover*. The episode featured a family who was in deep debt, and Oprah asked Dave to give them financial advice right on the spot. Now, if you've ever heard or seen Dave in person, you know that he has a great personality with a jovial laugh. Yet, as I watched him on Oprah, I noticed he didn't smile much. She asked him rapid-fire questions, but Dave's demeanor appeared negative. He didn't look confident, and it diminished the power of his interview. In Dave's defense, he's now a best-selling author with his own TV show. But his coming-out party wasn't as powerful as intended.

In contrast, I once watched an interview on *60 Minutes* with a Walmart executive who used smiling to her advantage. She was defending her company's position in a land-use lawsuit over the location of a new store. The reporter from *60 Minutes* was grilling her with harsh, accusatory questions. Yet, during the entire interview, this Walmart official never stopped smiling. She sat with a pleasant demeanor, patiently answered questions, and never once looked perturbed. Even if viewers disagreed with her position, she came across as credible and professional. I found myself liking who she seemed to be as a person. It was a strange interview to witness, but that scene reinforced the power of smiling on camera.

So always smile on camera during your author interview. Oddly enough, smiling can help improve your radio interviews as well. Hopefully, you'll never be questioned by an antagonistic reporter, but if it happens, you'll be ready to insure your credibility and boost your expert status.

SET PROPER GOALS FOR YOUR INTERVIEW

Once you've structured an interview around your main points and interesting sound bites, the next step is to set appropriate goals. By goals, I mean realistic measures to determine if your interview helped build your author platform and generate book sales. There are many factors to consider, but let's briefly look at four indicators of success: credibility, likeability, book purchases, and visitor signups.

INTERVIEW GOAL #1: CREDIBILITY—Most people will be hesitant to buy your book unless they feel like they can trust you, especially if you write nonfiction. So establishing credibility during your interview is critical. But don't make the mistake of letting your bio or your credentials carry that burden. The best way to establish credibility is provide listeners with information that improves their lives. Enable your listeners to solve a problem, overcome a struggle, or change their perspective. When your interview is over, you want the audience to walk away thinking, "Wow, that author really helped me today."

INTERVIEW GOAL #2: LIKEABILITY—Being liked by your audience is second to gaining credibility. That's because sometimes it's better to be credible and controversial, rather than likeable and boring. Nonetheless people are more likely to buy your book if they like you. So during your interview, concentrate on being pleasant. Feel free to laugh and act aware of your audience.

Don't just focus on the host and robotically answer questions. Show genuine emotion, and imagine your audience as a person sitting next to the host. Include them in the discussion by making comments, such as "I know many listeners today may feel this way..." or "Is it just me, or do we all seem to struggle in this area?"

INTERVIEW GOAL #3: BOOK PURCHASES—The obvious goal of any media interview is to help sell more books. The problem is that it can be difficult to monitor this result. You will never know how many listeners went to a bookstore and purchased your title. However, there are statistics that you can track.

First, you can check your book's Amazon ranking before and after your interview. Or you can monitor the Nielsen BookScan sales numbers for your title through your Amazon author account. Compare the figures to the date of your interview to see if there's a significant improvement in sales during that time period.

If you sell books directly from your author website, examine the success of your interview by checking for increased visitor traffic to your store page and orders placed on your site. And, if you conduct an interview in a specific city, you could even contact a few bookstores in that town and ask the manager if sales of your book picked up after your interview date.

INTERVIEW GOAL #4: VISITOR SIGN-UPS—Let's be realistic. Most listeners aren't going to rush out to buy your book based on a six-minute interview. However, you can still motivate a lot of people to want to hear more of your message. Capitalize on their interest by encouraging your interview audience to visit your website and register for a free newsletter, subscribe to your blog updates, or join one of your social networks (Facebook, Twitter, etc.). I'll tell you how to do this a little later in the chapter.

It's no small consolation for people to give you their contact information and invite you to stay in touch with them. You may not sell a book today, but those who register for your newsletter are more likely to buy from you in the future. Building a large database of newsletter subscribers, blog readers, or social network fans is a key component to growing your author platform. This fact is especially true if you find yourself with an active list of over 5,000 people.

Based on the four goals mentioned above, you have several ways to determine if your media interview is productive. But what if you conduct a few interviews and nothing happens? Suppose your book sales remain stagnant, or your website doesn't receive increased visitor traffic?

If you're not seeing results, something is wrong. Either your message is falling on the wrong kind of audience, or you're not giving your audience enough tangible value to excite them. The next section will offer some ideas to help remedy that situation.

LEAD THE AUDIENCE TO YOUR BOOK

Conducting an author interview doesn't always create more book sales. That's because most people in the audience tend to listen with an apathetic or skeptical mentality. It's the author's responsibility to educate and inspire the audience to take action. Below are some ways you can help motivate listeners to purchase your book.

1. NEVER SAY "MY BOOK" AS PART OF YOUR ANSWER—This may sound like a no-brainer, but it's a classic mistake too many authors continue to make. Whenever you conduct an interview, always say the full title of your book (you can skip the subtitle). If your book happens to have a long title, then mention a condensed version. But never say "my book." Why?

People usually need to hear your title at least three or four times before they can actually remember it. Plus, you can't expect everyone to listen to your entire interview. Some people will tune in for the beginning but leave before you've finished. Others may not tune in until your interview is already in progress. Saying your title a few times throughout the interview helps secure it into the listeners' minds.

2. OFFER A FREEBIE—It's unrealistic to expect most of the listening audience to buy your book immediately after an interview. However, it is realistic to expect a lot of people to take something that you give away for free. People love free stuff. Use this desire to your advantage by offering a free resource that builds rapport with your listeners and moves them closer to buying your book.

You can literally lead people to buy your book by creating an item of value and offering it as a gift. During your interview, mention the freebie to listeners and tell them it's available at your website. For maximum effectiveness, create interview questions and answers that allow you to naturally mention your freebie in the middle of your interview discussion.

For instance, you could end one of your answers by saying, "I know that people may want more information about what we've discussed today. To help out, I'm offering a free _____ (article/report/resource guide) to everyone listening. To get it, just visit my website at www..." Or, you could say, "I've enjoyed being on the program. To say thanks, I'm offering a free _____ to everyone who tuned in. Go to my website today at www..."

An effective freebie is something that motivates people to take action. Good examples could include an exclusive article, report, newsletter, quiz, audio CD, DVD video, accompanying study guide, special resource listing, or behind-the-scenes info. The possibilities are limitless. The key, however, is to make your item valuable and interesting enough that people truly want it.

Avoid lame freebies, such as sample chapters, coupons, trivial articles, recipes, and top ten lists. These ideas are cliché and usually fail to garner interest from your audience.

3. MENTION YOUR WEBSITE ADDRESS DURING THE INTERVIEW—Here's a little secret that some radio and TV shows don't want authors to know. Many media programs don't want to mention your author website address, and some hosts will refuse to say it on the air. I find this mentality ridiculous, especially when they're getting authors to appear for free on their programs.

However, here's the rationale behind their position. Some programs make a lot of revenue by charging for advertising space on their website. If they can boost their website's hits and visitor statistics, then they can charge more money for advertising space. So they'd prefer to not mention your website, because they don't want their audience to go to your website over theirs. This attitude can cause problems for authors. For instance, if you mistakenly say "my book" and never mention your website during an interview, then the audience could easily forget your book's title and never know where to get more information.

Fortunately there's a way to get around a host who is unwilling to help. Use your freebie item I just mentioned to bring your website up in the middle of conversation. When you offer a helpful resource that's free, it's hard for the host to prevent you from talking about it during the interview. Entice listeners with your freebie and drive the audience to you by telling them the only place to get it is at your website. Once they arrive, you can take steps to invite them into a relationship with you and your book (see Chapter 5 about author websites).

4. ATTRACT VISITOR SIGN-UPS—When listeners visit your website, ask them to subscribe to your free newsletter or sign up for blog updates in order to receive their gift. Doing so allows you to collect their contact information and build a growing database of people interested in your message. A sign-up box on your website's home page might say, "Sign up for my newsletter and get my (insert the name of your freebie)."

If you're uncomfortable making people sign up to get your freebie, you can still make it available from a special page on your website. When they click to that page, they can access your item without additional steps. Or you can have a newsletter sign-up box next to the freebie and invite people to sign up there.

Maybe you're thinking, why go through all of this trouble? Well, it would be nice if everyone listening to your media interview came to your website and purchased a book. But that's not going to happen. If you motivate them to provide their contact information, however, you increase the odds of a sale in the future. I know several authors who've written numerous books, but shortchanged their success because they never built a growing database of subscribers.

People who remain interested in your message are much more likely to buy your book. In addition, readers who buy your book are much more likely to tell their friends about it and even buy your next book down the road.

You can't sell books like wildfire if you don't know the people who appreciate your material.

By the way, taking these steps to gather contact information will not hurt your bookstore sales or your Amazon ranking. Many readers will still prefer to get your book through those channels.

If you want to grow your author platform, you need to create an ever-expanding database of interested readers. Media interviews can help you quickly grow your list. I know several authors who regularly pick up over one hundred subscribers per interview. These new sign-ups represent a lot of future book orders and word-of-mouth marketing assistance.

But don't take your database for granted. Stay in touch with these folks by sending newsletters or writing regular blog posts packed with helpful information that keep them interested in your message. For help crafting powerful newsletters, see Chapter 13.

If you're still not convinced about the need to create a growing reader database, consider that many publishers today will not accept a book proposal from an author who doesn't have a personal list with thousands of contacts. As marketing budgets get slashed, publishers are leaning more on the author for promotional support. When you show a publisher that you possess a large, legitimate database, they're more likely to show you extra attention.

Summary

By following the steps listed in this chapter, you should feel ready to take on the media world with confidence. You know how to prepare for an interview, control the discussion, determine real results, and turn listeners into customers. Don't waste the opportunity that an interview offers to capture hundreds, if not thousands, of new readers.

Act like the expert you are, and act like an equal to the host. Use the microphone to give away free advice, and use your website freebies to build a growing database of customers. Good media interviews get results, and they're one of the fastest ways to help you sell books like wildfire.

CHAPTER 8

FEED THE BEAST: HOW TO USE AMAZON TO SELL MORE BOOKS

Have you checked your book's Amazon ranking today? Nothing has mesmerized authors more than sneaking a peek at this ever-changing online number. Likewise, no company has tapped into the author obsession with their book's sales numbers more powerfully than Amazon.com, the world's largest Internet retailer. By creating a unique ranking system that constantly updates for every book, Amazon captured the attention of authors who are desperate to know if people are buying their work. Creating this fascination is one of the smartest business moves Amazon ever made.

Amazon is no stranger to controversy and making waves in the publishing industry. Its ability to influence book prices, maintain a massive selection, start its own publishing imprints, and monitor the buying habits of customers has established Amazon as the dominant force that every author and publisher must learn to manage. The company has emerged as the strongest, most powerful player in the industry. The organization represents the 800-pound gorilla that no one can ignore. Its growth is unprecedented, and Amazon is challenging Barnes & Noble for the position of No. 1 overall book retailer in America.

In addition, no other company has influenced book marketing like Amazon. Founder, Jeff Bezos, perfected the online shopping experience, pioneered the five-star book review system, created the book sales ranking feature, and single-handedly drove the explosion of e-books with the Kindle e-reading device. If you want to sell books like wildfire, you must learn how to navigate the online jungle that is Amazon. This chapter will explain how to use Amazon's promotional tools to maximize exposure for your books in the world's largest bookstore.

AMAZON RANKINGS EXPLAINED

A deep mystery exists over how Amazon calculates its book sales rankings. The algorithm used is as closely guarded as the secret recipe for Coca-Cola. How can authors tell how many books they're selling over time via their Amazon ranking? The truth is that no one knows for sure. In fact, even employees on the staff at Amazon report that the ranking system isn't completely accurate.

Therefore, your primary focus should be to stop obsessing over your book's Amazon ranking, because it's never a true indicator of sales. More important, the ranking only represents one channel of total retail book sales. Fortunately Amazon now offers a superior service to the sales ranking system, which I'll discuss in the next section.

Years ago, a few math wizards with a lot of time on their hands attempted to shed some light on the Amazon sales-rank issue. Here's an interesting summary of their study:

Your Amazon Ranking = Estimated Weekly Sales

10,000 = 30 books per week

100,000 = 6 books per week

1,000,000 = less than 1 book per week

(Source: Morris Rosenthal, 2007 http://www.fonerbooks.com/surfing.htm)

Using the table above, if you wanted to estimate your book's Amazon sales, you checked your ranking periodically over a few months. Once you'd gathered some numbers over time, you calculated the average number, and applied it to the chart above. For example, suppose you checked the ranking of your book once a month for three consecutive months. Those rankings were 5,500, 13,000, and 11,500. Over those three months, your average ranking would be 10,000 (5,500+13,000+11,500 / 3 = 10,000). If you apply 10,000 to the chart above, then you could guess that you're selling around thirty books a week. Remember, this is just a guess, no one knows for sure.

If you assume that your average ranking stays the same for a year, then multiply thirty books per week by fifty-two weeks, and you're only selling around 1,500 copies annually. Doesn't seem like much, does it? That's why your Amazon ranking shouldn't be something that stresses you out. It's not worth the emotional energy spent worrying about it.

So don't overanalyze your Amazon sales rankings. Look at it this way: An average rank of 1,000 means you have a successful title. An average rank of 10,000 means you're doing pretty good for a book that's not a bestseller. An average rank of 100,000 means it's not going to add much to your income. And an average rank of 1,000,000 or higher means you need to stop checking your rankings altogether and focus on your day job.

If you're average ranking is lower than 10,000, pat yourself on the back, because Amazon customers are probably buying over 1,000 copies per year. But that isn't enough money to pay the bills.

The reason I even mention this questionable Amazon research is to show how few books an author actually sells—even with a seemingly good sales ranking. In other words, you're wasting your time if you obsess over your sales rank. Fortunately Amazon provides a free service that takes the guesswork out of your book sales.

AMAZON'S "AUTHOR CENTRAL" SERVICE

In many ways, Amazon has positioned itself as a friend to the author community. The people at Amazon realized that authors are the best people to promote their books, because writers possess the closest and most passionate influence on readers. So Amazon launched a free service called "Author Central" (https://authorcentral.amazon.com), which provides several helpful ways for you to organize, promote, and track the success of your titles.

A big complaint among authors is that they have to wait up to six months to get royalty statements from their publisher to determine actual book sales. This delay keeps authors in the dark on the success of their promotional efforts (and keeps publishers in control). Amazon to the rescue! In an incredibly generous move, Amazon offers the official Nielsen BookScan sales data to all authors—for free!

This data is provided to Amazon by Nielsen BookScan and includes the actual nationwide book sales information from over ten thousand retailers, including Barnes & Noble, Target, Deseret Book Company, Hastings, Follett College stores, Buy.com, and Amazon's print book sales. Retailers currently not included at the time of this writing are Walmart, Costco, libraries, and religious retail chains, such as Family Christian Stores, Parable, and LifeWay. Nielsen estimates that BookScan captures around 75 percent of the total print book sales in the U.S. retail market. The numbers only reflect print book sales, not the e-book versions.

Besides this free sales information, Amazon also displays a geographic map that shows where your books were sold during the past thirty days with a lag time of one week. You can also view a list of the top cities across America where books are selling the most. In addition, you can see a graph of the Amazon sales ranking history for each of your books. This data lets you determine if sales peaked or dropped over time based on your promotional efforts.

Amazon's Author Central service is the closest data that authors can get to real-time aggregate sales numbers that's only available to publishers—and it's not cheap. Major publishers pay over $100,000 per year for this same information. So the fact that Amazon lets authors gain access to this data for free is amazing.

To review the sales data for your books, go to: https://author-central.amazon.com and set up a free author account. You will be asked to prove that you're the author of your books and create a bibliography of all your titles. Once you're account is set up, you can log in and find a tab at the top of the main page that says "Sale Info." Click on that tab and see your actual sales history for the past thirty days, which may be exhilarating or depressing. It's better to get the truth from Neilsen BookScan than it is to obsess over faulty sales rankings from Amazon.

AUTHOR PROMOTIONAL TOOLS
Besides updated sales info about your books, Amazon also provides several marketing tools that help authors bring more attention to their books. Here are four free steps that I encourage you to take:

1. Set up an author profile page
Amazon allows authors to create their own biography page, complete with a head shot and minibio around 100 words. The benefit of having an author profile page is that whenever someone searches for one of your books on Amazon, your profile page will usually appear near the top of the search results. This allows people to click on your page and learn more about you and all of the other books you may have written. For instance, if you're a novelist who's penned a trilogy or a nonfiction author who's written a series of related books, your Amazon author page can help cross-promote, raising awareness of all your titles.

2. Publicize your videos
Another beneficial feature of Amazon's Author Central service is the ability to post up to eight videos on your profile page. This service allows you to capture readers' attention by uploading book trailers, author interviews, or exclusive behind-the-scenes information about your titles. The formats currently supported include .avi, .flv, .mov, .mpg, and .wmv. Videos must be less than ten minutes long and smaller than 500MB.

3. List upcoming author events

Author Central also allows you to inform readers about upcoming events on your profile page. Let's say you're setting up a tour of book signings, media interviews, and speaking events to support a new book. Amazon lets you show the details for all of these events, including a description along with the date, venue, address, time, and even the individual book that you're supporting. Since Amazon garners more traffic than any other online retailer, this service is a great way to let your readers know when and where to meet you in person.

4. Display recent blog posts

If you're a consistent blogger, Amazon makes it easy to embed your blog via RSS feed into your author profile page. Author Central supports all versions of RSS and Atom blog feeds. Posts created before you add this feed will not be imported. If you want previous posts to appear on the author page, you will have to repost them on your home blog. However, connecting your blog to Amazon allows you to keep book shoppers informed on your latest thoughts, events, contests, and updates about future books. The following authors have great-looking Amazon profile pages: Lisa Gardner, Craig Groeschel, and Stephen King.

AMAZON CUSTOMER REVIEWS—THE COLLECTIVE VOICE OF THE READING WORLD

After reading thus far, you may be wondering, "What's the point of monitoring my book's individual Amazon page and maintaining an author profile if my sales rankings are inaccurate?" You should still keep an eye on this data, because there is a larger force at work on Amazon. This force is enormously influential and capable of directly affecting your book sales. The power of which I speak is known as the "collective voice," or in layman's terms—Amazon customer reviews.

When Amazon formalized a simple way for ordinary customers to review the books they purchase, the publishing industry was suddenly turned upside down. No longer did the stodgy literary reviewers, such as *The New York Times* or *Publishers Weekly*, hold sway over popular opinion. Now, the common man can exert just as much influence over the public's book-buying decisions simply by posting a five-star or one-star review on Amazon.

For example, when someone recommends a book to me, I typically search for that book on Amazon and read through several of the reviews. Based on those comments, I tend to form an opinion as to whether or not I want to purchase. If I read a majority of positive reviews that are thoughtfully written, I'll probably decide to buy. Ironically I may not actually buy the book on Amazon. Instead, I may get a copy the same day at my local bookstore. Yet those Amazon reviews are usually the first place I go to start my purchasing process, and they sometimes provide the motivation within me to buy. In contrast, if I read enough negative reviews on Amazon from people saying that a book is a waste of time and money, I'll probably pass on that title. Thus, that author misses a sale from me.

The power of customer reviews on Amazon has become a big factor over people's buying decisions. And Amazon's review system is more robust and influential than any other retailer. As an author, you cannot afford to ignore the persuasive force that's in play. That's why I recommend monitoring your Amazon book reviews and staying on top of the public's feedback. If you disregard what people say, you could needlessly lose a lot of book sales.

Reading through book reviews can be like listening to someone critique your newborn baby. It's easy to get emotionally involved when other people discuss something so personal. To help ease your soul, keep these points in mind:

1. Focus on quantity over quality
When it comes to Amazon customer reviews for your book, keep in mind that quantity trumps quality, regardless if most reviews are positive or negative. Why? Your book is better off when lots of

people are talking about it, even if their feedback isn't all positive. A big, loud discussion is better for generating public interest than a quiet, civilized discussion that no one ever hears. An author's worst enemy isn't negativity or piracy, it's obscurity. If only a few people are reviewing your book on Amazon, you've got a bigger problem than a few people giving you bad reviews.

For example, I'd much rather see one hundred Amazon reviews of my book with equally mixed opinions than only get five to ten total reviews who all say the book is great. When the conversation is that small, book shoppers tend to feel there's nothing interesting about your book. In contrast, some negative feedback can actually stoke stronger interest and generate sales for your title.

Therefore, if you want Amazon customer reviews to benefit your book, try to garner as many as possible. The best way to achieve this goal is by writing a great book, obviously! High-quality work ultimately stimulates the most feedback. That's why the quality of your writing still matters immensely to your book's success. If you churn out a boring, uninspired manuscript without solid research and editing, you will pay a price in the court of public opinion.

Having said that, it's okay to ask your friends and fans to support you by posting positive reviews on Amazon, as well as other sites such as BarnesandNoble.com, GoodReads, LibraryThing, Facebook, Twitter, and others. If you find that your book is struggling to get many reviews, here are some active steps you can take to address the issue.

- Send out a newsletter or an e-mail blast to your fans asking them to submit a review. Some of my clients who make *The New York Times* Best Seller List do this regularly.
- When someone sends you a letter or an e-mail thanking you for your book, respond quickly and ask that person to return the favor by posting a review.
- Ask people who have already given you a formal endorsement to post their glowing comments on Amazon.

- Never become desperate and pretend that you're someone else in order to post a review under another name. If Amazon catches you, your reputation will be damaged.

If you try these steps but still can't amass more than thirty reviews, your book may be the problem. Either it's not selling enough to generate positive reaction, or your content may be too boring to ignite a reader's desire to give feedback. A small amount of book reviews usually means a small amount of book sales.

2. Ask for help if you get antagonistic reviews

There may be times when you receive really harsh reviews. This is a common occurrence for most authors. Instead of stewing about it, ask your fans to assist. I know a distinguished author who received a slate of negative reviews because a group of people were jealous of his success. They immaturely took out their frustration by trashing his books on Amazon with angry, ridiculous comments. This author wisely countered the situation by sending an e-mail to his fans that politely explained the situation and asked for their help. Within a few days, he had received enough positive reviews to drown out the antagonistic party.

I'm not advocating that you fixate over what's said about your work. However, Amazon customer reviews can carry so much weight that you may need to wage an occasional "war of words" to protect the public opinion of your book.

3. Don't allow negative reviews to control you

If someone posts a negative review about your book, keep things in the proper perspective. Stay open to constructive criticism, because it can help you improve as a writer. There's a biblical proverb that says, "Plans go wrong for lack of advice, but many advisers bring success." Keep your ego in check as you monitor the feedback about your books.

Just like obsessing over your Amazon sales ranking is a waste of time, obsessing over your Amazon reviews is also unhealthy. People have a free will, and they're entitled to their opinions. You can't control what they will say, and fretting over someone criticizing your book will only put you on the fast track to getting an ulcer.

It's a good idea to discount most unsolicited feedback. In other words, don't let random comments get embedded in your psyche. Instead, pay attention to feedback from people whom you trust and those professionals who've walked the path ahead of you. Most unsolicited feedback usually comes from people who have an agenda. That person has an axe to grind, and they've decided to take it out on you. There's nothing you can do to prevent it.

One of the healthiest steps that an author can take is to adopt the mind-set of letting ridiculous comments roll away like water rolling off a duck's back. Yes, it's that simple. You are not indebted to give people your emotional or mental energy, especially when they don't deserve it. You can either ignore them or firmly tell them to back off.

In addition, just because someone may not like your book doesn't mean you're a bad person with no potential as a writer. If an Amazon review affects your self-esteem, then get into counseling or get out of publishing, because criticism is part of life as an author.

AMAZON MARKETING TOOLS FOR PUBLISHERS:
Thus far I've discussed several tools Amazon makes available to authors to help promote your books. However, there are some tools reserved just for publishers. You won't be able to access these services as an individual. But it's good to know about them. If you're traditionally published, ask your editor or marketing director if they plan to use these tools for your book's campaign.

1. Amazon Video Service
If a picture is worth a thousand words, then a video can be worth a million. If you have a good book trailer, ask your publisher to utilize Amazon's video service, which embeds trailers on your book page. These trailers can feature author interviews, behind-the-scenes clips, or fancy commercials that resemble a movie advertisement. Amazon typically positions these videos in a central location just below

a book's cover image. Visitors notice the video right away and can click on it to view.

Pricing for this service is not made public. Check with your publisher to request getting your book trailer placed on your Amazon page.

2. X+Y Program

Amazon also offers publishers a cross-promotion program that links similar books together at a discounted price. For instance, a publisher may use a new frontlist title to draw attention to a forgotten backlist title, and vice versa. When customers visit that book's specific page, they'll see a promotional area that says "Best value," which displays two book covers together and suggests "Buy together today" at a lower combined price.

The X+Y program can be beneficial by helping resurrect a backlist title during major promotions of a similar new book. As marketing efforts drive shopping traffic to see the new book, the X+Y promotion reminds them about the older book and encourages people to buy both for a significant discount. You can also reverse the process by using a strong backlist title that gets consistent traffic to highlight a book that recently launched.

Pricing for this service is not made public. If you have similar books that could work well in tandem, ask your publisher about using the Amazon X+Y program.

3. Amazon Vine Program

Publishers know the importance of getting a large quantity of customer reviews for their books. The more people buzz about a book, the more likely it is that sales will increase. Amazon has attempted to assist with this process by creating the Amazon Vine™ program.

According to Amazon, "The purpose is to enable a select group of Amazon customers to post opinions about new and prerelease items to help their fellow customers make educated purchase decisions. Customers are invited to become Amazon Vine™ Voices based on the trust they have earned in the Amazon community for writing accurate and insightful reviews. Amazon provides members with free copies of products that have been submitted to the program by vendors. Amazon does not influence the opinions of Amazon Vine™ members, nor do we modify or edit their reviews."

This program isn't without controversy. Some people have accused Amazon of allowing people to generate reviews just so they can get new products for free. Others feel that some individuals who review the products don't possess the expertise needed to make intelligent and unbiased feedback on certain items.

Publishers pay Amazon to use the service and provide free books that are distributed by Amazon to selected reviewers. In my own experience, I haven't seen enough reviews generated by this service to warrant the price. I've worked on a couple of book campaigns where the publisher used Amazon Vine, but those particular books received less than five additional reviews as a result.

As with the other Amazon services, pricing is not made public. So if you're interested in the Vine program, you'll need to talk with your publisher.

Summary

No other company currently influences the publishing industry as much as Amazon. The retailer continues to drive more book sales faster than any organization in history. Its growth rate is unprecedented, and its ability to set lower prices, dominate the e-book revolution, and capture enormous web traffic cannot be ignored.

Wise authors will take the steps covered in this chapter to make sure their books get the most attention possible in the world's largest online bookstore. Yet, Amazon accounts for only part of your book's online selling potential. The next chapter will discuss the world of social media and how to create a digital wildfire that rages through cyberspace.

CHAPTER 9

THE SKINNY ON SOCIAL NETWORKING

DISCLAIMER: Due to the rapidly changing nature of technology, many of the topics in this chapter are subject to change. Heck, things are happening so fast that by the time you read this, we could all be reading books on a three-dimensional holographic device that also makes the perfect cup of coffee. I can dream, can't I? Suffice it to say, the world of social media is constantly evolving. Therefore, I encourage you to visit this book's website for the latest information on technology and other marketing updates at www.BookWildfire.com

Social media, such as Facebook, Twitter, Google+, and YouTube, could possibly be responsible for the world's biggest time dump since solitaire came standard on personal computers. Yes, I'm coming down hard on technology, but not because I'm against it. Social media can be a very productive means to sell books. It can also be one of the biggest distractions that an author faces, and my perspective is based on the experience of coaching hundreds of authors.

For many people, Facebook, Twitter, and YouTube, are like the seductive sirens in Greek mythology who lured sailors to their shipwrecked doom by distracting them with enchanting music. A similar distraction affects our society as we spend hours each day posting comments on Facebook, following people on Twitter, or watching videos on YouTube. The problem isn't social media itself. Using these online networks can be a great tool. The trick is how you use the tools. Let's look at the good, the bad, and the ugly sides of this technology.

THE GOOD ABOUT SOCIAL NETWORKING

Social media is a good thing because it offers an inexpensive way to quickly communicate with thousands of people. Authors have an unprecedented opportunity to target specific types of readers, build lasting relationships, and start an online wildfire to market books at a rapid pace.

In addition, social media forces authors to learn how to be more concise. This need for brevity is good, especially when it comes to marketing, because people have no desire to listen to long sales pitches. The online world will not tolerate those who fail to distill their thoughts and content into pithy nuggets. Forget the literary snobs who prize flowery forty-word sentences. Twitter only allows you one sentence with 140 characters. Every author needs to learn how to be more concise, and technology forces you to improve that skill.

Even better, social networking transformed our society because it's essentially free to get involved. For the average struggling author, these free marketing tools are like a cool glass of water to a parched soul. We should thank the creators of Facebook, Twitter, and YouTube for making their tools available at no cost. Unfortunately free creates it own set of problems.

THE BAD ABOUT SOCIAL NETWORKING

A major downside to social media is that there are no barriers to entry. Anyone and everyone can have a voice on the Internet, which is exactly the problem. Social media has created an online version of worldwide cacophony. So many people are vying for the public's attention that it is extremely hard to cut through the noise and build a mass following from scratch. Thus, social media tends to unfairly reward those who already have a large platform, such as celebrities, athletes, preachers, and politicians.

Another problem with social media is that it can disguise genuine participation. For example, let's say you accumulate fifteen thousand "followers" on Twitter and ten thousand "friends" on Facebook. That's a large group of people, but it doesn't mean that all of them are real fans who will actually buy your book. You'll be lucky if 25 percent take action. Thus, you can't put much faith in the numbers that you accrue online. Social media lets people quietly monitor an author's activity without making any commitment to make a purchase.

As I mentioned earlier, social media can also become very time-consuming, because an author can't merely dabble in these online networks and succeed. If you don't maintain a frequent presence online, you will be ignored and forgotten. The time required to update your various profiles and follow other people can rob your ability to complete more important marketing objectives. Some of my clients have had to hire interns or assistants to stay on top of all of their online efforts. When you think of it that way, social media is no longer free; it brings an unseen opportunity cost, additional expenditures of time, and a hidden price tag.

THE UGLY ABOUT SOCIAL NETWORKING

Speaking of free, there's an ugly side of social media that can create problems for authors. People who follow you online expect authors to give away a lot of content for free. Ten years ago, no author imagined he would have to become a master of not only writing a book, but also creating consistent information for blogs, tweets, Facebook posts, YouTube videos, and online forums. Social networks demand authors provide a load of free material. And the quality of this material has to be good, or people will disregard you and follow someone else. If you're not prepared to present a lot of your expertise for free, you will be overlooked in the social networking world.

Now, I'm no literary purist, but it's also safe to say that social media has degraded the way our society communicates. Sure, some techno-gurus will argue that social media makes communication more authentic, real-time, and raw. But when I look at most tweets, Facebook posts, and YouTube comments, the level of writing is utterly sophomoric and inane. If aliens visited our planet and read through a typical person's social media posts, they'd probably be convinced that our civilization is regressing.

The shallow talk that's built into most social media platforms is ugly because it prevents authors from communicating their real value to fans. How can you explain the benefits of a book when you have to cram it into tiny phrases using broken English? "My buk iz gud 4 u. Plz buy it. $$ Thx."

Another ugly side of social networking is that it gives some authors a false sense of getting work done in the marketing arena, when really they're just wasting time. The problem is that promoting a book via social media is a passive approach. For example, you're hoping people will find you online and choose to "follow" you on Twitter, "like" you on Facebook, or join your Google+ "circle." These approaches are passive, because you don't have control over the process. People can come and go as they please. Their connection to you is very loose and noncommittal.

In contrast, if you take proactive steps to get face-to-face with people in the real world, create emotional rapport, and invite people to voluntarily give up their contact information, you generate a stronger connection that increases your ability to sell books.

Passive marketing tactics are fine but not at the total exclusion of proactive efforts, such as public speaking, media interviews, and things like monthly newsletters. The average author can't hide in a writer's cave posting information to the Internet and expect book sales to grow. Successful authors use a combined approach of both passive and proactive tactics.

HOW TO CREATE ONLINE COMMUNITY

If you want to build a following—either online or off—you must position yourself as someone who is worth following. The best way to attract a large group is to become an object of interest, which means drawing people to you with your expertise or charismatic personality. Celebrities in our society—actors, reality TV stars, musicians, athletes, best-selling authors, and politicians—are considered objects of interest because people are fascinated by their glamorous lifestyle, eccentric behavior, or award-winning achievements. Likewise, intellectual experts, such as scientists, doctors, lawyers, ministers, reporters, and counselors are also objects of interest because of their ability to help people discover new information or overcome personal challenges.

People won't become your fan unless you give them a clear reason to do so. I know this sounds obvious, but it's that simple. If you're engaging in social media and struggling to build a growing community, people probably don't regard you as interesting. You're lost in the mix of more appealing authors who are getting attention. So your goal should be to magnify the best parts of your book and your author expertise. Use your strengths to make people want to stay connected with you. Here's a list of ways to attract a following based on the genre of books that you write:

1. Nonfiction advice, how-to, textbooks: Deliver clear answers to common problems.
2. Biographies, reference: Provide insight into historical or current events.
3. Fiction, romance, chick lit: Generate intense feelings of emotion or passion.
4. Gift books, children's, religious: Serve as a constant source of encouragement.

5. Memoirs, comedy: Supply a unique sense of humor or wit.
6. Science fiction, young adult, crime: Create a feeling of fear, wonder, or suspense.
7. Business, political commentary: Express counterintuitive opinions that challenge the status quo.

This list is just a sample of the diverse ways that any fiction or nonfiction author could draw attention to their name and their books. You might choose to rely on one approach to build interest. Or you could combine several styles to help capture an audience. The point is to establish yourself as someone who is interesting and worth following. You don't have to change your personality, rather just be yourself. You do, however, have to give people a reason to like you, respect your skills, and want to learn more about who you are.

For example, I've established myself as an object of interest among author communities, because they know I can help them sell more books. By tapping into this felt need, I've drawn authors to me and assisted them by providing free instruction and encouragement. One way I keep people engaged is through my free weekly e-mail newsletter called, "Rob Eagar's Monday Morning Marketing Tips." Each Monday, I send out a brief tip that helps authors improve their book-marketing skills. As I send out my e-newsletter every week, I also post the tips to my blog and Twitter account. That way, I get maximum exposure via the Internet to establish myself as an object of interest. As I gain authors' trust, their interest grows beyond just following me. They eventually purchase my products and consulting services.

If you're still not sure how to make yourself an object of interest, try this exercise: List five authors whom you follow regularly on Facebook, Twitter, or their blog. Jot down the specific reasons these authors appeal to you. What makes them an object of interest? How are they able to hold your attention? Then make a list of ways you can copy part of what they do and apply it to your own approach.

WE ARE FAMILY: HOW TO MANAGE A THRIVING ONLINE COMMUNITY

Once you've defined yourself as an object of interest, you're only halfway to creating a growing community. The first step is to capture peoples' attention. The second is to keep people engrossed after you've attracted their interest. A community won't survive unless people stay connected. Therefore, you must keep people drawn to you by giving them a reason to return on a regular basis. This part of the process is where a lot of authors get frustrated, lose momentum, and burn out. Then they wonder why their platform remains small and their book sales suffer. Use the following ideas to help build and maintain your community using the major social media sites.

Be the Ringleader

Every community needs a hub and a leader who keeps it together. As an author, your job is to be the ringleader who acts as the central point for communication. You create this dynamic by setting up specific pages on Facebook, Twitter, and YouTube. These pages serve as the meeting point for followers to receive updates, new content, post their feedback, and converse with other members of your community.

Ideally you want online activity to revolve around you, rather than wait for someone else to set up and control the discussion. If you wait, you'll be on the outside looking in on a conversation about your own work. That's like waiting for someone else to throw a birthday party for you. It may never happen, and even if it does, it may not be your kind of fun.

Take the initiative to set up your own online presence and maintain it as the leader. This means checking in at least every few days to post new information, address comments, and wield your status as an object of interest to keep people connected. Feed the discussion with open-ended questions, articles, latest news, quizzes, and free resources. Serve as the nexus for people who are interested in your topic by providing links, research, and commentary on current events.

Dr. Henry Cloud, psychologist and author of the popular book, *Boundaries*, provides a good example of how to use social media to create an active online community. On Facebook (http://www.face book.com/DrHenryCloud), Dr. Cloud acts a leader who cares about his thousands of followers. He posts regular updates using a casual, friendly tone that shows his desire to encourage people. He also provides links to the sample chapters of his latest books. Even better, Dr. Cloud invites his fans to send him questions, and he personally answers them using short video clips. At the time of this writing, he had over forty insightful videos that meet the needs of his community. Thus, people view him as a leader who makes them feel connected.

Use Your Voice

In his book, *Million Dollar Speaking*, Alan Weiss, says, "You must blow your own horn, or there is no music." Likewise, if you want to build a growing community using social networks, you've got to express your individual voice. Don't try to copy other authors. Be yourself, and let your personality shine. Reflect on what makes you an object of interest and talk with authority about those issues. It's even okay if people don't agree with everything you say. Sometimes disagreements are the catalyst for the biggest discussions and produce greater awareness for your book.

Don't be afraid to state your opinions. Let people know why you love your genre and why you write the books you publish. Act like an expert on your subject who wants other people to "catch" your enthusiasm. Start new conversations by posting open-ended questions. Respond to your followers' comments and correct their misconceptions when necessary. Be the community leader who is devoted to caring for your fans and keeping their interest.

Leak Exclusive Information

One of the best strategies to grow an online following is to "leak" exclusive offers and content. The idea is similar to how political insiders within the government leak private information to reporters. The press gains an audience by broadcasting secret information to the public.

Authors can use this same strategy to leak information about their books. When people realize that there's only one way to get a secret deal or inside information, a twofold response typically occurs. First, natural curiosity is aroused, which keeps the attention on the "leaker." Secondly, the desire to tell others and leak the same information kicks into high gear. Everyone likes to be the first person to tell their friends about something cool. That's how ideas spread virally.

If you want more people to follow you on social media, create a regular stream of exclusive offers or inside information that can't be found anywhere else. By doing so, you tap into your followers' natural curiosity and entice them to stay connected. You might leak information on the following topics:

- Offer ultralow discounts to people who preorder your new book for a limited time.
- Leak sections of content from a new book you're writing.
- Reveal lost chapters, backstories, and spin-off products.
- Hold a "secret" contest with fans to help name key characters or come up with a title for your book.
- Give away limited-edition copies of your book that are only available for fans.
- Tell people about upcoming events and ticket information before anyone else.
- Give an exclusive behind-the-scenes look at your life as an author that includes pictures, updates, and musings.

People will join your online community when they know it's the only way to get exclusive information. In order to maximize this process, though, you must be consistent. If you leak special information only once a month or once a quarter, your community will lose interest. Get in the habit of leaking content at least every two to three weeks. Ask yourself, "What would make me interested in following me?"

If you travel frequently, share pictures and videos. If you're holed up in your writer's cave, leak little snippets of your manuscript to fans. If you create a new free resource, give it to your community before anyone else. Make people want to follow you because there's no other way to get the inside scoop.

Use social media to drive traffic to your author website

Facebook and Twitter serve as good tools to connect with a lot of people online, but these sites are no substitute for an author website. You need more than just a Facebook page or a Twitter account to build a community. You need a central location that houses information for all of your books. Only an author website can meet this objective.

To steal an analogy from the military, your author website should serve as your Internet headquarters, where everything about you can be accessed from one location. In contrast, Facebook, Twitter, and YouTube serve as online outposts. In essence, you're setting up little camps in other territories that give you representation and exposure, and drive people from those outposts to your headquarters (that's the goal). That way, everyone can get the full experience of learning about you and your books.

This step is important, because most social network sites are too limited to provide the kind of promotional experience prospective readers really need in order to understand the full benefit of your book. For instance, I'd much rather spend time on an author's website than look at their posts on Facebook or Twitter. On your website, people can read sample chapters, watch videos, access free resources, and make a purchase. It's also easier to capture contact information on your website than it is on social media pages.

Therefore, use your social media pages in tandem with your author website. The easiest way to do this is to provide hyperlinks back and forth between the various platforms. For instance, when you post a new comment on Facebook or Twitter, include a hyperlink back to your website for more information. Don't let your community get stuck following you only on social media sites. Drive them back to your website to see new content, such as pictures, resources, sample chapters, videos, and contests.

In addition, draw attention to your social media networks by placing links or icons in prominent positions on the home page of your author website. Encourage visitors to check out those pages and become a follower. Another option is to embed a widget from Facebook or Twitter onto your home page. This allows visitors to see your latest social media activity in an easy-to-read section that constantly updates itself.

Here's a time-saving tip: Instead of individually posting the same message to your separate Facebook and Twitter accounts, you can use free services found on www.HootSuite.com or www.Ping. fm to do it for you simultaneously. You can even draft posts and schedule them to release at a later date. Maximize your efforts on social media by minimizing your time.

SPECIFIC TIPS FOR USING FACEBOOK, TWITTER, AND YOUTUBE

At the time of this writing, there are three major social networks with large-scale global influence: Facebook, Twitter, and YouTube (Google+ is growing fast, but not at the same level as the other three yet.). Each site is different and provides a unique set of ways to help authors market a book. This section addresses these unique differences and provides specific tips to help you use these networks to your advantage.

THE SKINNY ON FACEBOOK

Facebook (www.facebook.com) is a social networking service launched in February 2004 by founder, Mark Zuckerberg. In July 2011, Facebook reported more than 750 million users. Each user creates a personal profile, then adds other users as friends, exchanges messages, and sends automatic notifications when they update their profile.

According to a survey by Netpop Research, the most active social media users are eighteen to thirty-four years old. They are mostly women (78 percent vs. 66 percent of men), and women in their thirties are the heaviest contributors. Thus, if you write books for women in their thirties, Facebook can be a marketing gold mine. How do you mine the gold?

Create an author profile page

If you're going to reach people on Facebook, you need to act like a regular participant. So you'll want to create your own page as an author that gives you a place to talk about the message of your book. Facebook calls the typical individual profiles a "Personal Profile," and they refer to the profiles created by an author as "Profile Pages." This set-up can get confusing, because they can look similar. But there are some big distinctions in how they work. You must have a Facebook personal profile first before you can create a profile page. So, if you're new to Facebook, you'll have to create that first. Once you have a personal profile, go to this link to set up an author profile page: http://www.facebook.com/pages/create.php.

Use the "Like" feature to give away a free chapter or resource

A clever way to use Facebook to promote your book is by creating a separate page on your profile that offers users a free sample chapter or related resource. In order for visitors to get access to your sample chapter, they must click on the "Like" button displayed on that page. Once they complete that step, a new screen will appear with a link to download your chapter. Using the "Like" feature allows you to increase the number of people who like your overall profile. In addition, you can track interest in your sample chapter by counting how many your total "Likes" increase over time. For more information about creating a "Like" button, visit: http://developers.facebook.com/docs/reference/plugins/like/.

Run targeted ads

One of the big problems with traditional advertising is that it's difficult to tailor your campaign to the people most likely to buy. Facebook, however, provides an inexpensive solution. Once you set up a profile, you can create small banner ads that appear only to the people you choose. You also get to select the cost you pay based on how many people click on your ad or how many total impressions you receive. Even better, you can set a budget limit to prevent spending more than you desire.

The best part about advertising on Facebook is the level of detail you can use to choose your specific audience. Facebook will let you narrow down potential viewers based on age, location, gender, and specific interests. As you set your parameters, you can watch a numerical counter literally determine the exact amount of users who fit your target.

I helped a client create a targeted Facebook ad for her book based on the topic of food struggles. We started with a daily budget limit of $50, uploaded an eye-catching picture, developed clever marketing copy, and included a link to the author's website. Then we used Facebook's targeting system to expose the banner ad only to women in America over the age of thirty who mentioned food, chocolate, or cupcakes in their personal profile. The ad experiment was a success, because we reached the author's $50 budget limit almost every day. This meant that numerous women were clicking on the ad and going to the author's website. (We also used Google Analytics to monitor the author's incoming website traffic to verify that Facebook was the referral source.)

Contests

Facebook makes it easy to create a contest with your book readers. You can do it yourself by posting the details on your profile wall, or you can use a separate page dedicated just to the contest. By continually mentioning the contest on your regular posts, you can help draw attention to it and build awareness.

If you'd prefer to run a top-notch contest with all of the bells and whistles, check out a company called Wildfire Interactive (www.wildfireapp.com—no relation to my company, WildFire Marketing). Wildfire Interactive is a leader at helping people build, implement, and monitor contests and sweepstakes on Facebook. They provide various templates and instructions that walk you through the set-up of your own contest campaign. Then they handle the responsibility of having the contest appear on Facebook and tracking the results.

Create a "Fan of the Week" campaign

Well-known companies, such as Oreos and Zappos, use a smart strategy on Facebook called "Fan of the Week." They invite fans of their products to change their profile picture in a way that shows them eating an Oreo cookie or holding a Zappos shoe box. Then these companies review their fan pictures and choose someone with the most creative picture. That person becomes their "Fan of the Week" and wins special recognition in the online community and a unique prize.

Authors can adopt this same idea to conduct a fun campaign with their community of readers. Ask your fans to submit a photo or change their Facebook profile picture to an image of them holding a copy of your book. Select a fan each week to win a prize and receive special acknowledgment in front of everyone else. This campaign is not only fun for fans, it also puts your book cover in front of everyone who sees your fans' profile pages, thereby multiplying awareness across Facebook.

Nobody likes to be sold. If you use Facebook to promote your book, be sure not to badger people to buy it. If you do, you will simply annoy them. Users want to communicate with friends and organizations that they trust. You can build that trust by using your Facebook page to give away free resources, updates, inside information, and prizes that encourage people to "like" you and join your community of electronic "friends."

A WORD ABOUT GOOGLE+

Google+ is a service meant to compete with Facebook. At the time of this writing, there are over 25 million users with rapid growth continuing. To date, Google+ offers some distinct advantages over Facebook, such as allowing you to group people into specific "circles" that better organize how you communicate. In addition, there's a free video chat feature that allows you to view and talk with up to ten people. This feature could work well with authors who want to be interviewed by members of a book club. Other features include a "+1" button that allows users to recommend items online to their friends, similar to the Facebook "like" button.

On the other hand, Google+ doesn't currently offer robust advertising and promotional opportunities, such as contests and inexpensive ad space. Therefore, Facebook still has the upper hand when it comes to book marketing. These issues are sure to change as the companies try to outdo each other. For updated information about marketing your book on Google+ and all the other major social networks, visit www.BookWildfire.com

THE SKINNY ON TWITTER

Twitter (www.twitter.com) is a social networking and microblogging service that allows users to send and read short messages called "tweets." Tweets are text-based posts of up to 140 total characters displayed on the user's profile page. Twitter was created in March 2006, and is estimated to have over two hundred million users who generate more than two hundred million tweets a day.

As an author, you can set up a personal account and use Twitter to broadcast messages and updates about yourself and your book. Your fans can select to receive your updates by choosing to "follow" you. The more followers you accrue, the more people you can use to grow your platform and market your books online.

However, too many authors use Twitter in a lackluster manner by posting random thoughts or predictable one-liners, such as book quotes or boring attempts at daily inspirations. This approach won't help you build an online community unless you're a celebrity. Here are some ideas that can work for the everyday author most of us are.

Pay With a Tweet

A great way to motivate your online community to help market your book is to incentivize their participation. A service called "Pay with a Tweet" (www.paywithatweet.com) makes this possible using Twitter. This service benefits authors by letting you give away a sample chapter or a free resource simply by asking people to "tweet" about it. The result is that you encourage other people to share awareness about your book with their community, thereby enlarging your promotional reach. In essence, you're getting other people to vouch for you to their followers.

Pay with a Tweet simplifies the process by creating the computer code that can be added to your website or blog as a "button." When people see that you're offering a free item, they click on the button and enter their Twitter information. Then a post about your book is automatically sent to their account for their followers to see. After they complete this step, a new screen appears that gives them access to download your free giveaway. And did I mention the best part? Pay with a Tweet is free.

Solicit questions for Q&A

Twitter can also be a great way to start a conversation with your community by letting people ask questions and share ideas. For instance, you can invite your "followers" to post questions by tweeting them to your account. Then you can answer the questions by placing a response on your website or blog, or you can post the reply on your Twitter feed. This way, your entire community can participate and follow along in the discussion.

THE SKINNY ON YOUTUBE

YouTube (www.youtube.com) is a video-sharing website that allows users to upload, share, and view their own videos. Three former

PayPal employees created it in February 2005. In November 2006, Google Inc., purchased YouTube and it now operates as a Google subsidiary. YouTube may not be as popular of a mass communication tool like Facebook and Twitter. Instead, it's the leading provider of online video hosting and streaming (Vimeo.com takes second place). In May 2011, YouTube reported receiving more than three billion views per day.

Due to a massive, constantly growing library of videos, YouTube also ranks as one of the world's top search engines. YouTube is much more than just a storehouse for movie trailers, music videos, and silly recordings that people upload. Millions of people also search YouTube each day to find well-crafted instructional videos that solve a plethora of issues. Authors can take advantage of YouTube's incredible traffic to provide answers and steer more people to their books.

It's easier than ever before for authors to create high-quality videos and share them with their readers. You don't need expensive equipment. Today, most smartphones have a built-in high-definition camera. Put your phone on a tripod or have someone hold it, and you're ready to record all kinds of useful videos. Use these tips to use visual technology to your advantage.

Create an author channel

To maximize the use of YouTube (or Vimeo), set up an account and build your own "channel." It's like having your own branded TV channel on the world's largest network. With a channel, you can organize and keep all of your videos in one place. This makes it easier to keep track of your content and to help your fans find your videos.

Book trailers

Movie studios rely on TV commercials called "trailers" to advertise their new films. Publishers and authors are using the same idea in the form of book trailers to advertise new books. And you don't need a big budget and fancy graphics to create a compelling trailer.

A trailer will work as long as you answer that big question readers are asking: "What's in it for me?" I've watched literally hundreds of expensive trailers that looked great but never answered that essential question. Which means that a lot of money and technology has gone to waste. In contrast, you can make an effective trailer on your own simply by focusing on the results that your book will provide. Professionalism is important but not at the expense of value. If you decide to create your own book trailer, keep these pointers in mind as you develop a script to follow.

NONFICTION TRAILER:

- Explain why your book is important: Define the problem, tell a compelling story, or provide a shocking statistic. Give the viewer a reason to be interested. If you fail at this first step, people will stop the video and never bother watching the rest of it.

- Explain why the viewer should trust you: State the case for your expertise by briefly describing your experience with your book's topic. You want to convince the viewer that you're worth an investment of their time and money. Don't brag about yourself or ramble. Simply present a few facts that provide evidence of your authority on the subject.

- List the results that your book can create: This is the crescendo of your video trailer. Prove to the viewer that they should buy your book by literally explaining the results it will produce. You could also include a brief success story that shows how someone else benefited from your book. State the obvious, because the viewer won't do it for you.

FICTION TRAILER:

- Describe the setting for your story. Introduce the main character and why the viewer should root for that person.

- Build the tension. Describe the scene in your novel that contains the highest level of tension-filled emotion. Show images that communicate the situation, and make viewers feel as much suspense as possible. This is the most important selling feature of the video. You must make the viewer feel fear, shock, drama, humor, or concern that connects to the main character. Build it to a climax. Then stop and leave the viewer hanging. Create a level of frustration that makes the viewer need to see the conclusion of your story.

- Tell the viewer what drove you to write the story and promise a fulfilling conclusion. Be bold about your novel. Challenge the viewer to buy a copy.

Post FAQ and behind-the-scenes videos

A great way to market your book and develop an author platform is by creating videos that help build a relationship with your readers. It's one thing for people to read your posts on Facebook and Twitter, but you add a dimension of interest when people can watch you talking to them.

Readers like to get to know their favorite authors, so give your audience a chance to pick your brain or get the inside scoop on your life. One way to do that is to record videos that provide a behind-the-scenes look at your typical writing day. Show a sneak peek of your office, your home, and your hobbies. Let people see what you do beyond writing books.

Mega-bestselling author, David Baldacci, provides lots of informative videos on YouTube. You can search through his channel (www.youtube.com/user/dbaldacci) and watch exclusive interviews, speaking engagements, and special looks into his office and writing life. Fans can learn more about his books, relate to him as a person, and build a stronger affinity to his stories.

You can also use the power of video to connect with readers by taking time to answer their personal questions. Readers appreciate an author who will address their concerns or curiosity. Gary Thomas, best-selling author of *Sacred Marriage*, does a great job handling frequently-asked-questions (FAQs) on his website at www.garythomas.com/videos. He provides answers to common questions that relate to each of his books. His videos provide an authentic response from Gary that shows concern for his readers.

For many authors, recording themselves on video can be a daunting process, so they avoid the technology altogether. I say, don't let your fear prevent you from connecting with your fans. Here are some tips that I've used with my clients to help them relax on camera:

- Treat the camera like a person. Pretend you're talking to a friend over a cup of coffee.
- Smile as much as you can—even more than you think necessary. A glum face will suck the energy out of a video, boring the viewer.
- Attempt to memorize your content. If you struggle recalling what to say, you can make a cue card and place it next to the camera. It's okay to occasionally glance at notes.
- Don't try to tell the viewer everything you know. Just tell them what they need to know.
- The more you practice and record yourself, the more comfortable you will be. It takes time to get used to staring into a glass lens.

A picture can tell readers what you look like, but a video can tell readers what your life is like. Harness the power of today's video technology to attract people and keep them connected to your books.

HOW TO MEASURE SOCIAL MEDIA SUCCESS

If you want to use social media to market your book, don't forget to keep the ultimate goal in mind—book sales. It's nice to get thousands of people to "like" you on Facebook or "follow" you on Twitter. However, it's all in vain if they never buy your books or spread word of mouth. Authors often think their social networking efforts are paying off without ever really knowing if books are being purchased. To make matters worse, it can take up to six months to get a royalty statement from your publisher to see how many books are actually sold. How can you tell if your online activities are bearing fruit? I encourage my clients to use the following indicators as a way to determine social media success.

Amazon ranking

To determine real-time book sales, the good ole Amazon ranking still acts as a decent gauge. Obviously the ranking doesn't reveal actual sales but it's one of the ways an author can tell whether marketing activities are having an immediate impact. If you promote a contest on Facebook and Twitter, for example, you could check your Amazon ranking before the contest starts and monitor it as the contest progresses. By tracking your ranking using the free service, TitleZ (www.titlez.com), and your book's individual page on Amazon, you're able to see if your promotional campaign moves the needle in a positive direction.

Amazon's Author Central BookScan sales

In Chapter 8, I discussed the various benefits that Amazon offers authors. You can log in to your author account and view an eight-week report of your sales history from Nielsen BookScan. This report doesn't include sales figures for all retailers, but it's enough information to see if your book is gaining or losing momentum. I recommend checking these numbers on a regular basis to see if your sales coincide with recent marketing campaigns that you've conducted, especially social networking activities.

Website sales and statistics

If you sell books from your author website, you can gauge the direct book sales in response to specific social media efforts. For example, you could put a post on Twitter or Facebook that includes a link to the store page on your site. Then you could track the actual sales to see if people respond. In addition, you'll want to review your website statistics (I recommend Google Analytics at www.google.com/analytics) to see if those social networking sites are among your top referral sources of traffic. If not, you can deduce that there's a disconnect between your social networking and author website platforms. In other words, people are reading your social media posts, but not taking action to visit your website and get more involved. In this case, you need to change your approach to a way that entices people to click and participate on a deeper level.

Utilize "Retweet" and "Like" buttons

It's easy to feel excited when you see lots of people signing up to follow you on Twitter or like you on Facebook, but it's even better to see those people telling others about your book. The good news is that these social networking sites provide free tools that make it easy for your readers to transform into word-of-mouth warriors.

Twitter offers a "tweet" button that allows people to "retweet" or tell their followers about you. Simply add a "tweet" button to your specific website pages, blog posts, online articles, and e-newsletter issues. If a reader appreciates your content, she can click on the "tweet" button. A new window appears that lets her add a caption and a hyperlink to your information that's immediately posted to their personal Twitter feed. Within seconds, she's given you a referral to her entire online network. This action boosts your credibility and creates a viral marketing effect that helps promote you to a wider audience. To learn how to add a "tweet" button to your content, go to www.twitter.com/about/resources/tweetbutton.

Likewise, Facebook offers a "like" button that lets users share your content with their friends. You can add "like" buttons to your website and blog for free. When the user clicks the "like" button on your site, a story appears in that user's friends' News

Feed with a link back to your website. The button acts like an approval and referral function for readers as they surf your online information. To learn how to add a "like" button to your content, go to http://developers.facebook.com/docs/reference/plugins/like/.

Summary

With the advent of Facebook, Twitter, and YouTube, it's easy to see why the world was turned upside down by social networking. The way that people interact and communicate will never be the same. Having said that, authors must remember that social media is not the savior of book marketing. You can have the most technologically advanced online strategy and still fail to sell books. That's because technology will never replace the need for value and life-changing information that people crave.

Therefore, if you want to succeed using social media, you must not become seduced by all of the bells and whistles. Don't let the techie nerds convince you that their online strategies are all you need. Social networking is still largely a passive approach to marketing, and passive approaches are no substitute for the proactive steps discussed in other chapters of this book. My clients who make the bestseller lists combine both online and offline activities into a balanced strategy.

Engage in social media because you want to, not because you have to. People won't follow you if it's obvious that you're a halfhearted participant. They can smell online fakers. There is no commandment that mandates every author must use Facebook and Twitter. The key to marketing success is to stay consistent. Be sure to conduct activities that you're able to commit to over time.

Above all, stay focused on the basics, which means concentrate on providing free content that entertains, inspires, or helps people solve a problem. Technology without value is a lifeless, robotic attitude to promoting books. On the other hand, when you combine the ideas in this chapter with real-life value, you can create an electronic wildfire that spreads faster than anything the forest has ever seen.

CHAPTER 10

WORKING WITH A PUBLISHER

One thing that most authors share is frustration with their publisher. One thing most publishers share is authors who sometimes drive them crazy. It's unfortunate that this problem exists, because the author/publisher relationship plays an important role in making books successful. You can't start a marketing wildfire if author and publisher are throwing water at each other.

Even if you're an author who's decided to pursue self-publishing, chances are that you'll consider working with a publisher someday. Many successful independent authors wind up cashing in on lucrative offers that eventually come from a traditional publishing house (I did). The fact is that at some point in your career, you'll probably face the task of working with a publisher. Most of the quarrels that authors and publishers encounter stem from misconceptions that people bring into the business relationship:

- Authors write their manuscript and then expect the publisher to do all of the marketing work.
- Publishers are short staffed and expect authors to shoulder more of the marketing burden.

- Both sides tend to blame the other when book sales don't meet expectations.

My intent for this chapter is to help reduce the conflict and maximize the communication that occurs between both parties. In order to give you a well-rounded perspective on this important topic, I've gathered a group of knowledgeable experts. In the coming pages, you'll read interviews I conducted with established veterans of the publishing industry. These people are marketing executives, acquisitions editors, literary agents, and very successful authors who have weathered enough storms and enjoyed enough sunny days that their insights can be trusted.

INTERVIEW—PHIL SEXTON
Publisher and Community Leader for Writer's Digest

Phil Sexton began his career as a bookseller for Waldenbooks in 1988. In the more than twenty years since, he has worked as the manager of a small chain of independent bookstores, director of book merchandising for a large book wholesaler, and vice president of sales for a major media company. Currently he holds the position of Writer's Digest publisher and community leader. He has authored or co-authored three books, many articles, and he co-founded the short-lived (but oh so much fun) literary journal, *Fresh Boiled Peanuts*. He lives, works, and writes in Brooklyn, New York.

1. In order to create a partnership with a publisher, what steps should an author take to maximize the relationship?

I'd advise writers to cultivate certain personality traits rather than execute any specific steps. Nothing makes an editor or publisher happier than to work with someone who is professional, courteous, dependable, and willing to collaborate. If you can do that and your writing is solid, they'll remember you as a good person to work with. In addition, put as much effort as possible into promoting yourself and your work. Publishers are desperate to work with writers who can help drive their own sales.

2. What are the biggest mistakes you see authors make when dealing with their publisher?

Many authors, particularly nonfiction authors, who have sold a book based on an outline rather than a finished manuscript, don't realize how hard writing really is. The incredible effort they put into crafting their query, their proposal, and their first few chapters is more difficult to maintain than they thought. Quality starts to fall as fatigue sets in and editors are left to do a lot of cleanup work on the completed manuscript. If you agree to write a book for money, make sure you're as enthusiastic and disciplined about crafting the middle and the end as you are the beginning. Even more so if possible. The less work you are for an editor, the more the publisher will want to work with you again.

Also, many authors—particularly new authors—don't understand how the business works. Therefore, they have false expectations once they finally get published. When things don't end up the way they anticipated, they get upset and sometimes take out their frustrations on the editors or publishers. The fact is, this is a business, and if you're a writer, you are, by default, a businessperson. Spend time learning what to expect and, if possible, negotiate for the things you want, rather than assuming they're going to happen.

For example, most authors are not given book or radio tours. Most books are not advertised in the *The New York Times Book Review*. (You'll be fortunate to get an ad in *Library Journal*—and even then you'll be one of several titles featured.)

Oh, and platforms? They're just as important as everyone in the business keeps telling you. They're more important today than they were yesterday. Tomorrow they'll be more important still.

3. What should an author do when there is a difference of opinion with the publisher over issues such as title, cover design, marketing plan, or some other such detail?

First, take a deep breath. It's not personal. You're working with professionals who are looking at your project from a somewhat more objective viewpoint than you are. Ask for the reason behind their decision. If the decision is a good one, there will be a good reason. If it's due to a whim, or a feeling, then it's no more valid than your own.

As far as titles and covers go, if you haven't negotiated for some sort of consultation or approval rights during the contract stage, you may simply be out of luck. If you want that sort of control or input, make sure you ask for it up front.

Titling, in particular, is a much more frequent issue with works of nonfiction. Many such decisions are based on what title conveys the most benefit for the customer. What title is most clear or most persuasive? What titles will most likely show up in a Google or Amazon search? What titles are easy for consumers to remember and/or spell? Also, what title is most easily read on the book's spine (which is what most consumers see first when they're browsing at their local bookstores)? What title will register most clearly when an online retailer reduces the cover to the size of a postage stamp?

Another consideration is that some covers and titles are considered in light of a buyer's preference. The publisher and the salespeople know what certain important buyers like. What opinions about covers they have expressed in the past. Sometimes a better buy can be secured if certain tweaks to the title and cover are made per the buyer's request. That may sound a bit like the cart driving the horse, but the publisher's job is to get your book the best distribution possible. Making alterations based on buyer feedback is one way to do that.

As for covers, unless you're a professional designer, sometimes it's best to leave design completely in the hands of the publisher. If you think that the design misrepresents you or your work, however, definitely mention it. For example, perhaps the typeface selected is playful and you want to be seen as authoritative. In that case, you have reason to say something. And, if you have a good relationship with your editor, he or she will be your advocate in cover design discussions. Regardless, don't nitpick. Choose your battles wisely.

The development and execution of a marketing plan is up to the publisher. If you want more control over this aspect of your book, then you need to negotiate for it at the contract stage. I've often provided a marketing plan as part of contract negotiations. Some publishers won't do it, but you'll never know until you ask.

Ultimately any differences of opinion should be handled in as professional a manner as possible. Stand up for yourself if you think the publisher is wrong, but be willing to listen to their argument and compromise where their reasoning is valid. There are often factors behind their decisions that you simply haven't considered.

4. When does it make more sense for an author to self-publish versus pursuing a traditional publisher?

Good question. I think the decision depends on a number of factors:

- How much control you want over the manuscript edit, the layout, the format, and the cover
- How much you're willing to manage the creation of the book

- How much you're willing to promote and market the book and yourself
- How much money you have to spend
- How many copies you want to sell and how much money you want to make
- How long you're willing to try to get published the traditional route

Self-publishing is often considered the easy way to get published. But it can be very labor intensive (as well as costly, depending on how you go about it). You need to ask yourself if you're willing to hire an editor and a designer. What about a proofreader? Some companies will provide all of these services, but they can cost a substantial amount of money.

Also, keep in mind that self-published books generally do not get national distribution in libraries and bookstores. You'll be able to sell it on Amazon.com and BarnesandNoble.com easily enough. But, it will be up to you to make enough noise to get people to realize that your book even exists.

If you are traditionally published, you'll receive an advance for your work up front, your book will be sold into most every major book retail and wholesale account, and you'll likely get at least a minimal publicity and marketing push. You also won't have to front any of your own money to make it happen. Alternatively, self-publishing gives you much more control over your book, a bigger royalty. And, if you're a savvy, tireless marketer, you get the potential to make a substantial amount of money on your own terms.

5. What should an author do when she realizes that initial book sales are under expectations?

First, if you haven't already done so, check with your publisher to see how well the book advanced to the major accounts. It may be that one of the big retailers (Barnes & Noble, Books-a-Million, Amazon) failed to carry the book in a meaningful way. If so, ask the publisher if there is anything you can do to help encourage a more robust shelf presence. Moving the needle here can be difficult, because once a book has been sold in, most buyers want to wait and see what kind of sales pattern develops before taking any additional stock. Additionally most publishers won't want to put more energy and expense into the marketing and promotion of a book that wasn't well received by buyers in the first place. So this presents you with something of a chicken-and-egg situation.

Thankfully you no longer need a publisher to manage all of the promotion associated with your book. If you have a strong platform and know how to leverage social media and more traditional publicity tools, you can generate your own buzz and drive people to seek out your book. This is hard work, but if you can start to build some buzz and drive traffic to retailers who provide sales detail to authors (Amazon, for example), then your publisher can use that information to repitch your work to other accounts. Keep in mind, a good publisher will have a plan to repitch your book already—but don't assume that's what they're doing. Keep up a dialogue with your editor to make sure that is the case.

If, however, your book is well represented in the retail market and still not selling, you may have an entirely different problem. Consumers may be able to find your book but are choosing not to buy it. You can compensate for some of this by using the same promotional efforts noted above—reach more people and you'll sell more books. However the failure to sell also may indicate that there's a problem with the product itself. Is the topic too narrow? Is the price too high? Is the print too small? The first issue can be overcome by making sure the target audience for the book knows it exists, which again relies on the promotional efforts of you and your publisher. Ask to speak with a publicist about how to best reach that group of consumers, if you don't already know.

The second and third issues are more difficult to overcome, as these are problems with the physical product itself and in some cases can't be corrected until the reprint stage (which may never come if the product isn't selling to begin with). Unfortunately that's one of the dangers of the print book business. Changes to existing product happen slowly. Thankfully there's no such issue with e-books. If an e-book needs to be repriced or the interiors need to be re-tweaked, it's simply a matter of updating and resending the file. Explore every option for improving the sales of your book with your publisher. Don't just focus on the print product.

6. As more and more people read e-books, how much does it matter for an author to get distribution in retail bookstores?

For now, print product sales are still the largest part of the business for traditional publishing houses, so it matters a great deal. It's likely, however, that the opportunities will continue to dwindle over time as the number of stores drop and the space allocated for books shrinks. Publishers are putting a lot of effort into finding new retailers into which they can place books—specialty retailers like card stores, gift shops, and housewares and clothing stores. All of these are being aggressively pursued.

7. Some authors may not realize the dependence that publishers have on the major retailers. Can you elaborate on this important relationship?

Until e-book sales become large enough to carry the cost burden associated with editorial, design, and production labor, plus author advances and other expenses, the major retailers of print product will always be incredibly important. The fewer major retailers there are, the fewer print books will be ordered for initial distribution. And since publishers don't want to carry a lot of overstock, they'll cut down the size of the print run to reflect the smaller up-front release. Once they do that, the cost per unit on the book goes up. This squeezes the publisher's margin. Each publisher has a specific target margin they want each book to earn. If it doesn't look like a particular title is likely to hit that target, the publisher may well cancel the project.

8. What are the best steps an author can take to grow his platform?

If you write nonfiction, do whatever you can to create a platform that presents you as an authority on the subject. You want to establish a presence that suggests without a doubt that you are a reliable resource of information on your chosen topic. Keep a blog, build a social media presence, line up speaking engagements, publish relevant articles, and offer yourself as a resource for media interviews on specific topics.

If you write fiction, building a platform can be a little more challenging. But if your fiction falls into a certain genre or category, keeping a blog or Tweeting about that genre or category can at least build an audience of people who share your interests. And if you're trying to publish a novel, consider building some name recognition first through online and print short story markets and e-book self-publishing.

These are all very basic things, and they represent some of the best, least expensive ways of building a platform. Once you've established these cornerstones, you can grow from there.

INTERVIEW—JOE WIKERT

General Manager & Publisher at O'Reilly Media, Inc.

Joe manages the sales and editorial groups and also co-chairs the O'Reilly's Tools of Change for Publishers conference (TOC). Joe has been providing his insights about the publishing industry on his Publishing 2020 blog (http://jwikert.typepad.com/) since 2005. Prior to joining O'Reilly he was vice president and executive publisher at John Wiley & Sons, Inc., in their P/T division.

1. You've witnessed a lot of changes in the publishing industry, especially in the area of technology. What changes have had the biggest impact on your role as a publisher?

It's hard to pinpoint one technology in general, other than saying "the web/internet." There are so many elements of the web that have enabled knowledge while also disrupting the publishing ecosystem. I tend to believe this is all for the best, despite the fact that it has led to a lot of painful change for many people and organizations. The fact that Google or Bing can so quickly provide you with free answers to questions that you used to have to pay for is incredible. In fact, I often say that my biggest competitor is Google, not another publisher.

2. In your experience, how has the process of marketing books transformed over the past five years?

Today publishers rely much more on authors with large followings or platforms. In the past, it was all about whether you're the expert or have an interesting story to tell. That's still very important. But another question that's asked almost immediately when we consider taking on a new book is, "How large is the author's platform?" The reason for this is that large author platforms often mean more for sales and success than any sort of publisher channel promotion from the past, such as endcap displays in bookstores or front-of-store placement.

Skeptics have pointed to this change as yet another reason why authors don't need a publisher. In some cases, that's true. In other words, if you've got an enormous platform, you could probably self-publish and make more money. However, most authors don't have such a large platform, so it's important to work with a publisher who can help you build one.

3. In order to create a solid partnership with a publisher, what steps should an author take to maximize the relationship?

I'd start by asking as many questions as possible. Before a contract is even signed, be sure to clearly determine the expectations of both parties. Besides writing the book, what's expected of you as the author? What sort of promotional efforts can you count on from the publisher? How have similar books performed for them in the past?

Choosing a publisher is just like a job interview, and you need to go in prepared. I also recommend taking the time to build a relationship with your editor. In fact, ask them for references. Will they put you in touch with other authors they've worked with? Beware of the publisher who declines this request, by the way!

4. As more and more people read e-books, how does that affect the marketing plan for a publisher or author?

These days marketing an e-book is similar to marketing a print book. That's largely because most e-books are simply quick-and-dirty conversions from the print edition. When we get to a much richer e-book experience, I think there will be many more ways to market other content. For example, what if your last book could suddenly offer readers a special one-day-only discount on the new book you're releasing tomorrow? Again, today's e-books don't lend themselves to this feature yet. But as we see more content in EPUB3 and HTML5 format, I expect to see more and more new and exciting marketing techniques.

5. What are the best steps you think an author should take to grow her platform?

It may sound lame, but "be yourself." Don't try to be someone you're not. Don't try to spin what you have to say just because someone with a larger platform does it that way. Also know that you probably won't build a significant audience overnight.

I've been blogging for six years (jwikert.typepad.com), and it's taken me a while to build my own platform. I'm not reaching millions of people, but I am read by thousands every day. That's a pretty significant number for the publishing industry, but I didn't get there overnight.

6. What is the single biggest factor that you think influences book sales?

I don't think you can point to just one thing. In one case, big book sales might occur because someone with a huge following recommended the title. In another case, Amazon (or another retailer) offered a book for a deep discount and promoted the heck out of it. In all of these cases, though, I think success starts with a terrific product. So, although you might sell a lot of copies of a bad product in a short period of time, you'll ruin your brand and won't have another chance to fix it.

7. Many people consider you a publishing futurist. What excites you most about the next five to ten years in the book industry?

I'm thrilled that we're in the midst of such radical change. It wasn't that long ago that the so-called pundits were saying e-books would never take off. That was before the Kindle, of course. What disappoints me most, though, is that we haven't even scratched the surface of what's possible with digital content. We're all just making some money off those quick conversions from print, and nobody has a sense of where this is all leading.

I like to say we're at the same stage the TV industry was in the early days. Back then, the first TV shows were nothing more than radio programs in front of a camera. That's what today's e-books are—digital renderings of the print product. Compare those early TV shows to what you can see today, not only on television but in the theaters. We've got a long way to go and all sorts of fun experimentation ahead of us. That's what gets me excited about this industry.

INTERVIEW—SANDY VANDER ZICHT

Associate Publisher & Executive Editor at Zondervan (HarperCollins)

Sandy has nearly three decades of experience acquiring nonfiction titles related to relationships, practical help, and spiritual growth. She has edited numerous *New York Times* bestselling books and holds a BA in English from Calvin College and a MA in English language and literature from the University of Michigan.

1. What is the editor's role in the publishing process?

As an executive editor, I have six roles that rotate constantly:

- **VISIONARY**—Assess marketplace opportunities and needs.

- **STRATEGIST**—Develop an acquisition strategy.

- **CULTIVATOR**—Nurture authors, concepts, and proposals prior to contract.

- **SALESPERSON**—Create alignment between the author and publisher, and also between the book project and all internal publishing departments.

- **CRAFTSPERSON**—Manage authors and projects under contract.

- **ADVOCATE**—Act as a champion for published authors and projects.

As an executive editor, my job in a nutshell is to acquire great books. Then I help the authors of those books say what they want to say in the most vivid way possible. I also articulate to the sales and marketing departments what is compelling and different about these books.

2. You've edited several *New York Times* best-selling books. From an editing perspective, what factors do you think help make a book become a bestseller?

I think great books need to have at least two out of the following three elements: 1) a great concept, 2) great writing, and 3) a great platform. For example, when the best-selling book, *Boundaries*, came out nearly twenty years ago, it was a brand-new, fresh concept for the marketplace. Too many people had trouble saying no. The authors, Henry Cloud and John Townsend, taught readers when to say no, when to say yes, and how to take control of their lives. Plus these authors had a great platform. They were psychologists, speakers, and co-hosts of a popular radio program. Their original writing needed work, but they have grown over time. So they had two out of the three necessary ingredients for success.

3. Are there common mistakes that you see authors make when working on their manuscripts?

The first mistake authors make is looking over their shoulder worrying about what their colleagues, friends, or family may say about what they are writing. Authors need to aggressively seek the truth and not worry about what others will say. The second mistake is handing in a draft that isn't really ready for an editor to see. A third common mistake is when authors write off their brand. In other words, they don't give their readers what they've come to expect.

4. What steps do you recommend authors take to improve their writing skills and manuscript quality?

Read, read, read, and write, write, write. Authors need to be reading good books, and they need to be writing every day. The more you stay consistent in these areas, the more you'll improve.

INTERVIEW—CURTIS YATES

Literary Agent at Yates & Yates

Curtis Yates has served as a literary agent and attorney at Yates & Yates since 2000. He provides counsel for top-tier authors, artists, and creative organizations. Curtis is a graduate of Westmont College and Pepperdine University School of Law. His services include author representation, expert legal advice, marketing guidance, career coaching, creative counseling, and business management consulting. Several of Curtis' clients are *New York Times* best-selling authors who have sold over a million copies of their books.

1. What role does a literary agent play in the publishing process?

My primary role as a literary agent is to work as an advocate for the author. If an author relies on someone inside a publishing house to be his sole advocate, he can wind up getting less than what is really needed. When an author selects a publisher, it's important to have a champion within that organization. But you also need someone on your side who understands your perspective and can balance that with an understanding of how publishing houses work.

Another aspect of being an advocate is by serving as a guide for the author. Agents should do more than just get you a book deal. An agent can and should be someone who can guide you through the publishing process. Plus agents can leverage the relationships and experiences they have had with lots of publishers and authors to help make your book project more successful.

Finally, agents also help authors by holding a publisher accountable on specific agreements about a book contract or executing certain parts of a marketing plan. Publishers will put things on paper, but sometimes important issues fall through the cracks. Someone has to be diligent about tracking those issues and making sure critical items are completed for the author.

2. How would you advise an author to maximize her relationship with a literary agent?

The two best ways an author can help his or her agent is through communication and involvement. Foremost, keep your agent in the communication loop. For example, copy your agent on every e-mail that you send or receive from your publisher. Sometimes authors forget to copy their agent on an important issue, then a problem arises, and the agent has to come in late to help resolve the situation. If you keep your agent involved throughout the book process, then he or she can help provide guidance during critical phases, such as cover design, creating a title, or working on the execution of a marketing plan.

3. How do you advise authors to set proper expectations with the publisher?

Actually I think it's more important to make sure that authors establish the right expectations for their relationship with their publisher. At the end of the day, publishers only do so much. Often today, the burden of marketing depends on the author more than it used to.

In today's tough economy, the onus falls on the author. You need to be prepared to bring several promotional ideas to the table. Don't expect the publisher to do all of the work. You will be disappointed.

Some marketers within publishing houses have too many preconceived ideas when it comes to what works in book marketing. This can create an environment of limited creativity where the marketing strategy is too formulaic and typical. Therefore, the author and the agent need to work together to bring their best ideas to the publisher and show how they plan to help execute a successful strategy.

4. When an author experiences a problem with the publisher, what steps do you recommend the author take to help resolve the situation?

The first step should be to call their agent. It's inevitable that problems will arise at some point between an author and their publisher. That's true for almost any business relationship. But this is another reason literary agents can be beneficial.

When an author keeps his or her agent in the communication loop, the agent can serve as a mediator when conflict arises. A good agent should be in the position to say, "Here's how we can handle this" and leverage their relationships within the publishing house to help resolve concerns diplomatically. Agents can help moderate a problem so that it doesn't exacerbate into a worse situation.

Occasionally an author will get upset with his or her publisher. When that happens, an experienced agent can go to bat for the author, navigate the discussion, and work with the publisher to create an equitable solution on behalf of the author.

There are two sides to every story. Inexperienced authors sometimes forget that many elements may be involved—elements that they may not know about or understand but are affecting a situation nonetheless. Even if the publisher is at fault or makes a mistake, it doesn't serve the author's purpose to go at the publisher with guns blazing.

Remember that publishers are people, and they're on your team. You want your publisher to work hard for you, so don't be a jerk. Each day, your publisher has numerous projects to consider. You want them to pick up your book project over someone else's, because they like you and believe in your book. So it's okay to speak up when you're not comfortable about something, but you want to handle it tactfully and preserve the health of the relationship.

5. What are the best steps an author can take to grow his or her author platform?

Every author is unique, so marketing a book isn't as simple as following three easy steps to build a killer platform. My advice is to be intentional, study your audience, and focus on forming long-term relationships with your readers. Then be diligent and consistent about connecting with your audience.

In addition, determine what marketing activities fit you and your personality. For example, some authors don't want to blog or do social media. Others fully embrace those tools. There's no right or wrong. The goal is to be yourself and stay consistent with your marketing activities.

If you want an audience that's loyal to you, then you can't be passive. Instead, you've got to be proactive and intentionally reach out to your audience on a consistent basis. An author can't say, "Marketing just doesn't fit who I am." Rather you've got find what activities fit you best and be disciplined about doing them.

For instance, you can't build a mailing list and then only contact people once a year when your new book comes out. That's totally ineffective. Put yourself in the shoes of your audience. Think about what they want from you and how often they want to hear from you. Then build a plan and stick to it.

INTERVIEW—RACHELLE GARDNER

Literary Agent at Books & Such Literary Agency

Rachelle Gardner has been in the publishing business since 1995, with experience in marketing, sales, international rights, acquisitions, and editorial. She was senior editor with NavPress, where she acquired and edited nonfiction, and developed and launched the fiction line, including three Christy Award finalists and an ECPA Award finalist in its first year. Rachelle has been a collaborative writer of eight published books. Rachelle's blog (www.RachelleGardner.com) has received the 101 Best Websites for Writers award from Writer's Digest numerous years.

1. What role does a literary agent play in the publishing process?

The agent is the author's advocate, a knowledgeable publishing professional whose job it is to navigate the relationship between author and publisher. When an author is entering into a contractual agreement with a large company—often a huge multinational corporation—it's a hugely unbalanced relationship, and an agent serves to help protect the author's interests.

Agents serve authors in numerous other ways. Many agents do presubmission editing work, helping to assure their clients' manuscripts and proposals shine before submitting to publishers. Agents seek out the right editors and publishers for each project, and do the actual submission. This is where the agent's relationships in the industry really make a difference.

Once there's an offer on the table, agents negotiate with the publisher to get to the best deal and then they read every detail of the contract and negotiate with the publisher to protect the author's interests. Agents help guide authors' careers through brainstorming book ideas, giving advice on which projects and publishers to pursue, and keeping the author apprised of industry trends. Ultimately agents help authors become more successful and work to advance their careers.

Agents have become increasingly important to publishers, too, because they prescreen projects, serving as a filter and thereby assuring a generally higher level of manuscript that comes in to editors.

2. Is it necessary for an author to have literary representation? Why or why not?

It all depends on what kind of publishing career an author wants. If you want to work with a large traditional publisher that pays advances and royalties (and probably has a contract that's ten to twenty pages of legalese), you really need an agent. If you're interested in a small niche publisher that accepts unrepresented authors, and you're comfortable navigating the world of publishing without an advocate, then you're free to go without.

I know several authors who are also attorneys and started out thinking they didn't need an agent because they're well versed in contracts, negotiating, and advocating. Eventually they all got agents, because they want to write and leave the business details to someone else.

3. What are the most significant changes you've experienced in publishing that affect authors today?

It's kind of funny to answer this question, because the publishing industry has changed constantly in the last decade. Plus the way consumers buy books is changing, the way they read books is changing, and the amount they're willing to pay for content is changing.

Also it's harder to get published traditionally, because there are fewer slots for "new" authors; and even when you do get published, it's harder to make much money. On top of all that, it's harder to market books, because the world of media and social media is so crowded—it's very challenging to be heard above the noise.

4. When an author experiences a problem with his or her publisher, what steps do you recommend the author take to help resolve the situation?

It's really important for the author to contact their agent first. Vent to the agent—yell, complain, curse, whatever you need to do. NEVER vent to the editor or anyone at the publishing house. Afterward the agent can address the problem with the publisher in a businesslike manner, thereby approaching a solution and saving the author/publisher relationship.

5. What are the best steps an author can take to grow his or her author platform?

First, authors need to assess what kind of writer they are, who their target audience is, and how that audience is typically reached. It's tempting to try to follow another author's advice for platform building, but every author is different, and you can waste valuable time and money if you neglect to evaluate what kind of platform best suits you.

Make a list of one to three marketing activities that you're willing to start doing. For example, is it a blog? Is it public speaking? Will it be a newsletter or a Facebook-based tribe? Choose where you'd like to start, then begin to get educated in that area. Don't start a blog without reading different resources on effective blogging. Don't attempt to start speaking without getting some coaching. For instance, start with Toastmasters or a local community college class. Preparation and education is key.

Most important, authors need to realize that a platform takes time to build. Many authors who seem like they suddenly became successful have been working at it for ten or twenty years. Your platform should grow out of who you are and feel natural for you. Otherwise, you'll never be able to sustain and grow it.

INTERVIEW—MIKE SALISBURY

Senior Marketing Manager, David C. Cook Publishers

For over five years, Mike has worked with numerous authors to promote their books at several publishers including Zondervan (HarperCollins) and David C. Cook. He lives in Colorado Springs, CO, and is currently an MFA candidate studying fiction at Pacific University. He considers himself lucky to surround both his professional and personal life with books.

1. What steps should an author take to help form a stronger partnership with the publisher's marketing team?

> First, I'd encourage an author to try to meet with their team in person, if that's possible. Once you connect, have a list of promotional ideas and tactics that you're willing to do on your own. This helps it feel more like a partnership. Many times a marketing team can help enhance and support these ideas, too. It also keeps the author from falling into that mode of "So, what are you going to do for me?" Marketers hate hearing that. Therefore, show up with some ideas, and you'll look like you're ready to go.

2. What aspects of marketing do you find that authors misunderstand the most?

> Social media. The best thing about social media is also the worst thing about social media—it's fluid. Social media is a constantly changing landscape that offers a lot of avenues to pursue. You don't have to start a blog, make a Facebook profile, or begin tweeting if you hate it. But you have to be somewhere. My advice to authors is, "Whatever you do to promote your books, do it well. You don't have to be everywhere. But, wherever you are, own it."
>
> Another author misunderstanding stems from the phenomenon called, "My book is for everybody." Someday it could be. But when you first start the marketing process, you must know your target audience.
>
> If you think your book is for everybody, then it's actually for no one. Seth Godin coined the term tribes as a way to define your audience. Likewise, as an author, you need to know your tribe and feed your tribe. If you continue to fan the flames, eventually we might celebrate the success of "everybody" reading your book.

3. What are the best ways that you've seen for an author to build a larger platform?

Be authentic. For example, own the social media channels that you use. Social media has made the world smaller. Think online "mom and pop" shops, and your blog, Twitter feed, or Facebook page is that shop. Everyone who interacts with you is a customer. Treat them well, and your platform will grow. Don't try to be someone online that you're not. People see right through it.

Building an author platform takes time. Be patient. Work on it a little every day. It doesn't happen overnight. I worked with an author who spent two years blogging before his book came out. He built that audience every day by figuratively hanging an "open" sign in the window. The people didn't come at first, but he kept hanging out the sign. He kept at it, and over time, the audience grew because he did the work.

4. What common mistakes do you see authors make when marketing their books?

A big mistake that authors make is thinking that their book will sell itself. It's not enough anymore to just write a book. You also have to promote it. The good news is that you're not alone. Every writer has to do the work. The best buzz for a book is writer based.

When writers connect with readers, they create a buzz that marketing can't buy. That buzz can make all the difference in the success of a book. It can be as simple as an event at your local library or a book signing. Building buzz is about meeting readers and making connections with fans.

5. What are the essential skills and strengths an author needs to maximize book sales?

Be kind. I know that may sound weird, but remember that in an online world, communities can be small. Thus, every interaction counts. So be kind to people. Be generous with your time. Take time to write back to fans. Treat people how you want to be treated. I know it seems simple, but you would be surprised how often it doesn't happen. There's a reason mom always said be kind to others. It works.

6. In your experience, how has the role of marketing changed for publishers over the last five years?

Book marketing has changed a lot. There are more marketing opportunities available than ever before due to online tools and social media. Yet I think one of the keys to success is not getting distracted by all the opportunities. You can't do everything. Pick and pursue the ones that best fit who you are as a writer. We need to remind ourselves of this mind-set every day. It's easy to become overwhelmed. Choose wisely where you put your time and energy into your marketing efforts.

7. What is the single biggest factor that you think influences book sales?

Write a book that matters. Yes, that may sound crazy, because who wouldn't strive to do that? But the opposite happens all too often. To me, books that matter come from writers who care more about the thing they are writing than book sales or bestseller lists. The internal need to create a book outweighs any external force. I like those kinds of books. When you read one, it has an undeniable quality. You can feel it enriching your life as you read it. And you can't help but tell others that they have to read it, too. In short, write a book that really matters.

INTERVIEW—CECIL "CEC" MURPHEY

Author and co-author of over 125 books

Cecil (Cec) Murphey is an award-winning author whose books include the *New York Times* bestsellers *90 Minutes in Heaven* (with Don Piper) and *Gifted Hands: The Ben Carson Story* (with Dr. Ben Carson). His books have sold millions of copies and have brought hope and encouragement to countless people around the world. Cec holds master's degrees in education and in theology, and received an honorary doctorate from Richmond Virginia Seminary.

1. You've written and ghostwritten more than one hundred books. What are the most significant changes you've experienced in publishing that affect authors today?

The biggest change I've witnessed is the increased level of author involvement required by publishers. If you don't use your legs to make the books sell, your book has no legs. You can no longer expect publishers to promote your books. They put their money behind the books that they're sure will sell or invest in authors who have proven they can sell.

Another big change is the focus on perceived needs. Whether fiction or nonfiction, people buy books that speak to them. They may want to relax, learn something new, or need a sensible answer to a perplexing problem. If you want your book to succeed, you need to avoid easy solutions that sound good but don't actually work.

2. As an author who has worked with numerous publishers, what advice would you give writers to make the most of that relationship?

Respect your editor. Remind yourself that their success as your editor is tied to your success as a writer. They want your book to be good. While a few overedit, most editors try to honor the author's voice.

If you don't agree with the changes your editor recommends, tell him or her. To do so is not to be adversarial. Writing a book is a joint project. If the book turns out well, the author gets the credit. No one will know how much your editor helped you.

3. Which battles do you think authors should fight, and which do you think they should let go?

Make sure it's a significant issue, and delete the word *fight* from your mind-set. I've never written a book where I didn't have a few differences with the editor. The editing process is a discussion in which both of you are attempting to make a quality product.

When I read a manuscript that my editor has edited, I make sure that each edit still sounds like me. If it does, then I let the edit go. If it doesn't, I mark it with a note that I disagree. If the editor misunderstood something I was trying to say, which sometimes happens, it may mean that I wasn't clear enough. Thus, I needed an editor to help clarify my thoughts.

4. One of your areas of expertise includes ghostwriting memoirs. What advice would you give an author to make their personal story more compelling to readers?

These days, it's difficult to publish your own story. Your experience needs to be truly significant. For example, when I wrote the manuscript for *90 Minutes in Heaven*, it was the first book on the topic. Since then, a lot of similar books have hit the market.

In 1990, I wrote the manuscript for *Gifted Hands: The Ben Carson Story*, which is the story of a young black boy who couldn't read in fifth grade. His mother intervened, and before he finished high school, he won a full scholarship to Yale. He is now one of the top pediatric neurosurgeons in the world. His story has inspired thousands of people.

If you want to make your story more compelling, ask yourself, "Why would anyone want to read my story? How does it differ from ten similar books? Keep in mind that there are no new topics, only new emphases. If you learned a lot of lessons in life, focus on them and illustrate your experience. For example, Edward Grinnan, editor-in-chief of Guideposts, recently published *The Promise of Hope: 9 Keys to Powerful Personal Change*. The book is a disguised autobiography; he uses at least one story about himself in each of the nine keys.

5. How would you advise someone who wants to move from free-lance writer to a full-time author?

Be careful and be sure. It's not easy to make a living as a writer. I've done it, but God gave me a vast amount of energy and a good dose of self-discipline. For example, I read at least a book a week in order to keep the ideas flowing.

Until you've published a few books, hold back on going full-time. I published ten books before I was ready to take the leap. The major impetus for me was an editor who liked my ghostwriting and said he would give me all the work I wanted, which he did for the next three years. Unless you can write and sell more than a book per year, you'll find it difficult to make enough income.

Another issue to consider is that writing is a solitary occupation. Unless you're highly self-motivated and willing to meet your deadlines, I recommend that you make your primary living in another field and just write part-time. Besides, what's wrong with being a part-time writer?

CHAPTER 11

THE FLAMMABILITY OF FREE: HOW TO DRIVE WORD OF MOUTH

With the advent of electronic books and reading devices, a lot of authors are terrified that someone will take their book's content, copy it, and share it illegally for free with the world. The idea of people blatantly stealing intellectual property makes some authors lose sleep at night. Yet there is a bigger problem than illicit piracy that every author should actually fear: the problem of anonymity.

No author wants her book to be ripped off. But a worse problem occurs when readers never find out that an author's book exists. Without awareness, there can be no purchase. In fact, piracy shouldn't be a concern, because some examples suggest that it can actually help boost overall book sales by spreading awareness to a wider audience. Some authors even judge piracy as an unconventional form of legitimacy. In contrast, the problem of obscurity means an author isn't selling many books at all.

I wrote this book as a marketing guide to help you avoid the dreaded fate of obscurity. However, one of the best ways to create a wildfire for your book is to steal a page from the piracy playbook by giving your content away for free. That's right. Give readers free access to your content. This doesn't mean that you encourage someone to steal your work. Instead the act of purposefully giving readers part of your book for free can be like throwing fuel on a fire. You activate a new level of excitement among readers by giving value that motivates them to want more and to spread the word.

The problem is that some authors mistakenly think they're good at this strategy, when they're only shooting themselves in the foot. For instance, they think that offering a complimentary sample chapter constitutes an exciting free resource for readers. This idea is severely limited, because the general public regards sample chapters as cliché. Almost every author offers sample chapters of their books, an act which is now run of the mill, and furthermore, expected. If you want your book to stand out in today's crowded marketplace, you've got to do more than offer a sample chapter.

This chapter will reveal how to provide flammable free content and creative tools that will help your wildfire burn a lot brighter. We'll examine the promotional power of pass-along resources, tools you can use to help spread awareness for your book, and how to create a fan club of readers who serve as your word-of-mouth warriors.

THE POWER OF PASS-ALONG RESOURCES

As I discussed in Chapter 2, a wildfire spreads when the intensity of a small fire ignites the surrounding trees and vegetation. The fuel within the kindling ignites and creates a fire that passes from one tree to another. Likewise, word-of-mouth spreads between people in a similar fashion. People read your book and feel a strong sense of excitement over it. Their excitement acts like a fuel that lights a fire within them and serves as a catalyst that compels them to tell someone else.

However, you can't expect people to read your book, fall in love with it, and immediately go buy ten copies to give away to friends. That's an unrealistic expectation. People aren't going to flock to bookstores and spend $100 to market your book for you. Yet this is what many authors anticipate. They subconsciously shift the burden of marketing to their readers (or their publisher) and expect other people to make word of mouth happen for them. But word of mouth doesn't work that way. Readers will, however, tell their friends about your book if you make it easy for them to do so. You have to remove the barriers of apathy, cost, and skepticism that people carry in their mind before they will take action.

I tell my author clients that readers will never buy copies of their book and give them away as gifts. That's unrealistic. On the other hand, it's fair to expect that people will read your book, appreciate the value in it, and use a free promotional tool from the author to tell several friends about the book.

The key phrase in this concept is "free promotional tool." It is the author's responsibility to provide tools that enable people to spread word of mouth about a book. You do this by creating free resources that are easy for people to pass along to someone else. You provide packaged content that delivers value to the reader and is simple to share with others. When it comes to book marketing, *free* is your friend. Offering parts of your book, or even the whole thing, for free can be one of the easiest ways to build buzz, grow your author platform, and generate sales momentum.

Some new authors bristle at this idea and complain, "If I give my book away for free, I'll never make any money." I can understand this concern, but look at the issue this way: If you offer your book for free, get a few hundred people to read it, and they generate word of mouth, you just built a fast-growing platform of nearly a thousand people—at almost no cost. That's an incredible risk-free way to get your name out in the public.

In contrast, let's say you give your book away for free, but very few people read it or tell their friends. That's still a blessing, because you found out that your book isn't very good without taking a huge financial risk. Rather than waste money on marketing efforts that would prove fruitless due to a bad book, you can save your money and use it to make your book better.

Several of my clients have successfully launched a new book by giving away free content. For example, I helped Lysa TerKeurst launch a new book entitled, *Made to Crave*. Part of our marketing strategy was to take 30 percent of her manuscript and turn it into a free resource called, "The Made to Crave—21 Day Challenge." This tool allowed readers to experience the value of Lysa's message in twenty-one daily nuggets. Lysa and her publisher turned this resource into a free e-book that was offered on Amazon for thirty days. In addition, Lysa posted this free resource on her author website and gave it away to a large radio network to share with its listeners.

Some people thought that giving away so much free content to so many people would cannibalize Lysa's book sales. Instead she sold over two hundred thousand copies in the first six months. Her book hit *The New York Times* Best Seller List and stayed there for over twenty-five weeks. Her success was due in large part to the power of this free resource. Lysa made it easy for thousands of women to test the concepts in her book, experience positive results, and get excited. Their excitement generated widespread word of mouth that led to incredible book sales—a blazing wildfire that swept across America.

Another client, Renee Swope, used a similar approach to launch her first book, *A Confident Heart*. Renee took content from her manuscript and created a free resource called "The 7-Day Doubt Diet." She promoted this resource to various groups of women that she knew and gave easy access to the information. All she required was that women sign up on her author website to receive the free resource by e-mail. Within the first thirty days, Renee received over twenty-six thousand sign-ups! Offering this free content built real buzz for Renee's new book, which launched shortly after and surpassed all of her publisher's sales expectations for a first-time author.

I've helped other clients take the concept of free resources and package it in other formats. For instance, Kathi Lipp used the power of free content to steal the show at a major convention with thousands of attendees. She purchased an exhibit booth to promote her new book, *The Husband Project*. However, Kathi needed a way to draw the leaders in attendance to her booth and generate interest in her message. Wisely she employed the giveaway principle and created a helpful free resource along with an enticing contest.

Kathi used content from her manuscript to make a helpful study guide that leaders could use to take groups through her book. She put this material onto an inexpensive CD-ROM disc as a pass-along tool. At the convention, Kathi displayed stuffed shopping bags from stores such as Target, Best Buy, and Victoria's Secret, on the table in her exhibit. The bags, which invited people to register to win a $25 gift card, attracted attention. The store bags and gift cards also connected to content in her book, and thereby opened the door to conversation about her book. As people registered to win her prizes, she also offered them her free leadership guide on the CD-ROM.

Kathi's strategy was so effective that she gave out all of her free CDs to leaders (over three hundred discs) within the first three hours of the convention. She drew so much traffic to her booth that she had to take down names and send CDs out after the event. She wound up gathering contact information for over six hundred key leaders of her book's target audience. Those contacts led to numerous paid speaking engagements for Kathi and bulk purchases of her book for small group studies. Kathi's book sold over twenty thousand copies in the first year, an impressive amount considering she did so as a first-time author in the middle of an economic recession.

Let's take the concept of free resources a step further. Suppose you're a first-time author with no platform, no fans, no awareness, no nothing. In this scenario, what would be the fastest way to build an audience of readers for your new book? Give your entire book away for free. Yes, that's what I said. Give the whole thing away for a limited time (thirty to ninety days) in order to gain a following and generate word of mouth. It's easier and cheaper than ever before to do this with e-books. For example, offer an electronic version of your book for free on Amazon. If a lot of people download it, you can switch to a paid version in both electronic and print formats, because you know that you have an audience who is hungry for your material.

When you give away free content from your book, it will rarely hurt book sales. Instead free resources serve as the catalyst to help capture new readers and boost word of mouth. As I said earlier, you can't expect people to buy your book and give ten copies to their friends, but you can expect people to take a high-quality free resource, share it with ten friends, and build the buzz you need for your book to succeed.

WORD-OF-MOUTH TOOLS THAT REALLY WORK

Have you ever read a book, really liked it, but never told anyone until someone else brought it up in conversation? Once you were reminded, then you evangelized that book to numerous friends. This situation identifies two common problems for authors who want to generate more word of mouth. First, most people won't tell their friends about your book unless you make an obvious request. Second, you must make the ability to tell friends as easy as possible.

Most people aren't against spreading the word about a good book. They're just busy or forgetful due to all the distractions in our hectic society. Thus, if you want more people to tell others about your book, you need to make it blatantly clear. Specifically tell people, "Please tell your friends about my book." Otherwise most readers will not think about forwarding your information to someone else.

In addition, people aren't interested in jumping through a lot of hoops to promote your book to others. That's why so few readers buy copies for their friends—it's expensive and time-consuming. Therefore, you can increase word of mouth for your book by making the process free and fast. This section covers some tools, online and off, that can help simplify the promotional process for you and your readers.

"Tell-a-Friend" website buttons

I'm a big fan of the free social media marketing service called "Tell-a-Friend" from https://secure.socialtist.com/signup. Their entry-level product is called Tell-a-Friend Free (TAF Free), and it allows people to share online information using more than eighty of the most popular social media channels. When you register for a free account, SocialTwist will give you the computer code to embed a cool-looking "Tell-a-Friend" button onto your website pages or blog.

When a visitor clicks on your "Tell-a-Friend" button, a little window appears on his screen that gives the option to instantly tell someone else about you. The visitor can choose to notify others via e-mail, instant messaging, a link to his blog, or he can share the word on a social network account, such as Twitter, Facebook, or LinkedIn, or bookmarking services such as Delicious and Digg. All you have to do is embed the "Tell-a-Friend Free" button into your blog or website. Then visitors who like your content can spread the word and recommend you to their friends, contacts, and networks using their own address books.

Even better, you can log in to your SocialTwist account and view a report that tells you how many times people have clicked on your "Tell-a-Friend" buttons. To improve your response rates, I recommend that you sprinkle these little buttons all over your website. Use them generously and make them easy to see.

I encouraged one of my clients to place these "Tell-a-Friend" buttons on her new author website. Within the first year, she received over five hundred referrals. That's a lot of free word of mouth that she would not have received otherwise. The results speak for itself.

Website banner ads

Another free tool people can use to tell others about your books are banner ads. A banner ad is a small image that serves as an advertisement for your book when someone copies the computer code and embeds it onto their website or blog.

Never underestimate the enthusiasm of your biggest fans. Some will gladly place a banner advertisement for your book on their website. The ad will draw attention and direct Internet traffic back to you. When a visitor sees your banner ad and clicks on it for more information, that's called a "click through," which means that a person clicked on your ad and was sent to a designated website page. This could be your home page or a specific landing page that relates to the ad.

The best way to improve your "click through rate" (CTR) is to use an eye-catching image along with a captivating headline. For instance, one of my clients created a banner ad that said, "Chocolate is my comforter" with an interesting picture of a woman sticking her head into a bright red refrigerator. The ad created a strong sense of curiosity in the viewer's eyes and made people want to know more, which led to above-average CTR results.

Keep in mind that most banner ads are small in size. Typical dimensions are based on the total number of pixels for the width and height, such as 180 × 150, 250 × 250, 160 × 600, or 728 × 90. Therefore, you need the text and image of your ad to be easy to read at small sizes. For instance, you may want to use only part of your book cover image, rather than try to cram the whole thing into the ad. Likewise, you must keep your marketing copy short and to the point. Don't oversell. Focus on using enticing language that gets the visitor to click and learn more.

If you want to add this promotional resource to your word-of-mouth toolbox, ask your website designer for help setting them up. They are easy to create and shouldn't cost much. Usually you just need to e-mail the image of your choice along with the marketing copy, preferred ad dimensions, and the designated website page that you want viewers to see. Your web designer can turn this information into a "clickable" picture file that can be placed on your website for others to copy. Once it's available, ask your fans to put your banner ad onto their website or blog and help you spread the word.

E-cards

Garth Stein, best-selling author of "The Art of Racing in the Rain," is a novelist who makes good use of e-cards. When you visit the "Fan Stuff" page on Garth's website (www.GarthStein.com), you can create a "Personalized E-card" that includes your comments and lets you choose a clever quote to send from his book. Then you enter a friend's e-mail address, and the card is automatically sent.

E-cards are an excellent way to let people spread the word about your books for free. For another good example of using e-card giveaways, visit the website for the best-selling book, *The Guernsey Literary and Potato Peel Society* (http://www.randomhouse.com/rhpg/guernsey/)

If you want to offer your website visitors a customized e-card, you will need to have a separate service added to your website. Talk to your webmaster about the cost and set-up procedures. Not many authors take advantage of this resource, so it can help you stand out from the crowd.

Printed postcards

Best-selling novelist, Liz Curtis Higgs, makes great use of oversize printed postcards to help her fans spread the word about her new books. The front side of her postcard features a large color picture of her book's cover, while the back contains promotional text and ordering information. Her postcards make a great promotional tool for direct-mail campaigns or pass-along tools to give away at book signings and speaking events.

If you want to use postcards as a promotional tool, make sure that the postcard does more than describe your book. You can boost word-of-mouth by giving people a reason to take action on the spot. For example, add these features to your postcard:

- Display an enticing coupon with a 15 to 20 percent limited-time discount.
- Show a website link connecting to an exclusive free resource that pertains to your book.

- Encourage the recipient to get exclusive info on your author Facebook or Twitter page.
- Place a QR code that links to a compelling video for your book.

Printed postcards may be an old-school idea compared to online tools, but they're inexpensive to make and still provide real promotional punch when combined with a value-laden offer.

Behind-the-scenes information and articles

Book readers, especially fiction fans, love to talk about their favorite authors. Make it easier for people to start a conversation about you by giving them interesting topics to discuss. For example, one of my clients wrote several novels set during the World War II era. She lived in England and traveled throughout Europe while conducting research for her stories. Because of her experience, she has a wealth of knowledge about the various European cultures and calamities that people experienced during wartime.

She knows fascinating information about the battlegrounds, prisoner camps, family support systems, and even wedding customs. I encouraged her to turn this knowledge into individual articles that would mesmerize the fans of her books. Likewise, you can use your research to write unique articles that people would like to share with their friends.

In addition, today's fiction fans want to know more about their favorite authors as everyday people. Even if they never meet you in-person, they want to understand your life as a novelist. Don't play hard to get in this arena. You don't have to divulge private information, but you can show people various sides of your personality and your interests outside of writing.

For instance, you could post a list of your favorite recipes, especially if they tie in to the food discussed in your novel. Offer a top ten list of your favorite movies, recommended travel spots, or favorite restaurants. You could even create how-to-style articles, such as how to hold a proper English afternoon tea, if your book takes place in England. Or if you write mysteries, you might write an article about how to assess the scene of a crime. Design and offer your resources in a way that encourages fans to pass them on to others.

Make your promotional tools available on your website, and remember to state the obvious. Tell people to help you spread the word. Besides the ideas listed here, don't be shy about asking your readers what kinds of pass-along tools they would prefer. Since you want them to feel comfortable taking the initiative to share your book with others, you should make it as easy as possible for them to do so by providing resources that fit their sharing style.

DEVELOP A MARKETING FAN CLUB

Any author can generate more word of mouth by offering helpful free resources and making them easy to share. But there's another way to generate even more word of mouth. Enlist a group of people to become your personal sales force. Imagine having your own promotional team that's obsessed with telling other people about your book. I call them "word-of-mouth warriors," and they can take your marketing efforts to a whole higher level.

If you're an author who has fans, and I mean truly rabid fans, you can harness the power of their enthusiasm to publicize your books. But rather than wait for them to mobilize on their own, which rarely happens in real life, you can proactively organize your fans into a focused team. Create a fan club specifically designed to help promote your books. In essence, invite your fans to join a special marketing group that conducts specific marketing activities on your behalf. In return for completing these tasks successfully, your fans receive special prizes or exclusive access to meet you.

Musicians and bands have used this strategy for decades with great success. In some circles, these fan clubs are known as a "street team," because the band enlists them to plaster the streets with posters advertising an upcoming concert. In addition, the fan club votes for them in popularity contests, request the band's songs to be played on their local radio station, give copies of the band's CDs to friends, or drum up buzz about a concert in order to help boost ticket sales.

As an author, you can create your own "street team" that augments your book-marketing efforts. The fan club concept may sound simple, but it must be executed correctly to get results.

The bottom line is that you can't build a fan club without fans. The word *fan* is short for the word, *fanatic*, which means "a person with extreme and uncritical enthusiasm for a cause or idea." A real fan is someone so passionate about your books that he is usually easy to identify. For instance, fans are not afraid to contact you. They feel no shame telling other people about you. They are quick to publicly defend you as someone they respect.

Popular musicians are known for having ardent fans, but authors can have fervent fans, too. They may look and act a bit differently, but they're just as committed. Examples of authors who have a devout fan base include novelists such as J.K. Rowling and Nicholas Sparks, or self-help gurus, such as Dave Ramsey and Dr. Gary Chapman.

Fortunately you don't have to be a perennial bestseller to utilize the power of fan clubs. You just need enough fans who are willing to work on your behalf. Use the following questions to judge whether a marketing fan club makes sense for you:

- Do you regularly receive fan mail and/or random e-mails from excited readers who praise you for your books?
- Do you have at least 2,500 subscribers to your blog, newsletter mailing list, Facebook account, or Twitter page?
- Would you consider yourself a mysterious or charismatic personality who can naturally attract the interest of others? You may be introverted, but you're mesmerizing to others.
- Are you willing to give true fans a little more personal access to you in return for marketing on your behalf?

If you can say yes to these questions, then you're probably in a position to build an effective fan club. If not, you're better off skipping this option and focusing on other marketing ideas listed in this chapter.

Creating a successful fan club is basically a two-stage process of "request and reward." You make a formal request to your fans by asking them to conduct certain marketing activities that help promote your books. Then you reward them for taking action. If your fans feel that the reward is worth the effort, you can repeat this process with them over and over.

Putting a fan club together is the easy part. You can add a page on your author website that explains what the club is about and invites people to join simply by filling out an online form requesting their e-mail or mailing address. You can gather the contact information into a database that you can tap into whenever you need to get the word out about your books. A simple e-mail blast can notify the group about an activity you want them to do and describe the reward that awaits them. I'll explain how to verify their participation in a moment.

REWARD YOUR WORD-OF-MOUTH WARRIORS

The hard part of managing a fan club is coming up with ways to announce your marketing requests in a manner that sounds appealing. That means offering a reward that comes across as worthwhile. You can lose a lot of fans if you bore them with requests and fail to deliver a tangible prize. People value their time, and they're not keen on wasting it to help promote you if they don't get something in return. Below is a list of rewards that some of my clients have used to thank their fans.

Free merchandise

You can thank fans for promoting your books by giving them free products such as books, CDs, DVDs, and T-shirts. If you take time to autograph these items, they're even more attractive. Rewarding fans with free merchandise can be a small investment that gains exponential levels of book exposure.

Exclusive access

If you poll most fans, the opportunity to personally meet and talk with a favorite author is deemed a major reward. With today's technology, it's easy to meet fans without leaving home. For instance, you can reward your fan club by setting up an exclusive teleconference call or video chat using Skype. Give twenty to thirty minutes of your time to say thanks, answer questions, and make fans feel special. Moreover, if you decide to go out on a book tour or hit the speaking circuit, you could provide the even better reward of backstage access. Who wouldn't love getting their picture taken with their favorite author?

Special discounts and inside information

This type of reward is as exciting as the previous two ideas, but there is value in offering your fans discounts and private information that they can't get anywhere else. Never underestimate the power of someone feeling like they're the first person to know. Knowledge is power, and fans love to wield that power in their circles of influence. Just don't skimp on the discounts or information. Otherwise your fans will feel like you're taking advantage of them.

For instance, you could give fans a secret 50 percent off sale for a short period of time. Or you could make them the first ones to hear about your next book. You could even enlist their involvement with creating the title or naming the central character. Make your fans feel like they're a special part of your writing process.

PROMOTIONAL ACTIVITIES FOR FANS

Now that you have enticing reward ideas for your rabid followers, what should you ask them to do? There is no perfect list of right and wrong activities. However, I recommend that you suggest tasks that either shore up your weaknesses or provide a large-scale promotional benefit. Here are a few ideas:

Post an online book review

Ask your fans to go online and post a favorable review at the major retail websites, such as Amazon.com, BarnesandNoble.com,

LibraryThing.com, and ChristianBook.com. The collective voice of numerous fans raving about your book can generate a persuasive buzz that boosts your credibility among skeptical book shoppers.

The number of reviews is just as important as the favorability of reviews. People are impressed when they see that a book has received over one hundred reviews—even if the reviews are mixed. The energy of a large conversation surrounding a book is more attractive than a quiet book with just a few five-star reviews.

In addition to retailer book reviews, encourage your fans to post a review about your book on their personal blogs. Due to the social media revolution, our culture tends to make decisions based on the influence of individuals we trust rather than corporate advertising. An influential blogger has the power to sway hundreds, if not thousands, of readers.

When you ask fans to post blog reviews, ask them to give more than just a simple explanation of your book. Urge them to include your book trailer video, book cover images, links to sample chapters, free resources, and/or where to purchase at online retailers. In addition, remind your fans to explain the emotional benefits that they personally experienced.

Promote via social media sites

Your fans can help spread word of mouth by mentioning your book on their personal social media accounts, such as Facebook, Twitter, Google+, and LinkedIn. Ask them to post a reference to your book using a casual, conversational tone and to provide a direct link to your author website or book's page on Amazon.

Sometimes your fans aren't sure what to say on your behalf. They sincerely like your book, but they're not adept at using promotional language. In this case, consider creating marketing hooks or interesting quotes ahead of time for your fans to use. I worked with a couple of authors who entered on their website a list of premade tweets that visitors could choose and automatically post on their Twitter account. This list helps remove the guesswork for their followers. They can simply choose an interesting quote and quickly tweet it to their social media network.

Give books to leaders

Another great way for fans to support your book is by giving copies to influential leaders whom they know, such as media personalities, celebrities, business owners, book club directors, librarians, church pastors, and politicians. This task is one of those unsung, but highly important, ways to build a grassroots marketing wildfire for your book. Social media marketing is good, but the face-to-face activity of fans conducting referrals and you (or someone else) physically handing a stranger your book carries a lot more clout.

Most authors find it emotionally uncomfortable to directly promote their book to a powerful leader. Thus, your fans can take steps to make these connections for you. It's the ultimate version of word-of-mouth marketing in the trenches. Always ask your fan club to consider this activity, and reward them well when they take action.

Get your book featured in a local publication

Even though our modern society has gravitated to online media, many people still read local newspapers, magazines, and newsletters. However, trying to contact every local media outlet is not the best use of an author's time. This is where your fan club can really help.

Ask them to get your book featured in their local publications. Promotional activities could include giving your book to the editor, sending an e-mail to an editor with a favorable review attached, or urging the publication to contact you for an author interview. The media world is constantly looking for interesting content, and they do listen to their subscribers. Therefore, ask your fans to flex their local muscle and use their excitement to get media attention for your book.

Host a book club discussion

Some fans may not have a large social media platform or rub elbows with big-shot leaders. However, their enthusiasm for your book may be just as strong. Invite those individuals to create their own discussion groups around your book. These fans might host a book club at their house, set up a lunch discussion group at their office, or formalize a reading group at their church.

Encourage your followers to go public with their zeal for your message in a setting that fits their personality and sphere of influence. Likewise, make it easy for fans to set up a book group by providing free tools on your website, such as downloadable discussion questions, book trailers, author videos, and promotional text.

MONITOR YOUR FAN CLUB

Once you've built a list of marketing activities and rewards for your fan club, you should monitor their actual participation. I encourage my author clients to keep the process very simple. The easiest way to hold fans accountable is by asking them to send you a brief e-mail with proof of the activity they've completed. You can even set up a special e-mail address just for this purpose and have someone else monitor the club for you.

For example, if a fan posts a review of your book on Amazon, Twitter, or Facebook, she can e-mail a link to that specific post for you to see. If someone gives your book to a leader, she can e-mail you that leader's contact information for potential follow-up. If he gets your book featured in a local publication, he can e-mail a link or a picture showing his success.

Requiring fan club members to verify their activity by e-mail prevents people from faking participation and allows you to reward authentic activity. Then fans will feel like you really appreciate their actions, plus you will be able to see how they spread the word.

One more word about fan clubs: Only try the above ideas if you really have a lot of rabid fans and you're sincerely ready to reward them. Do not make a halfhearted attempt to manipulate people because you're lazy and hoping others will do the hard work for you. You can lose readers for life if you abuse the love that fans bestow upon you. Be sure to avoid the following mistakes.

- Don't try to build a fan club for a month, then quit. Stick with it for at least a year.
- Don't expect everyone to participate. Be happy if 15 to 30 percent of your fans take action.
- Don't show anger if things don't go as planned.
- Don't give lame rewards. Give tangible gifts or exclusive access that's truly meaningful.
- Don't make vague requests about how to market your books. Clearly describe the steps that you want your fans to take. If you confuse them, they won't do anything.
- Don't let fakers take advantage of the system. Hold your fans accountable, but offer grace in the process. There's no need to be overly strict and potentially upset fans. You don't want them to turn their enthusiasm against you.

True fans want to help their favorite authors. But the author needs to organize and empower his fans in order to unleash their full potential. When you utilize an attractive request-and-reward system, you'd be surprised how far your fans will go to support your book.

Summary

Every author dreams of watching readers excitedly spread word of mouth about their book. But, if you want people to create a marketing wildfire, you must tap into the fuel of their inner fervor. The best way to capture their attention is by offering something of value for free. Free resources, both online and off, enable people to share their excitement with friends. As your author platform grows, add a new dimension to your marketing plan by organizing dedicated fans into your personal publicity team. Formalize a fan club, empower them, and make it fun for people to become your word-of-mouth warriors.

CHAPTER 12

SELL BOOKS THROUGH PUBLIC SPEAKING

A few years ago, I was waiting in a hardware store for a gallon of paint that was mixing. While standing in line, a man approached me and said, "Are you Rob Eagar?" Snapping out of my bored gaze, I shook his hand as he exclaimed, "Wow, I heard you speak at an event where you talked about your new book. Your message really encouraged me, and I bought copies for myself and some friends!" I was totally surprised and flattered. That was the first time I ever felt cool standing in a hardware store.

Getting recognized in public as an author is a fun experience. The sense of satisfaction that washes over you replaces the memories of toiling over your manuscript. While I have no desire to be famous, it's a privilege to meet strangers who appreciate my work. That great feeling, however, rarely occurs unless you get in front of people and speak about your book.

One of the best ways to sell your book like wildfire is by speaking in public. Not only can you make a lot of money from a speaking fee, there's usually an opportunity to sell books directly to the audience for a decent profit. No other avenue allows you to simultaneously connect with readers, build genuine relationships, generate word of mouth, and boost product sales. This chapter will reveal proven strategies to help you land author speaking events.

I can personally vouch for the ideas discussed here, because I've spoken as an author to over thirty-five thousand people at more than one hundred seventy events. I've faced the fear of standing in large auditoriums to address over one thousand listeners. Plus, I've given presentations in tiny rooms where only a handful of people attended. Every experience was different and beneficial, because speaking in public has played a large role in the success of my books and my ability to make a living.

Too many authors, however, suffer an intense fear of public speaking. Some surveys report that people would actually prefer to face death than speak in public. You don't have to let this anxiety be a hindrance. If you take steps to implement the information in this chapter, you'll be able to overcome the hurdles and secure more speaking opportunities, create an enjoyable presentation, and drive more book sales. Here's a list of the key topics we'll cover:

- Use the booking process to your advantage.
- Generate referrals from leaders.
- Create a professional demo kit.
- Establish and negotiate a speaking fee.
- Develop a powerful, focused presentation.

In addition, I'll share a few insights about how to work with a speaker's bureau and provide tips for authors who are just beginning to speak publicly.

USE THE BOOKING PROCESS
TO YOUR ADVANTAGE

Leaders of every stripe frequently request authors to address their organizations, such as business executives, nonprofit directors, trade show organizers, church pastors, book club hosts, and university groups. If you want to get the attention of these leaders, you must understand how the booking process works.

Most leaders choose a speaker based on one simple factor—trust. For instance, the average leader doesn't wake up in the morning and think, "Wow, it's a beautiful day to book a speaker!" Instead, most leaders think about the problems within their organization and search for solutions to fix those problems. Many times, the solution is an outside expert who can provide unique answers, inspiration, humor, or viewpoints. In other words, leaders aren't interested in booking a speaker, they want to book experts who happen to speak. Thus, if you position yourself as an expert rather than an author, you'll increase the trust factor and a leader's desire to seek you out.

For instance, many leaders are justifiably hesitant to bring in an unknown speaker. They have a reputation to keep. Plus they care about the needs of their members or employees. No leader wants to deal with the trouble of booking a bad speaker. So, if you want leaders to hire you and pay you fairly, you must enable them to trust you.

Note my emphasis on connecting with a true leader. This is an important distinction, because too many authors waste time talking to gatekeepers, such as secretaries, administrative assistants, or interns. These authors wonder why they don't get hired to speak at more events. Sure, it's much easier to talk to gatekeepers, but they have no decision-making power. They'll be polite and act interested, but they don't have the authority to select you and authorize payment. Thus, you are better off using your precious time and energy to directly pursue actual leaders.

In his book, *Money Talks—How to Make a Million as a Speaker*, Alan Weiss reveals the seven most common ways leaders book speakers. Look at his list below and see if you can detect an interesting pattern. Leaders usually make booking decisions in this order of priority:

1. Personally heard the speaker and was impressed.
2. Heard from a trusted peer that the speaker is excellent.

3. Heard from a trusted subordinate that the speaker is excellent.
4. Heard from a trusted third party that the speaker is excellent.
5. Heard from a speakers' bureau with whom there is a trusted relationship.
6. Heard or seen something about the speaker in the media.
7. Received promotional material from the speaker.

Did you discern a pattern? Notice how the top five ways leaders choose a speaker revolves around a relationship of trust. The highest priority is placed on seeing a speaker in action, which means your actual speech is your very best marketing tool to land more bookings. I've worked with several A-level speakers who confirmed that over 50 percent of their bookings came from leaders who had previously heard them speak.

In addition, many leaders lean heavily on recommendations they receive from peers, staff members, employees, friends, and speakers bureaus. Ironically I've found that most authors attempt to land bookings using the two least effective methods: chasing media interviews and blanketing the country with promotional kits. These tactics are a waste of money, because they fail to make a leader feel comfortable. And no leader likes to be sold.

The best way to secure speaking engagements is to get people to positively mention your name to leaders. This process is also known as "generating referrals," which is the next step in our discussion.

HOW TO GENERATE REFERRALS FROM LEADERS

Two kinds of leaders can book you for an event: leaders you know and leaders you don't know. Let's look at a few ways to connect better with both groups and use referrals to create new speaking engagements.

LEADERS YOU ALREADY KNOW

You probably know more leaders than you think. For example, you may have connections through these avenues:

- Leaders who booked you in the past year.
- Leaders who are personal friends or business acquaintances.
- Leaders who are friends with one of your friends.
- Leaders who manage organizations to which you belong as a member.

As you identify the leaders you know, determine who may share a trusting relationship with you based on past performance or personal connections. Then you can leverage that trust to your advantage in several ways.

Ask for names of other leaders

Leaders tend to run in circles with similar types of leaders. Many get together on a regular basis as friends, mentors, and peers. So, if one leader appreciates your message, she is bound to know five to ten other leaders on a similar level. Those connections can open new doors for you.

When you establish a trusting relationship with one leader, ask him for three names of other leaders you could contact or have them introduce you. Get permission to use that leader's name if you call or send an e-mail to the names provided. When you contact these referred individuals, mention your mutual acquaintance and describe how you helped his organization. Reiterate your value and the kinds of results you can produce for the referred company as well.

At best, the level of trust from the leader who knows you will transfer to the other leader and help mold a comfortable relationship on your behalf. At worst, you can add the referred names to your print newsletter list to build the relationship over time. (Don't add their names to your e-mail list unless they request to be added. Otherwise it's spam. For more information about how to create and send powerful newsletters, see Chapter 13.)

Ask for endorsements

If you did a good job for the leader who booked you in the past, don't be shy to request a testimonial. In order for the endorsement to be effective, however, ask the leader to write a specific example of how your message improved her organization. Testimonials are worthless if they don't point to an identifiable result. Other leaders are looking for proof that you've already helped one of their peers. This is how endorsements can work in your favor and create referral bookings.

For instance, list all of the influential leaders you've worked with in the last year. Give them a brief follow-up call and ask for an endorsement. Tell them you'd like to highlight your work with them in your marketing materials. Use their testimonial on your website, Facebook page, or as a book endorsement. When leaders see their peers vouching for your credibility, their skepticism will subside.

Ask for repeat bookings

Imagine that you just finished speaking at an event, and the leader is happy with your performance. While you're both in the throes of bliss and partnership, mention how you enjoyed the event and casually ask if you could speak there again in the future. Don't be forceful, but point out that you have other messages that could help the audience.

Sometimes the leader will be agreeable immediately. If so, get out your calendar and schedule a mutually beneficial date. Otherwise set a time within the next ten days to discuss a return engagement. For this step to work, you need to ask the leader soon after the event is over. If you wait a few weeks, after the emotion has died down, the leader can become distracted with other duties, and you'll diminish your opportunity to repeat.

CONNECT WITH LEADERS YOU DON'T KNOW

You may have solid connections with many leaders you know from the past. But, in order to land more events, you have to forge new relationships with leaders whom you don't know. When you initiate this process, remember that leaders book speakers primarily based on trust. Trust is primarily gained through relationship. Likewise, the most effective way to build relationships is through face-to-face interaction. Therefore, the best way to build relationships with new leaders is to meet where they gather and network with them.

Networking is a commonly misunderstood term among many authors. For some, the idea of networking conjures visions of smooth-talking salesmen wandering through a crowd passing out business cards to draw attention. But this scene is the furthest thing from real networking, and also a quick way to get blacklisted among leaders.

A better way to network is to attend events where leaders congregate, spend time getting to know them, and express an attitude of partnership. If you know a subject well enough to write a book, then you're probably familiar with the annual conferences, retreats, or trade shows that attract your topic's leaders and influencers. If not, conduct an Internet search or ask the leaders you know for a list of the major events they attend each year.

Attending a writers conference does not count as a speaking engagement for authors because you're not reaching new readers or expanding your platform at those events. You're preaching to the choir. If you want to be an author who is known as a legitimate speaker, you must address audiences that constitute your actual reader base or represents prospective purchasers of your book.

Consider attending at least three to five events per year for networking purposes. Even better, contact the event's host organization, and ask if you can teach a workshop and sit on a discussion panel. Look for ways to get your name in front of the attendees. If those efforts fail, you can still meet a lot of leaders by attending the event's sessions, dinners, or extracurricular activities. Don't go and hide in your hotel room. Walk around with confidence knowing that you offer real value to people.

Once you meet a leader, pay attention to this next step: do NOT jam a business card into his hand, talk about how great you are, and ask him for a speaking engagement. Instead, do the exact opposite. Keep the attention off of you, and focus on asking the leader questions about his group. Probe for issues that pertain to the value you can provide.

For instance, if you wrote a book about leadership skills and attend a leadership conference, don't mention your book unless you're asked. Instead, use probing questions to determine if a leader's organization is struggling with the issues that you handle, such as team-building concerns, mentoring new employees, or hiring and firing practices. Be cordial, try to find common ground, and seek to understand the problems that a leader faces.

When you determine that a particular leader could use the value of your message, implement this simple step: Ask the leader for her business card or contact information. Then ask if you may send them a helpful resource as a follow-up to your discussion. Note that I said "resource." Do not plug your book.

Before you network with leaders, put together some useful resources that might be helpful to them, such as a related article, special report, latest statistics, website links, or a book. Show that you care about the leader by offering to send your resource for free.

After you part ways, use the leader's contact information to follow up within twenty-four to seventy-two hours. Send a nice e-mail to say how you enjoyed meeting him and that you'll be forwarding the resource you promised. If you send a package, you can include a copy of your book with the resource you mentioned in conversation. If you e-mail a follow-up resource, you can include a link to your website for information about your book. Then wait one to two weeks to give the leader time to receive and look over your material. Follow up with a phone call to make sure they received your item, and ask if it was helpful.

If the leader doesn't respond or acts disinterested when you reconnect, don't try to sell yourself. Instead, say that you're glad you met and that you'd like to stay in touch. Ask that leader for permission to be added to your print or e-mail newsletter database for future mailings. It's better to wait for that leader to approach you later, rather than try to barge down their door.

If the leader's response is enthusiastic, you can share the fact that you speak on specific topics that could help solve one of her problems. Offer yourself as a partner who is looking to enhance the leader's organization. Start your relationship by looking for ways to help them, rather than use them to get a speaking engagement. Show more concern for the leader's needs than your own. Explain how your message could create positive results. Then ask if there are any upcoming speaking opportunities available. Wooing the leader with a partnership attitude will position you to get referrals and bookings in the future.

When a leader realizes you truly care about his needs, he will be more likely to reciprocate in the future. Leaders get approached by many people who have a selfish agenda, so you'll seem like breath of fresh air.

MAXIMIZE YOUR DEMO KIT

As you begin to make new connections and generate referrals, eventually a leader will contact you to inquire about a speaking engagement. The invitation will usually come out of the blue via a phone call or e-mail request. However, most leaders won't book a speaker without conducting a little due diligence.

This background check usually means a Google search, visiting your website, and requesting an audio or video speaking sample. Leaders test to see if you can overcome their skepticism and prove that you're skillful in front of an audience, thereby increasing their trust in hiring you. So it's important for authors to develop a professional-quality demo kit and keep it ready to go at all times.

Leaders can easily judge your speaking skills by watching a video that you post on YouTube or your website. But it's also wise to have physical items available, such as a CD or DVD with your speaking sample and related promotional materials that describe your expertise and value. Here's a quick rundown of the essential elements to include in you demo kit.

1. Describe the results you can produce

Leaders book speakers who can produce the kind of results their group needs, such as self-improvement, business results, entertainment, or a spiritual awakening. They're also looking for someone with a professional image, someone who can engage their audience, and preferably, someone whose name can attract a large audience. Thus, your media kit needs to reflect how you can meet these requirements. Your bio, speech descriptions, testimonials, and speaking samples should illustrate the ways that your message can improve people's lives.

Too many authors make the mistake of using promotional text that blathers on about their accomplishments, past book sales, and awards. Accolades are nice, but most leaders don't care about them. I urge you to write your text in a manner that focuses on how you enjoy helping other people. Let the results you've produced in the past shine, instead of your ego. See Chapter 1 for a review on this topic.

2. Audio speaking sample

Leaders choose speakers who they believe will do a good job. Once the trust is built, they'll book the same speakers for several years in a row. Therefore, you want to build trust by offering a speaking sample that shows you at your best. Your biggest ally is a brief clip that lets leaders hear you speaking confidently with a live audience.

If you're a novice or intermediate speaker, don't worry about creating a demo video. Use of video is generally reserved for advanced speakers with big budgets. On top of that, most leaders expect top quality when they watch a video. In fact, if your video isn't excellent, it will work against you. The good news is that a quality audio sample is adequate for most leader requests. Postpone making a video until your budget grows or you reach an advanced level.

Edit your speaking sample to make sure that it begins with a powerful section of your speech. Many leaders will only listen to the first 60 to 120 seconds to determine if they like you. So don't waste time by filling your demo with a long or boring introduction.

If you place a speaking sample on your author website, choose one of your most dynamic five- to ten-minute segments that highlights you at your best. You don't need a long segment. Nobody wants to sit at their computer and listen to a forty-five–minute speech. However, be prepared to send a full-length version of your best speech on CD or as an mp3 download to leaders upon request.

Before you make your demo speech available to the public, test its effectiveness by asking a few leaders that you know to evaluate it. Beg them to be honest, and don't rely on your friends for feedback. Leaders know what leaders are looking for, so listen to their judgment.

Above all, get your demo professionally recorded with good equipment. Even if you need to hire someone to help, the benefits outweigh the costs ($250 to $500 is a good range for audio recording). Nothing will kill your chances of getting booked like a bad demo with poor sound quality or distracting background noise.

3. Professional head shot

Your demo kit should establish trust with leaders who might pay money to let you talk about your book. However, nothing can ruin your credibility like a bad head shot. I've seen male authors display pictures of themselves wearing jeans, piercings, or unkempt facial hair. Worse, I've seen women authors use photos of themselves in wacky outfits or send shots of themselves at a family beach trip or wedding. Sure you want to display your personality. Nevertheless you don't want to exhibit a head shot that implies you might be a kook.

A good rule of thumb is to be professionally photographed in an outfit that you would wear when speaking. Wear conservative clothes that are a level higher than what your audience would tend to wear. It's hard for people to believe you're an expert if you look like you just walked in off the street. If necessary, spend the money to get a professional head shot by an experienced photographer, which can run around $250 to $750. Review their portfolio for samples of appropriate work before hiring a photographer.

4. Written promotional pages

Whether your demo kit is printed out or displayed on your website, you need to write text that covers the following information:

A. PERSONAL BIO PAGE—Create a bio on one page using less than 400 words. Keep all text focused on the results you produce for other people. You can include pictures of your book covers on this page.

B. TESTIMONIALS PAGE—Use another page to list at least five endorsements from other leaders and well-known individuals. Use testimonials that describe specific benefits you produced for past audiences. Focus on boosting your credibility.

C. SPEECH DESCRIPTIONS PAGE—Choose your best four to six speeches and describe each one using one introductory paragraph followed by three to four bulleted value statements for each message. The value statements should clarify the results you will produce for the listeners.

D. SUPPLEMENTAL RESOURCES—Include a copy of one or two relevant articles that you've written. You can also include the latest copy of your newsletter. These additional items should amplify your expertise by displaying your insights on a relevant subject.

You can post all of these necessary demo items in one place on your website. For your hard copy kit, use a nice-looking presentation folder with your logo or book cover on the front as the container for your materials. When you combine all of the ingredients discussed above, you should have a great demo kit that appeals to leaders. Keep a few kits in your office fully prepared and ready to mail at a moment's notice. In addition, give a few kits to friends who know influential leaders and can forward them on your behalf.

WORKING WITH A SPEAKERS BUREAU

Working with a bureau can be a great source of new speaking engagements. However, most reputable bureaus only work with advanced, in-demand authors. If you're new to the speaking profession and relatively unknown, you will find it hard to get on their rosters. These organizations tend to gravitate toward best-selling authors, well-known athletes, celebrities, and politicians. The best way for new authors to get the attention of a particular bureau is by showing how your message is different from any other speaker's message that they represent.

If you know a speaker who is already on a particular bureau's roster, ask that person to make an introduction for you. Schedule a meet and greet by phone or in person and give several examples of the results you've produced for audiences in the past. Be prepared to provide a top-notch video demo and several testimonials from nationally known leaders.

Some authors mistakenly believe that speakers bureaus do all of the marketing legwork and magically set up a ton of new engagements. This is a big misconception, because bureaus usually promote just the speakers in their top tier and let the lower-level speakers fend for themselves. If you're not a big-time personality, you will be lucky to get a promotional spot in their annual catalog mailing and a mention on their company website.

The benefit of bureaus is that they can provide access to high-profile events. Bureau agents work hard to build relationships with event planners and trade show directors. These relationships pay off as the event director contracts their speaker needs to the bureau. When the bureau receives a request, they will recommend you if you're considered the right fit for the event.

The price of working with a speakers bureau is usually a 15 to 20 percent commission that they take from your speaking fee. Therefore, I don't recommend that authors work with bureaus unless you're so busy that you need someone for administrative help. If you do go with a bureau, never sign an exclusive arrangement.

Always keep open the option to be represented by several bureaus at the same time.

WD **BONUS ONLINE CONTENT:** Download the article "Quick Tips for Beginning Speakers" at bookwildfire.com and writersdigest.com/book-wildfire-downloads

HOW TO ESTABLISH AND NEGOTIATE A SPEAKING FEE

Getting paid to speak about your book is a big boost to keeping your author career financially afloat. Yet setting and negotiating a fee can feel so awkward that some authors avoid speaking altogether. Use the following steps to navigate the process in a win-win manner.

Set a reasonable fee based on your value

People in Western cultures, such as North America and Europe, tend to attribute a lot of money to items or services that provide a lot of value. For example, we perceive a new Mercedes-Benz automobile as a luxury vehicle that's reliable and loaded with lavish technological features. Since everyone agrees that the car has much value, many people are willing to spend a lot of money to purchase one. Mercedes is a perceived symbol of quality, status, and comfort. Their high value equals a high price tag that thousands of car buyers are willing to pay.

This same principle applies to setting a speaking fee as an author. If you're a recent bestseller who has sold thousands of books, your perceived value will generally be quite high. Therefore, you can command a higher speaking fee. Many politicians, celebrities, and prize-winning authors, for example, routinely receive $10,000 to $50,000 for an individual speaking engagement. On the contrary, authors with little book sales and no name recognition sometimes have to speak for free.

Setting the proper speaking fee requires honestly assessing your value. If you have a history of helping people solve a problem, a reputation for being an expert, or a track record of attracting a lot of people to see you in person, then you can probably request a substantial fee, such as $5,000 to $15,000 depending on the type of event and audience size. However, if no one has ever heard of you and you're just starting to build your author platform, you may have to shoot for a fee in the $500 to $2,500 range.

Establish a speaking fee that's low enough to secure your first bookings. Then raise the fee as your value increases. For instance, if you become a better speaker, win an award, hit the bestseller lists, or become high demand in whatever way, you can increase your fee accordingly. Otherwise start at a level that allows you to gather experience and grow your track record. Ask other authors or professional speakers you know for a ballpark range that is appropriate for your level.

If you get a few paid bookings and no one balks at your fee, it's probably too low. Lack of resistance usually means you're leaving money on the table. Try raising your fee by 10 to 20 percent until you get a little resistance. Then you'll recognize a realistic range to request.

Get to the real decision maker

Once you establish a realistic speaking fee, share the number only with the person who can truly respect it—the actual event leader. Normally a gatekeeper, such as a secretary or administrative assistant, will make the initial speaking inquiry by phone or e-mail. In those cases, keep in mind that his primary goal is usually to get a speaker booked quickly and cheaply. By saving time and money, the assistant looks good in the eyes of their superior. The best way to avoid this conflict is to get past the gatekeeper and talk directly with the real decision maker. Only the true leader can share the actual event goals and budget limit. Ask the following questions:

- "Are you the person who is overseeing this event?"
- "Are you making the final decision, or are you recommending me to someone else?"
- "Are you in charge of the direction for this event?"

- "Who is in charge of making sure the goals of this event are met?"

If a gatekeeper resists connecting you with the leader, mention that your policy is to discuss an event with the leader before you can discuss money or accept an engagement. Use these statements if you need help:

- "I have to ensure that the event leader's objectives will be met."
- "It's a strict policy of my organization, and I can't consider any speaking invitation unless I talk with the event director first."
- "You and I can collaborate once I've received your leader's input."
- "I require talking with the actual decision maker to make sure that I can tailor an approach to meet his agenda and needs."

Remember that gatekeepers usually care about saving money and handling logistics. Leaders care about investing for long-term results and life change for their organization.

Emphasize your value

During an initial inquiry, always emphasize the value of your book's message to the leader interested in booking you. Start by asking, "How did you hear about me?" Then, recite some of your value statements (see Chapter 1) that apply to that person's needs.

Suppose you're an author of a nonfiction book and a business leader asks if you're available to address his group of employees. Direct the focus of your conversation to the problems that require your assistance. What issues are the employees facing? What type of results would the leader like to see you provide? Once you understand the needs of the organization, list some of your value statements that apply to the situation. For example, you could say, "It sounds like a lack of teamwork is the core problem that needs to be addressed. The message of my book and speaking presentation will help your company build teams that are unified in achieving their mission and create employees that solve problems faster and more thoroughly." Focus on the results you can create.

If you're a novelist, the same principle applies. Say you receive a request to speak at a fund-raising banquet, historical group, or literary society. Before you talk about money, ask questions to discern the leader's goals for that event. Then describe how you can specifically assist the leader in meeting those goals. For example, if you wrote a historical novel about the Civil War, you could say, "My presentation will include little-known research and insights that will transform your audience's perspective of our nation's history." If you write thriller mysteries, you could explain results, such as "Your audience will enjoy learning how to think outside the box in order to solve a crime."

On the other hand, if you realize that your value doesn't fit the needs of the speaking request, don't fake it. Turn down the engagement. Taking a gig outside your competency will usually backfire on you and harm your reputation. Instead, be honest and tell the inquirer, "I understand your problem, but that's not my area of expertise."

Sidestep initial questions about fees

When you receive a speaking invitation, soon you'll be faced with the inevitable question, "How much do you charge?" Before you reply, keep this tip in the back of your mind...the longer you put off saying your fee amount, the more time you have to build the other person's perception of your value. And, the better your chance of getting a higher fee.

If a leader pushes you early for a fee amount, sidestep the request until you get a chance to explain your value. Buy yourself more time to discuss the results you can create by saying, "I don't have a set fee. Instead, I offer options based on your needs. Tell me more about the goals for your event."

If you continue to get pushy requests about money before discussing value, cut to the chase and put the request back on the leader. Ask her, "What is your budget for this event?" Getting the other person to say a number first may actually reveal a fee range to your advantage. If they mention a higher number than you expected, accept it and enjoy the event. However, if they offer an unrealistic budget, politely say no, thank them kindly, and refer them to another speaker who might fit their lower range.

Build a partnership

The reason you want to negotiate a fair fee rather than accept anything you can get in desperation is because the best speaking engagements usually occur when the author and the event leader mutually respect each other. Your value as an author in the eyes of the organization is equal to your desire to work with that group. This balance of equal respect is known as a partnership, where each party mutually esteems the other.

During your initial conversation, treat the inquiring leader with respect. But test the waters to see if she's willing to appreciate your needs for a fair fee and an environment that's conducive for professional speaking. Ask the leader the following questions:

- What are the problems/needs of your group that I can help meet?
- Are there specific issues that you'd like for me to cover?
- What could I do that would make you the happiest?
- What steps are you taking to market this event in the community?
- If I have specific audio/visual/microphone needs, can you accommodate my requests?
- Will I be permitted to sell my books to the audience?
- Can you record my presentation and provide me with a copy?
- What authors have you booked in the past for this type of event? (It's okay to take any names given and contact those authors for a reference, if you're unsure about an event.)

Gauge the leader's answers to your questions to determine if he shows a sincere interest in your needs as an author. A partnership is a two-way street with mutual give and take. Avoid a one-sided scenario where you must meet all of his requests without getting assistance on issues important to you. If someone is willing to partner with you, you will sense an overall feeling of cooperation and admiration. Show the leader your willingness to help his organization and expect the same level of treatment regarding your presentation and selling your book.

Pursue a fair fee

Ideally you want to discuss your speaking fee after you talk about the leader's needs and confirm that you can meet them. Once you complete that conversation, you can mention an initial dollar figure, or ask the leader to be specific about the event budget for speakers.

Avoid the desire to bundle your value together just to get a booking. For instance, some authors try to appease event leaders by throwing in an extra Q&A session, breakout workshops, small group coaching, or discounted books for the price of their regular presentation. This mind-set works against you by cheapening your position as a peer.

Instead, look for ways to unbundle your services and charge a higher fee for additional value that you can bring to the event. If the other party benefits, so should you. Remember that you're seeking a partnership of equal respect.

I encourage my author clients to look in the mirror and practice saying their requested speaking fee out loud. Repeat the exercise until you can say your fee without hesitating, stuttering, or cowering. You must convince yourself that you're worth the money before you can convince someone else. Justifying your value in your own mind will help you explain it to someone else. When you begin the actual discussion about money (with the real leader), keep these pointers in mind:

1. Never reduce your speaking fee without reducing the value you offer. Otherwise you will come across as a shark trying to extract exorbitant fees. Always tie your fee to the value you can

provide. If the other party wants you to cut your fees, your response should be "What part of my involvement do you want me to cut?"

2. If the other party claims that your speaking fee is too high, politely state, "Other organizations pay this amount on a regular basis." Then wait while they struggle for an answer. Reverse the guilt tactic by identifying how they're making an unusually low request.

3. If the other party still doesn't want to pay your requested fee, it's usually due to one of the following three reasons:

- They don't understand your true value. Try explaining it to them again.
- Their budget is too low to be realistic. Part ways and move on amicably. You might even provide the name of another speaker you know who will accept their fee. This helps you look like a resource.
- They really don't want to be a partner with you. Instead, they're just looking for a cheap speaker to exploit. Say thank you and move on, satisfied that you avoided a lousy engagement.

4. If you and the leader agree on a fair fee, thank the leader and tell her how excited you are to work together. Put together a concise written contract and ask her to return a signed copy by fax or mail within thirty days. Request a 50 percent deposit to hold the event date on your calendar. Also schedule a follow-up call two to four weeks before the event to discuss final details and preparations.

Remember that the goal of the booking process is never to overcharge someone for hiring you to speak. Instead, your aim should be to create a partnership in which each side respects the needs of the other. In this environment, real results can happen for your audience, because both parties want to work together. When you focus on meeting the needs of the leader, you will usually be able to negotiate a higher fee and sell more books in the process.

HOW TO DEVELOP A POWERFUL PRESENTATION

An old adage among professional speakers says "The brain can only absorb what the 'behind' can withstand." This means that the longer you talk, the less information your audience tends to remember. When a speaker covers too much, the information tends to run together and cancel itself out in the listener's mind.

Worse, when you rush through a ton of content, it sends a signal that you're more concerned with covering your material than trying to help the audience. In essence, you generate an emotional cue that says, "I'm more concerned about selling my book than helping you." Unless you're a popular celebrity with rabid fans, this selfish approach will hinder sales.

The reality is that most people can only retain about 5 to 15 percent of what they hear when listening to a speech. Therefore, your job as an author is to concentrate your message in a way that allows you to control whichever part of your speech you want people to remember. This point is crucial, because if the focus of your message wanders, your audience will also wander. And, bored or confused audiences don't usually buy many books.

Thus, if you want to use public speaking as a springboard to book sales, you would be wise to create a concise presentation with one main point.

Some people will argue that a speech with one point doesn't cover enough material to convince people to buy your book. In certain cases, that may be true, such as when you're giving a day-long seminar where people specifically attend to learn as much information as possible. Those situations are less frequent than a typical keynote presentation, where you have only thirty to forty-five minutes to motivate a large group of people. Let's assume you're not giving a full-blown seminar or workshop. The following discussion shows how to create a powerful, one-point message that can make your book appealing to the masses

10 QUESTIONS TO BUILD A SPEECH BACKWARDS

The hallmark of a great speech is when the audience takes action based on what the speaker said. Therefore, it's better to develop a speech that focuses on the result you want the audience to experience, rather than with the opening story you want to tell. Build a new speech starting from the end and work to the front. The following list of ten questions will help you create an outline for a presentation that keeps your material focused and memorable. Start with the first question and work your way down the list in order.

1. What specific action do you want the audience to take after hearing your speech?

2. What story or example can you tell at the end of your speech that will inspire the audience to take action and follow your recommendations?

3. What application step can you ask the audience to take that applies the solution of your message? (If the audience likes your solution, they'll think, "What can I go do about it?")

4. What hurdles might prevent the audience from employing your solution? Provide an answer for each hurdle or misconception. (Remove the mental walls that may prevent action.)

5. What is the solution to the problem that you will raise at the beginning of your speech?

6. What are three to four examples you can share that describe how various groups in the audience are struggling with the problem? (Your goal is to make people feel the frustration, create tension, and build a desire for your solution.)

7. What examples from your own life can you share that show how you've personally wrestled with the problem? (This step helps build credibility with your audience.)

8. What major problem is your audience facing that you can help them overcome? (You need to define why your speech is necessary.)

9. What is the main point for your message that ties everything together and makes your speech easy for the audience to remember?

10. What visual objects or interesting images could you show from the stage to keep your audience engaged and help your main point stick in its mind?

By working backward to construct a speech, you can build a presentation that leads your audience into life-change. When they experience the power of your message, your book becomes an attractive resource for follow-up or a souvenir from the experience. In addition, people are more likely to spread word of mouth when they believe the author expressed genuine caring for the audience.

SELL YOUR BOOKS AT EVENTS WITHOUT BEING OBNOXIOUS

Speaking in public offers several benefits to authors, including the chance to travel the country, meet fans face-to-face, and make a healthy speaking fee. Even better, there's the opportunity to sell a lot of books to a captive audience. However, some authors squander the occasion by acting too timid or too crass when trying to promote their book from the stage. Thus, I offer the following tips to help increase your book sales without coming across as a pushy salesman.

Incorporate your book into your presentation
People can't buy your book if they don't know it exists. So take a moment during your presentation to make the audience aware of

your new title. However, making people aware doesn't mean shoving it down their throat. Nobody likes to feel like they've been sold. And audiences don't appreciate the bait-and-switch method of an empty speech that only offers answers if you buy the book. If you try too hard to promote your book, you will simply make the audience mad. They won't buy anything unless they think it's in their best interests.

The best way to appeal to an audience's interest is by showing the value of your book. Let listeners see the benefits you offer in the context of their current situation. You can make this possible by incorporating part of your book into your presentation. For example, I've found that reading aloud from a small part of my book creates much better results than giving the audience a promotional pitch. When listeners see that your book offers answers they can readily apply, they'll be more likely to purchase. Here are some sample scripts you could use to integrate part of your book into your presentation:

> "Based on what I've talked about the last few minutes, allow me to give you an example of what I mean by reading a brief section from my book ..."

> "I don't have enough time during this presentation to go into all of the details. But I provide a lot more information in Chapter __ of my book. Allow me read you a short section to give you a sneak peek."

> "I wrote my novel because the problem that my main character confronts is important to me. Let me read you a brief section to show how the primary issue in my story affects all of us here today."

When you read aloud from your book during a presentation, you send a subtle message to the audience that validates the need to purchase. Listeners won't feel like you are trying to sell them something. Instead, they'll feel you are offering a resource that can help them.

That distinction alone can lead to a higher percentage of sales at the live events you attend.

Show the book's cover

Imagery serves as a powerful tool to motivate and remind audiences to take action. Therefore, you should always attempt to show the cover of your book to everyone in the room. You could hold up your book while you read from it during your presentation, or you might display your book's cover on a video screen before, during, or after your message. Telling people the title of your book isn't enough. Whereas showing the cover locks the image of the book in the listener's mind.

Some of my clients pass out free postcards with their book's cover on the front side and promotional text on the back to all attendees at their events. This gives people a chance to see the book cover repeatedly (every time they see the postcard). It also reminds them of the purchase opportunity and can be used as a pass-along tool to share with friends.

Mention your resource table

This step may sound obvious, but it's important to let your audience know that you have resources available. Many things vie for attention, and it's easy for attendees to miss your book table or feel apathetic about taking a look. To combat against these issues, always have a giveaway, such as a recent newsletter issue, free resource, article, handout, recipe list, or contest prize, at your resource table. Mention these freebies and give every person in the room a legitimate reason to stop by your booth before they leave.

Charge full retail

Have you ever attended a music concert and seen T-shirts on sale for over $25? How can musicians get away with these ridiculously inflated prices? Emotion can trump logic when it comes to pricing. In other words, the emotional experience of a great performance makes people feel less concerned about price. Fans enjoyed the concert so much that they'll gladly pay an inflated charge to take home a souvenir to remember their good feelings. The greater the emotion, the less they see price as an issue.

As an author, you can enjoy this same dynamic. When readers hear you speak, they get to feel an emotional connection to you as an author. If they're fans of your material, that connection can run incredibly deep. Look at the intense followings of big bestsellers such as J.K. Rowling, Malcolm Gladwell, and Stephenie Meyer.

Furthermore getting a signed copy of your book can feel like a personal treasure to a fan. Thus, price isn't top priority when most people visit your book table. You can easily charge the full retail amount for individual copies of your book, especially if you sign them in-person.

Offer a combo pack

Most people will pay full price for your book at an event, but if you want to move large quantities, consider offering volume discounts or discounts for purchasing different resources together. For example, I used to sell individual copies of my paperback books for $15 and a four-disc CD audio set for $20. Together the full retail was $35. But at my events I would offer these two products together as a combo pack for $25, which was a 30 percent discount. People bought this combo pack like crazy, and my event sales increased dramatically.

If you have a lot of products to offer, such as books, CDs, DVDs, and workbooks, and study guides, put them together at a deep discount (40 percent plus) and promote a special price to buy one of everything on your resource table. You may not get many takers, but you won't get any if you don't make the opportunity available. For those who do purchase, you'll get a high ticket sale that adds a lot to your revenue.

Always accept credit cards

Whenever you sell your books in public (or on your website), always accept credit cards. Research has shown that people will purchase

30 percent more product when they can pay via credit card rather than cash or check. If you don't accept credit cards, you're leaving a lot of money on the table.

Fortunately there are numerous inexpensive ways for people to buy your products without cash. Typically I ask people to supply their credit card information on an order form, and then use Pay Pal's "Virtual Terminal" feature (www.PayPal.com) to enter the data and process a customer's card. PayPal wires the money to my bank account whenever I want it.

If you own a smartphone, you can use a credit card swipe reader that automatically processes customer information in real time. For instance, check out Square Up (https://squareup.com/) for an affordable service that works with any iPhone, iPad, or Android device. You pay only a 2.75 percent fee to accept all major credit cards.

Summary

The opportunity for more speaking engagements will happen when leaders are convinced you can benefit their organization. To reach those leaders and get paid to speak, you must learn to generate referrals and use those connections to your advantage. As leaders begin to trust your reputation, inquiries will naturally occur. These opportunities will benefit you only if you give a presentation that benefits the audience. When leaders see that happen, they will gladly reward you with a speaking fee. And the audience will gladly reward you with book sales.

Some authors say there is little to be made from words written on a page. But there is a nice living to be made for authors who take their books to the stage.

CHAPTER 13
CREATE NEWSLETTERS
THAT GET RESULTS

When I teach seminars at writers conferences, people frequently ask me, "What is the single best book-marketing tool that any author can use?" That's a tough question, because you can make good arguments for all kinds of options. But based on my experience, only one tool creates more bang for the buck than any other tool I've recommended to my clients, and that's newsletters.

Every one of the authors that I've helped launch a new print newsletter has landed at least one paid speaking engagement from their very first issue. That's real money and the opportunity to sell a lot of books in person. Yet too many authors view newsletters as an archaic marketing tactic. Why send out an old-fashioned newsletter when you can join all of the cool hipsters on Twitter and Facebook?

I've dedicated this chapter to one of the most overlooked tools in an author's marketing arsenal. A big benefit of newsletters is that they offer a proactive way to connect with book buyers on a continual basis. In contrast, most social networking and Internet-based marketing tools are reactive, because you're waiting for readers to find you.

Here's an overview of the details covered in this chapter:

- What makes a newsletter effective and ineffective?
- Who should receive your newsletter?
- When is the best time to send out your newsletter?
- What content should be in your newsletter?
- How do you make your newsletter look professional?
- How do you build a growing database of subscribers?

Sending out a good newsletter will get results, whether you're a beginner or a best-selling author, whether you write fiction or nonfiction. A few years ago, an author asked me to analyze her marketing plan and suggest new tactics to help her sell more books. I noticed that she wasn't proactively reaching out to influential leaders. Instead, she was waiting for leaders to contact her, which was an unrealistic expectation. I suggested she start a quarterly print newsletter. My client was skeptical, but agreed to give it a try. After the very first issue, she immediately received two new speaking engagements. And then something even more interesting happened.

Several months later, this client received an invitation to speak near my office, so I stopped by to attend her presentation. Backstage, we bumped into the event director, and I asked, "What led you to book this author for your event?" She replied, "Her great newsletter! I've been receiving it for almost a year. Earlier I didn't have the budget to book a speaker. But I always thought to myself, 'I love this author's newsletter. And, as soon as I have the money, I'm booking her for my first event.'" I flashed my client one of those I-told-you-so looks, and she grinned sheepishly.

Later that month, my client calculated that sending out her newsletter had directly generated more than $25,000 worth of speaking fees and book sales. This was money she would have missed otherwise. Sending her newsletter to a targeted group of prominent leaders created numerous speaking engagements, substantial book sales at those events, and ongoing purchases of her group study materials. Another one of my clients made more than $8,000 in one weekend, which he attributed to his first newsletter issue. You can't argue with these results.

The bottom line is that newsletters work. Consequently, if you've never sent one out, it's time to get off the fence. Or, if you've already been sending newsletters, I'll show you how to make your next issue even more productive.

Here's why newsletters are so important to your book's success. Marketing research has shown that the average American is exposed to over 3,500 buying impressions every day. This is a total of all the billboards, website ads, TV and radio commercials, plus all of the product choices one encounters when walking through a store. That's 3,500 today. Tomorrow you'll get hit with another 3,500 impressions, and so on. When you add it up, there is no way that our brains can keep up with all of those choices.

Add to this problem another interesting statistic: There are over 1,000,000 new books published each year. How do all of these numbers apply to you as an author? The average book shopper is bombarded with too many choices to manage. There's no way people can remember all of the books they see advertised.

Therefore, it's your job to remind your reading audience that you exist. Otherwise they will literally forget who you are. Consider the familiar phrase, "Out of sight, out of mind." This is certainly true for your book. If you don't take proactive steps to remind people you exist, they will forget you're on the planet.

This is why newsletters can be so helpful in growing your book sales. It's a powerful tool to keep you in front of your readers, so that they remember to buy your book and recommend it to friends. If you don't think newsletters are cool by now, check your pulse.

NEWSLETTER MISTAKES AUTHORS MAKE

For the diehard cynic, maybe you're thinking, "I tried newsletters in the past, but they seemed like a waste of time. I didn't experience the results that your clients did. What's the problem?" Usually there are two mistakes that derail an author's success with a newsletter.

Mistake #1: Writing newsletters about yourself, rather than for your audience

The most common mistake authors make is sending what I call a "you-letter" instead of a newsletter. A you-letter is a newsletter that's all about Y-O-U. In other words, a letter that is self-absorbed and annoys people. For example, you're probably sick of getting e-mails and junk mail in which someone writes about nothing but himself. It's like that person is saying: "Hey, I know you're busy, but I want you to just sit there and read a bunch of selfish blather about me."

When I was writing this chapter, I happened to receive an unsolicited e-mail newsletter from a new author plugging her first book. To my chagrin (and her loss), her newsletter content contained six different promotional ads for her book. There wasn't one helpful article or piece of information that benefited me. Ironically her book was all about how to overcome stress and work more efficiently. Yet her newsletter was the picture of inefficiency. Furthermore it made me want to avoid all of her future newsletters.

If you want to kill the power of your newsletter, then use it to talk about yourself and ignore the needs of your audience. Make that mistake a couple of times, and people will throw everything you send to them in the trash.

Here's a good rule of thumb to remember: Keep 80 percent of your newsletter content focused on the audience and only 20 percent of the content about yourself (product promotion and personal updates). Stick to that 80/20 rule, and you'll see better results.

Now I know that some of you may have innocently mistaken the word *newsletter* to mean that you're supposed to share about all of the latest *news* in your life. While that's true to a degree, you must keep personal stuff to a minimum. Instead, focus on providing beneficial material to your readers. Content is key, as you'll see later in this chapter.

Mistake #2: Sending your newsletter to the wrong people

A newsletter will work against you if it's sent to people who don't care about the topic you write about. It's better to send your material to a smaller targeted group who will be excited to read it than to shoot it out like a shotgun aimed at a random mass group. Most people hate junk mail and spam. You don't want get on anybody's bad list. Therefore, write specific articles and content that fit the needs of the reader who will receive them.

If you send a newsletter about parenting issues to a group of business leaders or church pastors, for example, they will likely ignore you because it's not a good fit. You must tailor your message to a group of moms and dads who need your expertise.

WHO NEEDS TO RECEIVE YOUR NEWSLETTER?

After considering the two mistakes discussed above, the next logical question is: Who needs to receive your newsletter? It's a waste of time and money to blindly send out hundreds of copies with no target. As I mentioned, your recipients should be people who are genuinely interested in your expertise or the topic of your book. Many authors fail to realize that there are two different kinds of groups who need your newsletter. I refer to these two groups as "leaders" and "readers."

Leaders are influential people with the power to quickly spread your name and book on a large scale. Their leadership position grants them the authority to recommend your message, hire you for a speaking engagement, or buy your books in quantity. If a leader gets excited about your message, she could quickly tell another one hundred or one thousand people about you. Examples of true leaders are individuals like the senior executives of a business, pastors of a church, directors of a non-profit, newspaper reporters, and radio producers. In today's Internet-based society, a leader can also include a high-profile blogger or the organizer of an online social network.

Readers, on the other hand, represent a completely different group. They are fans of your books, past customers, friends, family, and the general population. Readers have referral and buying power, and they make up the core of your word-of-mouth army, however, their influence is generally smaller than a leader's.

It's important to differentiate between these two groups, because influential leaders have different needs than readers do. That's because leaders are generally busy people with assistants who screen their mail and even their e-mail. For instance, if you randomly e-mail your newsletter to a corporate executive, he will rarely see it. In contrast, your readers group is more forgiving and usually has a personal connection to you. So they're more likely to read your newsletters.

How do you reach both groups effectively? Create and send two separate newsletters. That's right, send two separate newsletters. Before you tune me out, listen to my rationale. If you really want to reach influential leaders, then you must do it on their terms. Here's the rub: Many leaders receive over two hundred e-mails per day. Their e-mail in-box is inundated. If you try to reach them via a simple e-mail newsletter, they'll never see it. Your newsletter will disappear forever. Worse, if they never requested your e-newsletter but you send it anyway, you will be labeled *spammer* and blacklisted. Do it repeatedly, and you could face legal action.

Fortunately you can prevent this sad fate by sending a professional-looking print newsletter. Mailing a print piece increases the chance that it will hang around a leader's office and maybe even draw that leader's interest. A print newsletter can serve double duty as a great promotional piece to give away at your book signings or speaking events.

There's a catch, though. You must tailor the content of your leader newsletter to meet the leader's needs concerning the management of people. Consider how your book's information can make her job as a leader a little easier. Offer tips and statistics that can improve her situation, thereby increasing the chance that she'll promote your message.

Sending a one-sheet, front and back print newsletter to leaders is sufficient. Use thick paper, and print both sides in full color. I know this costs more than e-mail, but you increase the likelihood that leaders will read it. Even better, you can send out thousands of print newsletters without getting labeled as a spammer. To find the mailing address for a specific leaders, Google their names or visit their organizations' websites.

Remember that leaders and readers are two distinct book-buying groups who have different needs. A print newsletter to leaders and an e-mail newsletter to readers with tailored content for each group will help cover your promotional bases.

WHEN TO SEND YOUR NEWSLETTERS

Now that you know who needs your newsletters, it's important to know when and how often to send them. If you're hard-pressed for time, you might push off your leader newsletter for a month or two but keep it on your priority list. In the meantime, send out an e-mail newsletter to your reader group. Generally an author will have a larger database of readers than leaders. It's more cost-effective to use e-mail if your list has thousands of names. Here are some timing guidelines based on whether you're sending to readers or leaders:

For Readers: At least once a month via e-mail

The best day of the week to send e-mail newsletters is usually Tuesday or Wednesday. In addition, a good time to send them is around 2 p.m. Eastern time, so that people in every time zone can receive it around their lunch hour. However, there is no magic time to e-mail your newsletter. The main factor is that you stay consistent. Nothing will hurt your effectiveness more than skipping a month or two and allowing people to forget you exist.

For Leaders: At least once a quarter via snail mail

The best time to send print newsletters is when leaders are in the middle of making their booking decisions for speaking engagements, purchasing decisions for annual curriculum, or special purchases for Christmas gifts. Don't forget that your book can apply to all three of these decisions. Therefore, send your print newsletters in January, April, August, and November. Avoid sending around the summer break, Thanksgiving, and Christmas holidays, because most leaders are distracted or out of the office.

EIGHT ELEMENTS OF EFFECTIVE NEWSLETTERS

So far, we've answered the who, why, and when aspects to your newsletter. The next question is: what content should you put in it? Look at these eight key elements that will make your newsletters appealing to readers.

Newsletter element #1: Feature article

First, we'll start with the centerpiece, which is your feature article. Keep in mind that people don't like to read long, wordy newsletters. Shoot for a word count of around 500 words. More important, pack your article with helpful information for the reader. Provide information that is immediately applicable, thought provoking, or perspective changing. You don't have to be deep or intellectual, but your article needs to help people. No one is interested in reading about stuff they already know, so don't bore people. Instead, be contrarian and get their attention, or give them fresh tips they can really use.

Make your article easy to digest by breaking the text into bulleted points or lists. The more you can separate your text into small chunks, the more your reader's eyes will thank you. The goal is to be brief, pithy, and able to solve a reader's problem.

Pause for a moment right now, and ask yourself, "What problems does my book help people solve? How can my expertise make people's lives better?" Keep that question in your mind at all times, and make a list of topics or issues that you could address in future newsletters.

If you're a fiction author, you may be thinking, "But, I just write stories. My books don't really solve a problem, and I can't put together a nonfiction-type of newsletter." That's not true. If you write fiction, your book still helps people. At the least, you provide enjoyable entertainment and an escape for the reader.

If you're a novelist you can write newsletter articles about the problems your stories and characters encounter. For example, if you write romantic fiction, create articles about the power of love, the inner workings of relationships, or the differences between men and women. If you write historical fiction, you could cover little-known facts about your book's time period or historical era. You could offer travel tips that apply to the cities or regions where your stories are set.

Take fascinating research from your book, and use it to engage your readers. If you write mysteries, provide information about home security tips, travel safety, or insight into how law enforcement protects our lives. Don't tell me you're a fiction author who has no reason to write newsletters.

Likewise, if you're a nonfiction author, your articles need to display your expertise. If you're a published author, the public regards you as an expert. Give people advice, techniques, and inspiration to overcome the issues they face. You can write about how to deal with conflict, handle finances, organize priorities, or work more efficiently. The possibilities are only limited to your wisdom and experience.

The idea of creating consistent articles may have some of you wondering, "How can I send out one newsletter per month? I'll never be able to generate enough material to keep up, especially with my busy schedule." Those in search of good material for the newsletter can try these tips:

a. Take your book, find a helpful 500-word section, rewrite the beginning and ending paragraphs, and voila ... there's your article.

b. If you hit writer's block, recruit another author to provide free content from their book for your newsletter. But only use this option as a last resort. You should always focus on letting your own expertise shine. If you consistently provide your readers with helpful information, though, most won't care if some of it doesn't come from you. They'll still be glad you sent it, and you'll get the goodwill from recipients. Be sure to name your source if you get material from someone else.

Newsletter element #2: Extra section of value

Your feature article is the main item of value for the reader, but remember the rule of thumb: 80 percent content about helping the reader, 20 percent content about you. One main article isn't enough. You need to include another item of value. This section should be brief. No more than 200 to 300 words. Take your expertise and boil it down to a useful nugget.

For example, you could offer an interesting statistic, resource listing, unique recipe, or even an insightful opinion on current events. Some of my author clients use this element to display one of their popular blog posts. Others use it as a Q&A section where they answer hard-hitting questions from readers. They tackle problems regarding relationship difficulties, corporate politics, family conflict, and life as a novelist.

Newsletter element #3: Brief bio with value statements

Your next element is a brief bio with at least three value statements. The reason for this is twofold. First, some people may sign up for your newsletter weeks or months before they get your next issue. Second, others may have forgotten who you were or the basis of your expertise. You need to quickly remind them why your message is important. Otherwise they may think, "Who is this person?" and ignore your newsletter.

I recommend creating a two to four sentence bio that sums up who you are followed with a few value statements. As mentioned in Chapter 1, a value statement is a short sentence that describes a specific result you produce for readers. Don't talk about what you do. Instead, list the ways you help make people's lives better. If you can't do that, no one will feel drawn to your message. Some random examples from some of my clients follow:

- Boost profitability with less wasted inventory.
- Say no without feeling guilty or being used.
- Increase your confidence to deal with difficult people.

- Create havenlike environments that make your kids excited to come home.
- Experience a deeper sense of God's peace during a time of loss.

Since communicating the "value" of your book's message to the reader is such an important issue, I suggest putting this information near the top of your e-mail newsletter or on the outside page of a print newsletter. Doing so helps increase the likelihood that a skeptical reader will see this helpful text first and feel attracted to the rest of your information.

Newsletter element #4: Testimonial from a leader

The next important element is a powerful testimonial about your book. The key to this element is to use an endorsement from someone with a well-known name or title. Readers care *who* said it, just as much as *what* was said. That's why you want to get into the habit of asking leaders you know for a two- to three-sentence testimonial that mentions how you've helped his audience.

If you don't have a leader's testimonial to use, then recruit fans of your book to offer their endorsements. Regardless of whether it's a leader or reader, be sure to ask for a specific example of the results your message produced for that person. Shy away from endorsements that sound vague, because those can hurt your credibility. Display testimonials that communicate the specific benefits you provide people. Here's a comparison between a bad and good endorsement:

Bad example:

"I highly recommend Steve's book as an outstanding resource for any organization."

—John Doe, VP of Sales, Acme Inc.

Good example:

"Since we started using The 5 Languages of Appreciation in the Workplace, we haven't lost any co-workers in our department, the team is happier and more positive, and we hired back two employees that used to work in the division. We are so thankful for this book."

—Susie Smith, Human Resources Director, Acme Inc.

Do you see the difference between a vague and specific endorsement? Urge leaders to be as specific as possible. Tell them that other leaders need to see the results you helped bring about.

Newsletter element #5: Upcoming events calendar

Once you have a strong testimonial to display, you're ready to add another key component to your newsletter—an upcoming events calendar. This is usually a small box or an area of text that lists where you'll be appearing in the next three months. Your events calendar should include all of your upcoming speaking engagements, radio or TV interviews, and book signings.

Include the date, location, and contact name for each event. It's quite common for someone to see your event listing in your newsletter and make a point to come see you in person, which adds your event attendance.

If you have only one to two events scheduled over the next ninety days, stretch your calendar to include six months. You don't want it to look thin.

By the way, if you don't have any events lined up for the next six months, leave off the calendar section entirely ... and get to work lining up speaking and media events. Reread my discussion on those subjects in Chapters 6 and 12.

The goal of your events calendar is to show your newsletter recipients that you're an active author, which reinforces the fact that other leaders request you. Your calendar helps build credibility by implying that your message is dynamic and requested. A secondary benefit is that your calendar shows people that you're more than just an author. You're also a professional speaker, a media personality, and a desired expert.

Newsletter element #6: Featured product

Once you've created your feature article, extra section of value, bio with value statements, testimonial, and events calendar, it's okay to talk about yourself. This is the area where you can advertise your new book, seminar, or spin-off.

Show a small color picture and provide a brief description of your featured item. Then create a sense of urgency in the reader's mind by offering a discounted price, but only if they order quickly. For instance, you could say, "Order in the next ten days, and get a 20 percent discount." That encourages your readers to take action.

Avoid beating readers over the head with your products or begging them to buy something. Nobody respects an author who acts like a used car salesmen. However, this doesn't mean you shouldn't advertise your materials. Rather, first mention the results that your book provides, then state how to order it. For example, you could say, "Available in bookstores everywhere"…"Buy on Amazon.com," or list a link to your author website.

Newsletter element #7: Contact information

I've received some excellent newsletters from authors who still made a major mistake: They forgot to include their contact information! That's like tripping just before you cross the finish line. Never underestimate the importance of letting your readers know how to contact you.

Your newsletter recipients are potential word-of-mouth warriors who can make or break your book's success. They can request you for speaking engagements, forward your newsletter to friends, and purchase your book in bulk quantities. If they can't reach you, you'll miss out on those opportunities.

Give people several ways to reach you, including your business phone or cell phone number, e-mail address, website URL, and your mailing address. If you're concerned about privacy issues, limit your contact information to an e-mail address and a post office box number. But don't get so worried about stalkers that your prevent everyone from reaching you.

Newsletter element #8: Professional layout

A great way to guarantee people will ignore your newsletter is to send something that looks homemade. Doing so makes you look incompetent, and all your newsletter efforts will be wasted. In contrast, a professional-looking layout helps you look like an expert—even if you're doing everything out of your home. The goal is to enhance your credibility so that people take you seriously. Use these tips as you design your next e-mail or print newsletter:

1. If you can afford to hire a graphic designer to create a newsletter template for you, by all means do so. You can reuse the template for future issues by simply swapping out the content. The extra level of style can really impress people and make them more likely to forward your material to others. You always want to enhance the possibility of getting more word of mouth, and image plays a big role in your credibility.

2. If you can't afford to hire a graphic artist, try using standard software, such as Microsoft Word or Publisher. Personally I use Word to design and print my newsletters for leaders. I've found the "Text Box" feature an easy way to lay out pictures, colors, and fonts that look great.

3. Whether you're creating a print or e-mail newsletter, here's a great design trick: Use the banner from the top of your website's home page as the header for your newsletter. Obviously this will only work if you have a professional-looking website. By using your home page banner, though, you keep your branding and imagery consistent across various marketing tools.

4. If you'd rather not attempt to design a newsletter yourself, consider using an outside service. For e-mail newsletters, I recommend Constant Contact (http://wildfire.constantcontact.com). They offer a free, sixty-day trial and their system lets you choose from over four hundred great-looking templates. Plus, they help automate your subscriber database, taking care of things such

as new sign-ups and unsubscribers. Another reputable service is MailChimp (www.MailChimp.com).

- Both services provide helpful reports that tell you how many people have read your newsletter and how many times readers clicked on any of your promotional web links. From a marketing perspective, this is incredibly useful information. They also provide great customer service and easy-to-understand tutorials to help you learn how to use their system.

- To design a print newsletter, you can buy professional-quality, ready-made templates from companies such as Stock Layouts (www.StockLayouts.com). They offer more than fifty different templates that you can customize. You can preview, purchase, and download a template to your computer in a wide variety of software formats. Insert your newsletter text and images into the template, print it, and you're ready to mail to your recipients.

- Speaking of printing, I recommend going to a FedEx Office or local office supply store, such as Staples or Office-Max. It's a waste of time to babysit your printer all day while it spits out hundreds of copies and eats up your ink cartridges. Plus these stores usually offer price discounts on color copies as low as $.25 per side. That's a deal, and a much better use of your time. Also, if they make any mistakes, you can hold them accountable, rather than worrying about fixing a print problem yourself.

HOW TO BUILD YOUR NEWSLETTER DATABASE

Now that you know about the eight essential elements every newsletter needs, let's discuss how to build an ever-growing database of subscribers. The larger your database, the larger your potential for word of mouth and increased book sales. In fact, publishers adore authors who have a newsletter following of five thousand subscribers or more. A number that large gives publishers confidence that you have a growing, influential platform to help sell your books. Therefore, I suggest you set a goal to add at least one hundred new subscribers to your database each month.

Sounds simple but there's a catch. People are very concerned about privacy. Nobody wants to receive a newsletter they didn't request. In general, people have a more lenient attitude toward print newsletters, but that's not the case for e-mail newsletters.

You would be smart to send your e-newsletters only to people who specifically request it. This request process is known as "Opting-In." If you don't require people to opt-in, you could be considered a spammer and your e-newsletter could be shut down. How do you convince people to willingly offer their name and e-mail address? Here are a few easy ways:

First, as discussed in Chapter 5, ask your website designer to place a newsletter sign-up box on the home page of your website. Make sure that it's easy for visitors to see. I prefer to use a small sign-up box that hovers over the upper part of your home page. Sure it's distracting, but my experience has shown that done this way, you will get 10 to 30 percent more sign-ups.

One of the best ways to get more subscribers is to give people an incentive to sign up. Offer a free article, report, resource guide, recipe list, or short story that your audience would genuinely appreciate. Make it an exclusive item so that the only way to get it is by registering for your newsletter. You want people to think, "Wow, I can't believe they're giving that away for free. I'll gladly give my e-mail address to get it." You must offer something truly appealing to get results. Otherwise people will ignore your sign-up request, and you'll miss out on a lot of new registrations. For example, I used to give away an exclusive article called, "Marketing Mistakes Authors Make" as an incentive to attract subscribers. Many of the authors who follow my newsletter have told me that wanting that article was the impetus to join my database.

Another way to increase newsletter sign-ups is by raffling a prize at your book signings or speaking engagements. For instance, whenever you speak, give away an item that everyone would really want, and make the audience register to win it. Be clear that if they sign up, they'll be added to your newsletter list. Many of my clients get creative and give away prizes that tie in to their book's theme, such as a spa gift certificate, Home Depot gift card, or food gift baskets.

When I was promoting my first book, I used to raffle off a five-pound Hershey's chocolate candy bar. It drove audiences wild. During my main presentation, I used the candy bar as a visual illustration, and then told the audience they could register to win it. Sign-up slips were provided to each attendee with the option to request my newsletter, and I collected them at the end of my event.

Giving away the giant candy bar was a huge success. On average, over 80 percent of my event attendees signed up for my newsletter. Within a couple of years, my e-mail subscriber list grew to over eight thousand people. Developing such a large database sure made promoting my book a lot easier.

Summary

I hope this chapter has inspired you to use the power of newsletters to promote your book. If you send articles and information that really help your subscribers, you'll get good results. Remember that you need to reach both leaders and readers. Follow the eight essential elements to create a template you can use to create each issue. The key is to be consistent and provide real value to your readers. Set a goal to capture at least one hundred new subscribers a month through your website and event giveaways. Over time, you will build a loyal following that looks forward to hearing from you. If you want to sell your book like wildfire, newsletters should be a regular part of your marketing plan.

CHAPTER 14

MARKETING TIPS FOR FICTION

"Informing the reader about facts and events is an important part of what I do. But ultimately that's not enough: I also want you to care. A history book can educate you, but oddly, a novel is much more likely to move you to tears, because it creates empathy. That's the amazing power of fiction."

Barbara Kingsolver—New York Times best-selling author

If you're a fiction author who picked up the book and immediately turned to this page, my warmest welcome. I think you'll find the previous chapters just as helpful as this one. The principles I discussed in those chapters apply regardless of whether you write romance novels, cookbooks, memoirs, self-help, mysteries, children's books, fantasy, or science fiction.

However, my experience has shown that fiction authors sometimes see themselves as a different animal within the publishing community. Many of my clients who are novelists initially bristled at the idea of becoming world-class marketers. For some reason, they harbored the idea that fiction authors shouldn't, or couldn't, promote their books. I've heard excuses, such as:

- "Novelists should just stay home and write. Leave the marketing to the publisher."
- "Radio and TV programs hate interviewing fiction authors and prefer nonfiction."
- "Marketing corrupts the purity of writing, so authors shouldn't promote their work."
- "I'm too introverted to promote my books in public."
- "A few book signings ought to be enough."

If an author holds these kinds of beliefs, it's no wonder she might view book marketing as the emotional equivalent of getting a root canal. Fortunately the process of boosting your book sales doesn't have to be a painful experience. There are plenty of activities to choose from and at least a few should fit your personality.

Having said that, I do agree that there are some distinct differences that separate how you promote fiction versus nonfiction. For example, successful fiction tends to rely more on word of mouth than nonfiction does. Thus many publishers put less emphasis on a novelist's marketing platform and focus more on his skill as a writer. The assumption is that if the story is compelling enough, the book will sell itself.

I partially agree with this idea. My concern is that the publishing industry churns out so many new books each year, even great ones sometimes get crowded out by all of the hubbub. That's why a solid marketing plan is just as crucial for selling fiction as it is for nonfiction.

Another difference in marketing fiction is that the value of a book may be less apparent when compared to nonfiction. For instance, a science fiction story about mankind fighting evil robots could be seen as less beneficial to everyday life than a nonfiction book that helps readers overcome a battle with cancer. Yet that science fiction novel may outsell the medical self help resource by a margin of ten to one. Why the difference? Because the definition of value takes many forms in the mind of the marketplace.

A nonfiction book that helps people manage cancer deserves recognition for its value. However, a novel that provides readers with an enjoyable escape or stimulates the mind can also be defined as a beneficial book. The point isn't to determine which books are noble and which are not. If people are willing to buy a book, they do so because they're convinced they will get ample value for the money required to purchase.

Therefore, if you write fiction, don't assume your books are inferior in value to nonfiction. Some of the best teaching in the world occurs through the power of stories. For instance, the stories of the Bible teach the ways of Christianity through colorful parables, rather than didactic sermons. J.R.R. Tolkien showed how anyone can be brave and make a difference in the world through his *Lord of the Rings* trilogy. Through her popular romance novels, Jane Austen helped redefine the way millions of women view relationships.

It's important to make sure that you identify your book's value and include it in your marketing strategy. As I discussed in Chapter 1, people buy books, both fiction and nonfiction, primarily on the basis of self-serving interests. Thus a novelist must be able to answer the reader's ultimate question, "What's in it for me?" Readers will always have different definitions of value. But if you never understand how your target audience defines value, you'll never be able to sell your books like wildfire.

Aside from the concept of value, there are other nuances that apply to marketing fiction. Thus I put together the following list of tips that specifically focus on promoting novels. If you're an introvert, you will be glad to find that most of these tips don't require you to leave your writer's cave or interact with people in public.

1. CREATE EMOTION WITH YOUR AUTHOR WEBSITE
In Chapter 5, I explained the critical role that your author website plays to help boost book sales. It's to every author's benefit to achieve these four main goals with their online presence:

GOAL #1: Credibility—Establish your expertise

GOAL #2: Content—Offer value-laden information for free

GOAL #3: Community—Create a reader fan base

GOAL #4: Contact Information—Ask visitors to let you stay in touch

However there is one important aspect about websites that affects fiction authors more than nonfiction writers. The difference is the ability to create an emotional experience with your website. A fiction author's website should be more than just a boring group of pages that lists facts about you and your book. Your website should provide a visual and emotional connection that relates to the stories within your books.

More often than not, people buy novels based on the desire to satisfy an emotional need, such as the desire to escape their everyday routine, to feel inspired, to explore fantasy, or to imagine being transported to another era. This emotional impetus is sometimes the biggest factor in a purchasing process. Logic makes people think, but emotion makes them act. Therefore, emotion needs to be a key component of your marketing strategy. Your website is one of the best ways to communicate emotion to your fiction readers.

For example, I helped *New York Times* best-selling novelist, Wanda Brunstetter, transform her author website (www.WandaBrunstetter.com) from a lackluster catalog of books into a vivid experience of her novel's unique settings, that is, the beautiful Amish farm country. Wanda's original website contained a lot of information, but navigating the various pages was a dry and bland experience. Instead, of feeling transported into an Amish village, visitors received a bunch of information that left them without any emotional connection to her books. Essentially her website prevented readers from experiencing the picturesque, calming locations that comprise the backbone of her novels.

Wanda and I solved this problem by revamping her website with evocative imagery, video, and text. We even included a subtle audio soundtrack that helps set an Amish country air. When readers visit Wanda's new website, they're drawn into the Amish world. Our goal was to make visitors feel the way they would standing in the middle of Wanda's books and seeing what her main characters see. By doing so, we injected a deeper sense of emotion into the website experience, which makes it easier for visitors to feel drawn into purchasing Wanda's books.

As a fiction author, take an honest assessment of your website. Is it emotionally appealing? If not, use pictures, color, video, and audio to transport your website visitors into the setting of your books. Make them feel like they're really there. Below is a list of fiction author websites at the time of this writing that evoke real emotion:

> www.PatriciaCornwell.com
> www.DanBrown.com
> www.MoWillems.com
> www.StephenKing.com
> www.RandomHouse.com/rhpg/guernsey
> www.DeborahHarkness.com
> www.ThinkPinkalicious.com
> www.WandaBrunstetter.com

Don't let your website become a boring catalog for your books. Leave that mistake to the publishers. Instead, use your website as an emotional tool to connect with your readers and immerse them in your stories.

2. OFFER CONTESTS

People love to win stuff. Likewise, whenever a lottery starts reaching an obscenely high number, such as $200 million, people naturally start to talk about it. You can tap into this same principle by creating a contest that really excites people.

The key is to avoid the desire to be cheap. You don't necessarily need to spend a lot of money, because you could get someone else to donate a nice prize. But if you want to create a big buzz, you need a big grand prize. An autographed copy of your book won't suffice. Think bigger, such as a free trip to a resort location, a one-year's supply of a specific product, a huge gift basket filled with numerous items, or a chance to meet you in person for a private dinner.

Sometimes companies will contribute the prize for free if they're convinced your contest will reach a large group of their target audience. If you see a likely fit with a specific organization, don't be shy to contact them and ask if they'd like to get involved. Be prepared to show tangible numbers about the size of your platform. Tell them that you have a newsletter list, Facebook page, or Twitter account with over five thousand followers, and you're likely to get their interest.

Once you've settled on a prize, the next step is to design a contest that feels interactive. Don't just ask people to register to win by sending in their name and contact information. That's too boring and hinders word of mouth. Instead, base your contest on people's input or actions. For instance, try these ideas:

A. NAME A CHARACTER: Ask fans to help name a key character, choose your next story setting, create a title, or submit a book cover idea. You choose the best idea, and that submitter wins the prize.

B. WEBSITE SCAVENGER HUNT: Post a unique question that contestants must answer, and then provide hints throughout your website. This encourages fans to visit your website in depth. For an added dimension, you could include hints on your Facebook and Twitter page. Don't make the answer too difficult, but make people work a little to figure it out.

C. SUBMIT A PICTURE: Have your fans upload pictures of themselves with your book in strange locations. You could also choose winners based on different categories, such as the most artistic, funny, or unique.

D. AUTHOR TRIVIA: Put together a list of twenty questions, then ask contestants to e-mail their list of answers or to fill out a form on your website. You can use this strategy to help build a larger newsletter mailing list. Simply ask them if they'd like to opt-in when they submit their answers. The users who get the most correct answers are entered into a drawing for the grand prize.

E. WHY DO YOU DESERVE TO WIN?: Ask fans to post a short response that explains why they deserve to win your prize. Are they your biggest fan? Are they the most unique fan? Give people a chance to prove their desire to have for your prize and your books. Really interesting entries can lead to increased word of mouth.

F. BEST MAIN CHARACTER IMPERSONATION: Ask people to impersonate the main character in your story. This can be a fun way for fans to show their excitement and demonstrate their creative side. Via e-mail, contestants can send pictures of themselves dressed up as the character. The closest to the real McCoy wins the prize.

Now that you have several contest formats to choose from, here's how to boost the viral marketing potential. Offer the grand prize in a way that the winner can share with friends. For example, you could say, "Invite five friends to join you if you're the winner of the grand prize" or "Invite your friends to enter this contest, and if one of them wins, you get to share the prize together." By getting contestants to name or enlist the help of their friends, you increase the likelihood that they'll talk about your contest.

One final tip about contests. At the time of this writing, a company called Wildfire Interactive (www.WildfireApp.com—no relation to my company, WildFire Marketing) offers a great, affordable service for hosting contests on social media sites such as

Facebook and Twitter. You create an account and fill out the details about your contest or sweepstakes. Then a customized template and web page are automatically created and serve as your contest hub. You can also use their system to manage a contest on your website. Several of my clients have used this service with positive results.

3. ACTIVATE THE POWER OF BOOK CLUBS AND DISCUSSION GROUPS

One marketing technique particularly useful to fiction authors is to tap the power of book clubs and discussion groups. Millions of readers congregate both in person and online to discuss their favorite novels. Promoting your books to these groups can quickly boost sales by increasing the number of volume orders placed. Below are some ways to get started:

Provide spicy discussion questions

Encourage groups to dive into your novels by getting them talking. First, create a list of interesting questions and post them in the back of your book or on your author website or your publisher's book page. The important thing is to make it easy for people to find and download these questions.

Second, don't put a book club to sleep by giving them boring questions. Simple yes or no answers fail to generate curiosity and dull questions, such as "Did the main character seem scared in Chapter 3?" don't inspire discussion. Instead, push your audience to shake things up with deeper questions such as:

- If you were in the main character's position at this point, how would you respond?
- Do you feel as if this book changed your views on the primary subject of the story? Why?
- The main character's adherence to social customs can seem controversial to us today. Pick a scene where you would have acted differently. Why?

- If you could change something about this book, what would it be and why?

Turn your book into an event

Another way to get book clubs interested is by providing a context for groups to interact within. Can your book be used as the basis for a mystery dinner, field trip, supper club, or service project?

You might provide a list of specific recipes that pertain to the primary locations in your novel. If your book is set in New Orleans, for example, supply ideas for music and local recipes akin to the region, such as shrimp gumbo, jambalaya, crawfish, and beignets. Music options offered could be Dixieland jazz, big band, zydeco, or Harry Connick, Jr. Make your story come alive by inviting book club members to cook and eat what the main characters cook and eat.

In contrast, you could encourage a book club to conduct a service project based on your novel. For instance, if your book deals with difficult social subjects, such as soldiers fighting overseas, children at risk, or abandoned animals, you could invite the group to send letters and care packages to servicemen or to read to kids at an after-school program or to volunteer at a local humane shelter.

Look for ways to make book clubs view your novel as an experience they can share, rather than just a book to read. Positioning your book as the catalyst for meaningful activity is great way to generate excitement and boost word of mouth.

Offer a "virtual meeting" to book clubs

Book clubs thrive on debating how a novelist creates and masterfully tells a poignant story. A sense of awe overwhelms the way some readers feel toward their favorite writers. As the author, why not offer to remove some of the mystery? Allow book clubs to meet you privately by scheduling short phone calls to answer some of the members' biggest questions. Just hearing your voice can be a major thrill for some literary fans. In addition, you can use technology, such as Skype, Facebook Chat, and video conferencing, to make virtual appearances with readers around the world. Imagine no longer having to endure miserable book-signing events where nobody shows up. Now you can be the life of the party!

Several of my clients offer free thirty-minute phone calls to book clubs, because they like getting to know their readers without having to leave home. These phone calls allow authors to build stronger relationships with fans, understand why readers appreciate their books, and recharge the writing soul after a long day working on their next novel.

Never underestimate the desire that readers have to meet their favorite authors. Offer a free phone call, chat session, or video conference to book clubs on a regular basis, during your next major book launch, or as the prize for a special contest. Promote this opportunity on your website and social media pages. Plus, notify your publisher, literary agent, and publicist about your availability.

4. CREATE TOOLS FOR BLOGGERS AND SOCIAL MEDIA

Book reviews can mean life or death to a novel. Getting praise from influential critics is a crucial aspect to promoting fiction. Before the Internet, though, major newspapers, magazines, and Oprah's book club controlled the literary review world. If you couldn't get a book review from the establishment, you were out of luck.

Fortunately the Internet came along and revolutionized the book review process by allowing anyone to evaluate a book and post comments for the world to see. The major sources of influence are no longer consolidated to just a few industry critics. Today there are book review bloggers and social media mavens who have bigger followings than the old "experts." This change has helped level the playing field for authors of all kinds.

It easier than ever before to market your novel to large audiences. The key is to make it as painless as possible for bloggers to get access to your book. That's why I recommend novelists create a free "toolkit" on their website that simplifies the process for bloggers and social media reviewers. (It works great for nonfiction books, too.) Fill your toolkit with these resources:

- Cover art images of your book in various sizes.
- A brief author bio of around 100 words.
- A one-paragraph synopsis of your book.
- A website link to your video trailer, if you have one.
- A website link or PDF file to download your first chapter.
- A short "Q&A with the author" article that a blogger can use.
- Your contact information for bloggers to reach you and request a review.

Creating a toolkit for bloggers simplifies the review process on both ends by serving as a one-stop shop for your novel. Bloggers can quickly access all of the information without having to track you down. That kind of speed and convenience makes it easier for them to post a review without waiting to get your information and possibly losing interest. Likewise, there's less work on your part, because the necessary tools are premade and ready to go.

Once you've composed your toolkit, don't sit back and wait for bloggers to find you. Use online search engines to find bloggers that address your book's genre. At the time of this writing, there is a unique page on Google that lets you search for book reviewer blogs at this link: http://www.google.com/cse/home?cx=0179979 35591651423304%3A5fpbgt6-tou&hl=en

Most book review bloggers post their contact information and review guidelines. And they are adamant about not accepting books outside of their preferred genres. So don't waste your time if your novel doesn't fit. Find bloggers who focus on your genre, and politely e-mail a request for a review. Be prepared to send a finished print copy by mail. Many reviewers prefer to read paper over electronic versions.

If a blogger agrees to review your book, don't harass him about when it will post. Most reviewers are flooded with offers, so it may take months to get to your title. Just send the requested information, make him aware of your blogger's toolkit, and move on. Concentrate on other marketing activities instead of pining away for reviews. If a blogger decides to review your book, he'll usually contact you by e-mail with an update.

One option that may help you gain the favor of high-level blog reviewers is to offer exclusive content or unique information. Like journalists, bloggers like to be first to publicize inside news or special access. For example, you could offer a new book trailer or a behind-the-scenes author video to entice a big blogger to give your book coverage. You could include influential bloggers on your advanced reader copy (ARC) list to receive books before they're available to the public.

If searching out and contacting bloggers doesn't appeal to you, there are companies and publicists who will set up blog review tours for your book. These services can cost $500 to $2,500 depending on the amount of bloggers they contact and length of time devoted to your title. Essentially you're paying the company to interact with their network of preapproved bloggers who agree to review any books they are sent.

For the money, purchasing a blog tour isn't a bad option. Keep in mind, that some of these companies may advertise a huge number of bloggers within their network, but many of these bloggers have a small readership. So their actual influence may be smaller than expected. Before you decide to go with a particular blog tour outfit, ask for references and speak to some of the authors on the list. Ask the authors if they have statistics that show the tour actually created book sales. Otherwise you might be wasting your money.

Moving away from the blogger world for a moment, remember that your blogger toolkit can also come in handy for social media networks such as Facebook and Twitter. If you already have the tools posted on your website, it's easy for others to grab them and share with their friends and followers. Encourage your fans to post links to your sample chapters, videos, and author interviews on their social media accounts. Word of mouth can't spread unless you give people a reason to talk.

Here's another idea I've seen used successfully to market fiction in the social media segment. Create a fake account on Facebook or Twitter for the main characters in your novel, and act like they're real people. Post fake updates that let readers interact with the characters and get involved with your story. For example, best-selling author, Laurie R. King, created a fake Twitter account for her main character, Mary Russell (http://www.twitter.com/mary_russell). The Twitter posts make Mary sound like a real person, and over five thousand book fans find this continuous interaction very amusing.

This idea has worked well especially for authors of young adult fiction. Readers feel like they're able to engage and follow their favorite characters. And even if it's fake, it can create a big buzz. Only try this idea is if you're already a serious user of Facebook or Twitter. If you're not familiar with the system and style of these social networks, then your inexperience will be apparent and kill the wow factor. In some cases, you may be better off hiring a young intern who's well versed in the technology to manage a fake campaign on your behalf.

5. MAXIMIZE THE USE OF VIDEO

An old adage says that a picture is worth a thousand words. If that's true, a video is worth a million words. That's why the use of video trailers as book commercials has become so popular in the publishing industry. The point of using video isn't to overwhelm the viewer with a million words about your book. Instead, the goal is to generate as much emotion as possible within the viewer. Video can be one of the most powerful marketing tools in a fiction author's toolkit. To maximize your results with video, keep the following factors in mind.

Don't just tell the plot. Create videos that build excitement for your book.
If you create a video as a promotional device, your biggest goal should be to make the viewer feel something about your book. Emo-

tions act like a mental hook that catches the viewer's mind, just like a hook catches a fish. It's harder to forget something when you feel deeply about it.

Therefore, don't use video to simply tell people what your novel is about. Use the power of video to emphasize what the reader will feel. The key is to look for the most suspenseful, passionate, or scary part of your book, and showcase that element in your book trailer. Show your viewers enough information about your plot to get their interest, build towards a climax, and then suddenly leave them hanging in suspense. For some great examples of fiction book trailers, go to YouTube and watch these compelling videos:

> http://www.youtube.com/watch?v=Bvo_RokPp_U
> (*Dead or Alive*—Tom Clancy)

> http://www.youtube.com/watch?v=U0mGCBvcOaI
> (*Rules of Vengeance*—Christopher Reich)

> http://www.youtube.com/watch?v=AKFwfYwZoWA
> (*Scarpetta*—Patricia Cornwell)

If you can't do video well, then don't do it at all.
I'm amazed by the thousands of dollars authors and publishers waste on creating cheesy book trailers that are flat out boring. I'm talking about videos made with a camera moving over a bunch of still shots while a faceless narrator drones on about the story. It's the equivalent of reading a boring sales brochure. The author seems to think, "Hey, at least I've got a video—that's better than nothing." Actually nothing is sometimes better than something. A bad video can actually work against you, because it can prevent people from making a purchase or spreading word of mouth. It would be better if the video was never made in the first place, especially considering the cost and time involved to make it.

If you want to produce a successful video for your book, you don't need to hire a high-priced production company. But you do need to put real thought into the style and production format. The point isn't to show off that you have a video for your book. The point is to sell more books because the video convinces people that they need to buy your book—right now!

If you decide to hire a video production company, check out their portfolio first. Have they created compelling book videos in the past? Don't risk being a twenty-something's guinea pig just because she brags about how good she is with technology. The young techno-crowd may understand how to use a fancy camera, but they don't always understand how to market books. The result is a video that makes viewers think, "Wow, I like the cool graphics." Great for the videographer, but not so great for your book.

If you want to make a homemade book trailer, use an HD video camera on a tripod. This level of quality is now standard on most smartphones and small video recorders. So you don't have to spend much to get good quality. Above all, pay attention to the lighting and make it look professional. Certainly try to make a good video on your own, but don't be afraid to hire someone if you find it's beyond your range of skills.

Above all, you're better off not doing a video at all if the alternative is a poor attempt. Your book doesn't need a book trailer to be successful, but I do highly recommend using this tool. When it comes to video, people will judge you against the big boys and girls so make your shot count.

Use low production videos to create mystique as a novelist

Another powerful use of video is to show readers behind-the-scenes clips of your life as a novelist. Think of it like giving your fans a visual backstage pass to your writing studio, book-signing events, research trips, and hobbies. Give people a chance to see what it's like to live as a writer.

With today's technology, it's easier than ever to create decent videos with inexpensive equipment. For example, my iPhone has a built-in high-definition camera that can record video at a professional-quality level. Most new DROID smartphones and tablets, such as the iPad, have this capability as well. When I record a video, I either put my device on a tripod or have someone hold the camera steady. I recommend keeping videos brief, such as two to four minutes in length.

Once you're finished recording, you have a couple of options for what to do next. You can either upload the video directly to YouTube, share the link with followers, and embed the video on your website, or you can transfer your video file into video editing software that lets you add graphics and effects before broadcasting it. Either way, it doesn't take much time or technical knowledge to make nice videos that connect with your readers. Don't be shy about giving this marketing idea a try.

6. DEVELOP BACKSTORIES AND UNPUBLISHED WRITINGS

In Chapter 5, I referenced a Codex Group survey of twenty-one thousand book shoppers, which found that exclusive, unpublished writing was the most preferred content that would make them return to a fiction author's website. Examples include short stories, backstories, lost chapters, and alternative openings or endings. This desire for content is especially popular with women readers. So if you want to drive more people to your website, posting exclusive, unpublished writing is one of the most effective ways to do it. The good thing is that it's easy to make this exclusive material available.

As a novelist, your task of writing a book is essentially to create one big story out of several smaller stories that involve different characters and settings. During the writing and editing process, you have probably generated interesting material that didn't fit into your book or didn't connect with the main narrative. Or maybe you touched on an interesting character who didn't warrant full development in your story.

Hollywood is famous for using this process to create movie prequels, sequels, tie-ins, and spin-offs. Original movies, such as *Star Wars, Rocky, Batman, Star Trek*, and James Bond have been expanded far beyond their initial story lines. Literary phenom Stephenie Meyer developed a novella called *The Short Second Life of Bree Tanner* based on her Twilight book series. She offered the novella as a limited-time free gift to her fans before officially publishing it. The buzz over the story was huge and kept readers engaged with her books.

Likewise, you should look through the parts of your novel that were left on the cutting room floor. Many times, you'll find material that you can turn into short stories or novellas. Consider these examples.

a. You could write a prequel or a short back story about your main character that explains the history or events leading up to your novel.

b. If you're writing a series of novels, create short stories that cover the material in between two consecutive books. Fill in any gaps or take a different look at another character who deserves more attention.

c. Develop a "lost appendix" or a "Where are they now?" story that looks at a character's life after the original story ended. Listen to fan feedback about secondary characters they may want to know more about.

Once your short stories are crafted, you can use them in a variety of ways to generate buzz for your books. For instance, put them on your website, and use your social media networks or newsletter to build awareness and direct traffic. Create these stories as special promotional tools, such as freebies or premiums that are included when someone buys your novel. Offer them as a free resource to audiences at your book signings, speaking events, or media interviews. Keep your publisher abreast of these items as well. In many cases, the publisher might want to incorporate them into the overall promotional plan.

You're a novelist, so creating backstories can be one of the easiest ways to turn your natural skill into an effective marketing strategy. Use these ideas to reignite past books, and keep them in mind as you write your next novel. Save a few interesting parts of your story to use as exclusive bait that draws readers to you.

7. MASTER MEDIA INTERVIEWS

Many fiction authors complain that there is a media bias against their genre. In some cases it's true, because it's easier for a self-help nonfiction author to offer material that fits most radio and TV programs. Plus some novelists worry that they won't have anything to talk about on the air. After all, they don't want to spoil the book for readers.

Still, I believe fiction authors can provide a more interesting interview than a didactic self-help nonfiction author. Keep in mind that fiction routinely outsells nonfiction, and the reading public is enamored with great storytellers. Readers want to see the quirky person who writes the novels that touch their hearts.

I encourage you to avoid a negative mentality, and never rule out the possibility of good media coverage for your fiction. It is possible to get media interviews, but you may have to adopt a different approach to get a radio or TV producer's attention. A detailed explanation of how the media industry works can be found in Chapter 6. Most of the principles I cover there apply, regardless of whether you write fiction or nonfiction. A few differences that novelists should recognize will maximize their chances in the media world:

Apply the thread of reality in your fiction to current events

Even though you write fiction, a thread of reality most likely runs through every story you write. If you write historical novels, for instance, there may be a message about the pioneer spirit to discover new lands, the mistreatment of women and slaves, or the greed of kings and governments. If you write romance, your book may have themes of overcoming relational conflict, trying to understand the opposite sex, or the search for true love. If you write fantasy, your stories may focus on the desire to do heroic deeds, utilize new technology, or triumph over evil empires.

All of these themes point to a reality that readers face today. As humans, we try to understand relationships, to perform heroic deeds, to cope with new technology, and to manage social inequality. These issues dominate the headlines and current events within our society. Therefore, look at your novel and define the nonfiction theme within. Then connect that theme to current events, and use that connection as your media hook. You appear more interesting to radio and TV producers when you show how people in real life wrestle with the same issues that the main character faces in your novel. In some ways, your character serves as a case study in how we approach a difficult situation.

Will this approach work for every book you write? Probably not. But it's a much better approach than not pursuing media coverage at all. You can't win if you don't play. And you can't increase your media exposure if you don't try to get in the game.

Present yourself as an expert

Once you've identified the nonfiction theme in your novel that connects to current events, present yourself as an expert to the media. Yes, I said "expert," because I'm assuming that you either conducted research for your novels or you based your story on a similar life experience. If you've taken time to research a subject or you have experienced a situation personally, then you're in a position to speak with authority. That makes you an expert in the media's eye. Producers aren't looking for weird writers who freeze in front a microphone. But they are hungry for interesting experts who can provide their audiences with fascinating information.

Several of my fiction clients spend an incredible amount of time traveling, researching, interviewing, and gathering data for their novels. They're like walking treasure troves of unique information about their genres. For instance, best-selling author, Wanda Brunstetter, regularly spends several weeks every year visiting and researching Amish communities. She can tell you insightful details about the history, customs, and modern-day challenges of the

Amish people. The Amish even regard her as a trusted spokesperson on their way of life. Wanda's firsthand knowledge makes her a great interview when the media needs an expert to handle Amish-related issues or topics related to simplifying overbusy lives.

If you've taken time to write a story with painstaking detail, you may be more of an expert than you think. I'm not encouraging you to stretch the truth about your knowledge, but your background and understanding as a writer can make you a solid candidate for the media. If you know your stuff, don't sell yourself short. Connect your fiction to the nonfiction reality in the world, and offer yourself as an expert.

Help the audience feel the emotion of your story

Once you land a media interview, use the following technique to grab the attention of the audience: Draw them into your novel by explaining the story line and then asking questions like, "How would you respond if faced with the same challenge as the main character?" or "What would the main character look like in your world?" In other words, don't just explain your story, challenge viewers to get involved.

Patricia Cornwell, the megabest-selling author of forensic fiction, does a great job at challenging an audience to solve her mysteries. She literally toys with viewers by saying, "I've dropped some tricky little clues throughout the pages of my book, but I dare you to figure out the story. You know what? You're not going to, because I'm still gonna fool you." How can you resist that kind of emotional bravado?

Likewise, take steps to help the audience immerse itself into the settings and struggles of your novel. Don't give away anything important to the plot during your interview. But do make people feel what it's like to walk within the pages of your book. Logic makes people think, but emotion makes them act. If you can get listeners to feel the power of your fiction, you will move them much faster toward making a purchase.

Summary

I hope this chapter has helped remove any hesitation you previously felt about marketing your fiction. There are just as many good strategies for promoting novels as there are for nonfiction. The major difference is to focus your efforts on maximizing the emotion that you want readers to feel when they hear what you have to say. Facts may get attention, but feelings get action. Use the concepts I've provided in this chapter to inject new life into your marketing plan.

- Create Emotion with Your Author Website
- Offer Contests
- Activate the Power of Book Clubs and Discussion Groups
- Create Tools for Bloggers and Social Media
- Maximize the Use of Video
- Develop Backstories and Unpublished Writings
- Master Media Interviews

Show the world that novelists can be just as good at marketing books, if not better, than their nonfiction counterparts. Sell your story like wildfire!

BONUS ARTICLES, UPDATES, & EXTRAS

Don't miss out on the great bonus articles highlighted throughout *Sell Your Book Like Wildfire* as well as the following extras:

- **MIXING MARKETING WITH FAITH:** All too often marketing a book gets misconstrued as a selfish attempt to draw attention to the author or a shallow means to make money off of others. This helpful article can help you learn to balance your religious beliefs with your business strategy.

- **SELF-ESTEEM AND THE SUCCESS OF YOUR BOOK:** You must believe in your own message strongly enough to promote your book above the noise of all the competition. Yet this can happen only when you feel an ardent confidence in your message accompanied by an enthusiasm to tell other people about it. This article can help inspire your confidence.

- **TIPS TO MARKET E-BOOKS:** E-books are here to stay and they make up the fastest growing part of the publishing industry. Every day, more and more people choose to consume content via an electronic means. Learn to promote your e-book with these great marketing tips.

 BONUS ONLINE CONTENT available at bookwildfire.com and writersdigest.com/book-wildfire-downloads

ABOUT THE AUTHOR

 **ROB EAGAR** is the founder of WildFire Marketing, a consulting practice that helps authors and publishers sell more books and spread their message like wildfire. Rob has consulted with numerous publishers and trained over 400 authors. His client list includes several *New York Times* bestselling authors, such as Dr. Gary Chapman, Wanda Brunstetter, and Lysa TerKeurst. Rob is also a successful author who has spoken to over 35,000 people and appeared on the *CBS Early Show*, CNN Radio, the *Los Angeles Times*, and the ABC Family Channel. He resides with his wife, Ashley, in Atlanta, Georgia.

For more information about Rob Eagar and his consulting services for authors and publishers, call 1-800-267-2045, email: Rob@ startawidlfire.com or visit: www.StartaWildfire.com

COACHING SERVICES AND RESOURCES FOR AUTHORS FROM ROB EAGAR

Rob offers a wide range of instructional resources and coaching services for authors at any level. For more information on the resources listed below, visit: www.BookWildfire.com

FREE BOOK UPDATES – Since marketing and publishing constantly change, Rob will provide free updates to the topics covered in this book. Visit the book website to access these free updates.

FREE RESOURCES – Access Rob's free library of articles, videos, and weekly marketing tips.

INSTRUCTIONAL RESOURCES FOR AUTHORS – Purchase templates, tutorials, and resources from Rob that help walk you step-by-step through the process of marketing your book, such as:

- Marketing Plan Template for Fiction and Non-Fiction Authors
- Bestseller Website Tutorial for Fiction and Non-Fiction Authors

AUTHOR COACHING PROGRAMS – Rob offers personal coaching that teaches authors how to implement essential book marketing skills, such as building a brand, creating a website, engaging in social media, writing newsletters, landing media interviews, securing speaking events, etc. His coaching programs can be customized to fit your individual needs.

WRITERS CONFERENCES AND WORKSHOPS – Rob speaks at writers conferences, publishing events, and conducts specialized workshops for authors. Visit his speaking page to view his schedule or request him to speak at your event.

For more information about these resources and services, visit: www.BookWildfire.com

INDEX

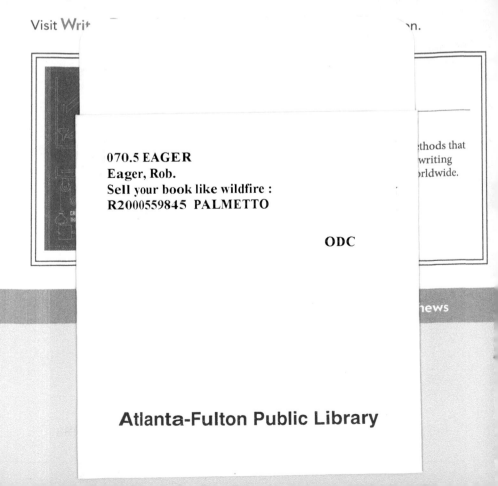